THE M. & E. HANDBOOK SERIES

THE LAW OF CONTRACT

THE M. & E. HANDBOOK SERIES

THE LAW OF CONTRACT

W. T. MAJOR, M.A., LL.B.
Barrister-at-Law
Principal Lecturer in Law at the
City of London Polytechnic

FOURTH EDITION

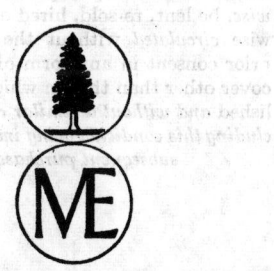

MACDONALD & EVANS LTD
8 John Street, London WC1N 2HY

First published January 1965
Reprinted February 1966
Second Edition November 1967
Reprinted March 1969
Reprinted April 1970
Reprinted April 1971
Third Edition March 1973
Fourth Edition June 1974
Reprinted June 1975
Reprinted January 1976

©

MACDONALD AND EVANS LIMITED
1974

ISBN: 0 7121 1230 2

This book is copyright and may not be reproduced in whole *or in part* (except for purposes of review) without the express permission of the publishers in writing.

HANDBOOK *Conditions of Sale*

This book is sold subject to the condition that it shall not, by way of *trade or otherwise*, be lent, re-sold, hired out or otherwise *circulated* without the publisher's prior consent in any form of binding or cover other than that in which it is published *and without a similar condition including this condition being imposed on the subsequent purchaser.*

Printed in Great Britain by Richard Clay (The Chaucer Press), Ltd, Bungay, Suffolk

PREFACE TO THE FOURTH EDITION

ALTHOUGH little more than a year has elapsed since the Third Edition of these study notes, it has become necessary to bring out this edition so as to incorporate the changes brought about by the *Supply of Goods (Implied Terms) Act*, 1973. I have taken the opportunity to include the important contract law decisions of 1972–73, in particular, *Holwell Securities* v. *Hughes, Ashmore, Ltd.* v. *Dawson, Ltd.* and *Jarvis* v. *Swan Tours, Ltd.*

I am grateful to the Senate of the University of London, the Associated Examination Board, the Chartered Institute of Secretaries and the Institute of Bankers, who were generous enough to allow me to use past examination questions in this book. Questions from the Contract paper in the intermediate examinations for the LL.B. degree are designated *Intermediate Laws*; those from the "A" level General Principles of Law examinations are designated *A.E.B.*; those from the Institute's examination in General Principles of Law are designated *Bankers*; and those from the Mercantile Law examination of the Chartered Institute are designated *C.I.S.*

WILLIAM T. MAJOR

London, January 1974.

NOTICE TO LECTURERS

Many lecturers are now using **HANDBOOKS** as working texts to save time otherwise wasted by students in protracted note-taking. The purpose of the series is to meet practical teaching requirements as far as possible, and lecturers are cordially invited to forward comments or criticisms to the Publishers for consideration.

P. W. D. REDMOND
General Editor

CONTENTS

	PAGE
Preface to the fourth edition	v
Table of Cases	xi

CHAP.
- I. Introductory ... 1
- II. Offer and acceptance ... 5
  - The offer must be definite ... 5
  - Communication of the offer ... 7
  - Acceptance must be unqualified ... 9
  - Acceptance of a tender ... 11
  - The communication of acceptance ... 12
  - Revocation ... 16
  - Lapse ... 18
  - Rejection ... 19
- III. Intention to create legal relations ... 22
- IV. Consideration ... 26
  - The nature of consideration ... 26
  - Waiver must be supported by consideration ... 31
  - The doctrine of equitable estoppel ... 32
- V. The terms of a contract ... 37
  - Express terms ... 37
  - Exemption clauses and fundamental breach ... 40
  - Implied terms ... 49
  - Conditions and warranties ... 58
  - Collateral contracts ... 62
- VI. Matters affecting the validity of a contract ... 67
- VII. Mistake ... 69
  - Mistake—its effect upon agreement ... 69
  - Mistake at common law ... 70
  - Mistake in equity ... 82
- VIII. Misrepresentation ... 89
  - Representations distinguished from express terms ... 89
  - Misrepresentation may be innocent or fraudulent ... 92
  - Where non-disclosure constitutes misrepresentation ... 98

vii

CONTENTS

CHAP.		PAGE
IX.	Duress and undue influence	103
	Duress	103
	Undue influence	104
X.	Capacity	109
	Contractual capacity	109
	Infants as contracting parties	109
	Contracts made by insane or drunken persons	119
	Contractual capacity of corporations	119
XI.	Illegal contracts	123
	Contracts illegal in inception	123
	The consequences of illegality	129
	Illegal performance of a lawful contract	130
XII.	Void contracts	133
	Void contracts generally	133
	Contracts made void by statute	133
	Wagering contracts	134
	Contracts void at common law as being against public policy	137
	Consequences where a contract is void as being against public policy	144
	The *Restrictive Trade Practices Acts*	145
XIII.	Contracts unenforceable unless evidenced by writing	155
	Unenforceable contracts	155
	The statutory provisions	156
	Formal requirements under the *Hire-Purchase Act*, 1965	159
XIV.	Privity of contract	161
XV.	Assignment	168
	The assignment of contractual rights	168
	Statutory assignment	168
	Equitable assignment	170
	Assignment by operation of law	171
	Assignment of contractual obligations	171
	Negotiable instruments	172
XVI.	Agency	175
	The principal–agent relationship	175
	The position of principal and agent with regard to third parties	179
	The position as between principal and agent	180
	Breach of warranty of authority	182
	Termination of the agency relationship	183

CONTENTS

CHAP.		PAGE
XVII.	Discharge	185
	The end of a contract	185
	Discharge by performance	185
	Discharge by agreement	189
	Discharge by acceptance of breach	192
	Discharge by frustration	196
XVIII.	Remedies for breach of contract	206
	Remedies	206
	Unliquidated damages	208
	Liquidated damages	216
	Claim for a specific sum as damages	219
	Quantum meruit as a remedy for breach	220
	Recovery of a reasonable price for goods	221
	Specific performance	222
	Injunction	223
	Limitation of actions	225
XIX.	Quasi-contract	231
	The meaning of quasi-contract	231
	Actions in quasi-contract	232
	APPENDIXES	
	I Examination technique	236
	II Examination questions	239
	INDEX	279

TABLE OF CASES

(Where the facts are noted, the page number is in italics)

A

	PAGE
Addis v. Gramophone Co., Ltd., [1909] A.C. 488; [1908–10] All E.R. Rep. 1	209
Akerhielm v. De Mare, [1959] A.C. 789; [1959] 3 All E.R. 485	*93*
Alexander v. Rayson, [1936] 1 K.B.	25, *126*, 127
Allcard v. Skinner (1887), 36 Ch.D. 145	*104, 105, 106*
Anderson, Ltd. v. Daniel, [1924] 1 K.B. 138	131
Andrews v. Hopkinson, [1957] 1 Q.B. 229; [1956] All E.R.	*63*, 64
Appleson v. Littlewood, [1939] 1 All E.R. 464	22
Archbolds, Ltd. v. S. Spanglett, Ltd., [1961] 1 All E.R. 417	23, *125*
Armstrong v. Jackson, [1917] 2 K.B. 822; [1916–17] All E.R. Rep. 1117	81
Ashington Piggeries v. Christopher Hill [1971] 1 All E.R. 847	*55*
Ashmore, Ltd. v. Dawson, Ltd., [1973] 2 All E.R. 856	*131*
Attwood v. Lamont, [1920] 3 K.B. 571; [1920] All E.R. Rep. 55	*44*, 145
Avery v. Bowden (1855), 6 E. & B. 953, 962	93

B

Baily v. De Crespigny (1869), L.R. 4 Q.B. 180	200
Baker v. Jones, [1954] 2 All E.R. 553	137
Balfour v. Balfour, [1919] 2 K.B. 571; [1918–19] All E.R. Rep. 860	22
Ballett v. Mingay, [1943] 1 K.B. 281; [1943] 1 All E.R. 143	12, *113*
Beatty v. Ebury (1872), 7 Ch. App. 777	*90*
Behn v. Burness (1863) B. & S. 751	60
Bell v. Lever Bros., [1932] A.C. 161; [1931] All E.R. Rep. 1	*72*, 98
Belvoir Finance Co. v. Stapleton [1971] 1 Q.B. 210; [1970] 3 All E.R. 664	129
Benaim & Co. v. Debono, [1924] A.C. 415; [1924] All E.R. Rep. 103	15
Bentley (Dick) Productions, Ltd. v. Harold Smith, Ltd., [1965] 2 All E.R. 65	38, *39*, 92
Beresford v. Royal Insurance Co., Ltd., [1938] A.C. 586; [1938] 2 All E.R. 602	*127*, 128
Beswick v. Beswick [1968] A.C. 58; [1967] 2 All E.R. 1197	161, *162, 163, 164*
Bettini v. Gye (1876), 1 Q.B.D. 183	*59*
Beverley Corporation v. Richard Hodgson & Sons (1972), 225 E.G. 799	192
Bigg v. Boyd Gibbins, Ltd., [1971] 2 All E.R. 183	7
Bigos v. Bousted, [1951] 1 All E.R. 92	130
Bissett v. Wilkinson, [1927] A.C. 177; [1926] All E.R. Rep. 343	*90, 91*

TABLE OF CASES

	PAGE
Blackburn Bobbin Co., Ltd. v. T. W. Allen & Sons, [1918] 2 K.B. 467	197
Blay v. Pollard and Morris, [1930] 1 K.B. 628; [1930] All E.R. Rep. 609	78
Boulton v. Jones (1857), 2 H. & N. 564	8, 73
Bowmakers, Ltd. v. Barnet Instruments, Ltd., [1945] K.B. 65; [1944] 2 All E.R. 579	130
Bradbury v. Morgan (1862), 1 H. & C. 249	19
Branca v. Cobarro, [1947] K.B. 854; [1947] 2 All E.R. 101.	*11*
Bridge v. Campbell Discount Co., Ltd., [1962] A.C. 600; [1962] 1 All E.R. 385	218
British Basic Slag, Ltd's Agreements, *Re* [1963] 2 All E.R. 807	146
British Reinforced Concrete Co., Ltd. v. Schelff, [1921] 2 Ch. 563; [1921] All E.R. Rep. 202	*42*, 143
British Waggon Co. v. Lea & Co. (1880), 5 Q.B.D. 149	72
British Westinghouse Electric and Manufacturing Co., Ltd. v. Underground Electric Rail Co., Ltd., [1912] A.C. 673; [1911–13] All E.R. Rep. 63	215
Brooks Wharf and Bull Wharf, Ltd. v. Goodman Bros., [1937] 1 K.B. 534; [1936] 3 All E.R. 696	*232, 233*
Brown & Davis v. Galbraith, [1972] 3 All E.R. 31	52
Byrne v. Van Tienhoven [1880], 5 C.P.D. 344	*17*

C

C.H.T. Ltd. v. Ward, [1965] 2 Q.B. 63	136
Camillo Tank Co. v. Alexandria Engineering Works (1921), 38 T.L.R. 134	234
Carlill v. Carbolic Smoke Ball Co., [1892] 2 Q.B. 484; [1891–94] All E.R. Rep. 127	5, 8, *13*, 14, 134
Carlisle and Cumberland Banking Co. v. Bragg, [1911] 1 K.B. 489	*80*
Carlton Hall Club v. Laurence [1929], 2 K.B. 153	136
Casey's Patents, *Re*, [1892] 1 Ch. 104	*30*
Central London Property Trust, Ltd. v. High Trees House, Ltd., [1947] K.B. 130; [1956] 1 All E.R. 256	*33, 34*
Chapelton v. Barry U.D.C., [1940] 1 K.B. 532; [1940] 1 All E.R. 356	*41*, 44
Chapple v. Cooper (1844), 13 M. & W. 252	115
Chillingworth v. Esche, [1924] 1 Ch. 97; [1923] All E.R. Rep. 97	*11*
Christoforides v. Terry, [1924] A.C. 566; [1924] All E.R. Rep. 815	181
City and Westminster Properties, Ltd. v. Mudd, [1959] Ch. 129; [1958] 2 All E.R. 733	*62, 63*
Clarke v. Dunraven, The *Satanita*, [1897] A.C. 59	*63*
Combe v. Combe, [1951] 2 K.B. 215; [1951] 1 All E.R. 767	*33, 34*
Compagnie de Commerce et Commission S.A.R.L. v. Parkinson Stove Co., Ltd., [1953] 2 Lloyds Rep. 487, C.A.	*15*, 16
Cooper v. Phibbs (1867), L.R. 2 H.L. 149.	*82, 83*
Couchman v. Hill, [1947] K.B. 554; [1947] 1 All E.R. 103	*38*, 40, 92
Coutts & Co. v. Browne-Lecky, [1947] K.B. 104; [1946] 2 All E.R. 207	111

TABLE OF CASES

	PAGE
Cowan v. Milbourn (1967), L.R. 2 Ex. 230	130
Coxhead v. Mullis (1878), 3 C.P.D. 439	118
Craddock Bros., Ltd. v. Hunt, [1923] 2 Ch. 136; [1923] All E.R. Rep. 394	85
Craven-Ellis v. Canons, Ltd., [1936] 2 K.B. 403; [1936] 2 All E.R. 1066	234
Cumming v. Ince (1847), 11 Q.B. 112	104
Cundy v. Lindsay (1878), 3 App. Cas. 459	75
Currie v. Misa (1875), 1 App. Cas. 554	26
Curtis v. Chemical Cleaning and Dyeing Co., [1951] K.B. 805; [1951] 1 All E.R. 631	42, 43, 44
Cutter v. Powell (1795), 6 Term Rep. 320	185, 186, 189

D

D. & C. Builders, Ltd. v. Rees, [1965] 3 All E.R. 837	32, 190, 191
Dakin & Co., Ltd. v. Lee, [1916] 1 K.B. 566	187
Davies v. London and Provincial Marine Insurance Co. (1878), 8 Ch.D. 469	99
Davies & Co. v. William Old (1969), 67 L.G.R. 395	9
Davis Contractors, Ltd. v. Fareham U.D.C., [1956] A.C. 696; [1956] 2 All E.R. 145	198
De Bernardy v. Harding (1853), 8 Ex. 822	221
De Bussche v. Alt (1878), 8 Ch.D. 286	181
Denny, Mott and Dickson, Ltd. v. Fraser (James) & Co., Ltd., [1944] A.C. 265; [1944] 1 All E.R. 678	200
Derry v. Peek (1889), 14 A.C. 337; [1886–90] All E.R. Rep. 1	92, 93, 94
Diamond v. Campbell-Jones, [1961] Ch. 22; [1960] 1 All E.R. 583	213
Dickinson v. Barrow, [1904] 2 Ch. 339	158
Dickinson v. Dodds (1876), 2 Ch.D. 463	16, 18
Diplock, Re, Diplock v. Wintle, [1947] 1 All E.R. 522; [1948] 2 All E.R. 318	231
Doyle v. White City Stadium, Ltd., [1935] 1 K.B. 110; [1934] All E.R. Rep. 252	117
Duff's Executors' Case (1886), 32 Ch.D. 301	19
Dunkirk Colliery Co. v. Lever (1878), 9 Ch. D. 20	216
Dunlop Pneumatic Tyre Co., Ltd. v. New Garage and Motor Co., Ltd., [1915] A.C. 79; [1914–15] All E.R. Rep. 739	217, 218
Dunlop Pneumatic Tyre Co., Ltd. v. Selfridge & Co., Ltd., [1915] A.C. 847; [1914–15] All E.R. Rep. 333	29, 152, 161, 162

E

Ebbw Vale Steel Co. v. Blaina Iron Co. (1901), 6 Com. Cas. 43, C.A.	187
Eccles v. Bryant and Pollock, [1948] Ch. 93; [1947] 2 All E.R. 865	11
Edgington v. Fitzmaurice (1885), 29 Ch.D. 459; [1881–85] All E.R. Rep. 856	93
Edwards v. Carter, [1893] A.C. 360; [1891–4] All E.R. Rep. 1259	114, 115
Ehrman v. Bartholomew, [1898] 1 Ch. 671	224
Ellen v. Topp (1851), 6 Ex. 424	194
Ellesmere v. Wallace, [1929] 2 Ch. 1	134

TABLE OF CASES

PAGE

Entores, Ltd. v. Miles Far East Corporation, [1955] 2 Q.B. 327; [1955] 2 All E.R. 493 15
Errington v. Errington and Woods, [1952] 1 K.B. 290 . . 5, *16*
Esso Petroleum, Ltd. v. Harper's Garage, Ltd., [1968] A.C. 269; [1967] 1 All E.R. 699 . . . . *143*, 144

F

F.M.C. (Meat) v. Fairfield Cold Stores, [1971] 2 Lloyd's Rep. 221 44
Felthouse v. Bindley (1863), 11 C.B. (N.S.) 869; (1863) 1 New Rep. 401 . . . . *13*, 14
Fibrosa Spolka Akcyjna v. Fairbairn Lawson Combe Barbour, Ltd., [1943] A.C. 32; [1942] 2 All E.R. 122 . . *202, 203*, 232
Fisher v. Bell, [1961] 1 Q.B. 394; [1960] 3 All E.R. 731 . . *6*
Fisher v. Bridges (1854), 3 E. & B. 642 . . . . . *129*
Fitch v. Dewes, [1921] 2 A.C. 158; [1921] All E.R. Rep. 13 *140,* 141
Foakes v. Beer (1884), 9 App. Cas. 605 32
Foley v. Classique Coaches Ltd., [1934] K.B. 1; [1934] All E.R. Rep. 88 40
Ford Motor Co. Ltd. v. A.E.E.F.U. & T.G.W.A. [1969] 2 All E.R. 481 23
Foster v. Driscoll, [1929] 1 K.B. 470; [1928] All E.R. Rep. 130 . *128*
Foster v. Mackinnon (1869), L.R. 4 C.P. 704 . . . . *80*
Frederick E. Rose, Ltd. v. Wm. H. Pim & Co., Ltd., [1953] 2 Q.B. 450; [1953] 2 All E.R. 739 . . . . *85*

G

Galloway v. Galloway (1914), 30 T.L.R. 531 . . . *72, 73*
Gaussen v. Morton (1830), 8 L.J. (O.S.) K.B. 313 . . . *184*
General Billposting Co., Ltd. v. Atkinson, [1909] A.C. 118; [1908–10] All E.R. Rep. 619 . . . . . *195, 196*
Glasbrook Bros. v. Glamorgan C.C., [1925] A.C. 270; [1924] All E.R. Rep. 579 27
Goodyear Tyre and Rubber Co., Ltd. v. Lancashire Batteries, Ltd., [1958] 3 All E.R. 7 . . . . 164, 165
Gordon v. Gordon (1821), 3 Swan. 400 100
Great Northern Railway v. Witham (1873), L.R. 9 C.P. 16 . *12*
Greenwood v. Greenwood (1863), 2 De G.J. & Sm. 28 . . 100
Grist v. Bailey, [1966] 2 All E.R. 875 . . . . . *83, 84*
Guthing v. Lynn (1831), 2 B. & Ad. 232 5

H

Hadley v. Baxendale (1854), 9 Ex. 341 . . *209, 210*, 213, 214
Hands v. Simpson, Fawcett & Co., Ltd. (1928), 44 T.L.R. 295 . *99*
Harbutt's Plasticine, Ltd. v. Wayne Tank Co., Ltd. [1970] 1 Q.B. 447; [1970] 1 All E.R. 225 . . *46, 48, 49, 193*, 212
Harris v. Nickerson (1873), L.R. 8 Q.B. 286 . . . . *6*
Harrison & Jones, Ltd. v. Bunton and Lancaster, Ltd., [1953] 1 Q.B. 646; [1953] 1 All E.R. 903 70
Hartley v. Ponsonby (1857), 7 E. & B. 872 27

TABLE OF CASES

xv

	PAGE
Hartog v. Colin & Shields, [1939] 3 All E.R. 566	78
Harvey v. Facey, [1893] A.C. 552	6
Head v. Tattersall (1871), L.R. 7 Ex. Ch. 7	192
Hedley Byrne & Co., Ltd. v. Heller & Partners, Ltd., [1964] A.C. 465; [1963] 2 All E.R. 575	98
Heilbut, Symons & Co. v. Buckleton, [1913] A.C. 30; [1911–13] All E.R. Rep. 83	38, 39
Henthorn v. Fraser, [1892] 2 Ch. 27; [1891–84] All E.R. Rep. 908	14
Herman v. Jeuchner (1885), 15 Q.B.D. 561	128
Hermann v. Charlesworth, [1905] 2 K.B. 123	145
Herne Bay Steamboat Co. v. Hutton, [1903] 2 K.B. 683; [1900–3] All E.R. Rep. 627	200, 202
Heron II, The [1967] 2 Lloyd's Rep. 457; [1967] 3 All E.R. 686	213, 14
Heskell v. Continental Express, Ltd., [1950] 1 All E.R. 1033	213
Higgins, Ltd. v. Northampton Corporation, [1927] 1 Ch. 128	86
Hillas & Co., Ltd. v. Arcos, Ltd., [1932] All E.R. Rep. 494	31, 50
Hirachand Punamchand v. Temple, [1911] 2 K.B. 330	32
Hoenig v. Isaacs, [1952] 2 All E.R. 176	87, 188
Holland v. Manchester & Liverpool District Banking Co. (1909), T.L.R. 386	98
Holman v. Johnson (1775), 1 Cowp. 341	123
Holt v. Markham, [1923] 1 K.B. 504; [1922] All E.R. Rep. 134	233
Holwell Securities v. Hughes, [1973] 2 All E.R. 476	15, 16
Home Counties Dairies v. Skilton, [1971] 1 W.L.R. 526; [1970] 1 All E.R. 1227	141, 142
Hong Kong Fir Shipping Co., Ltd. v. Kawasaki Kisen Kaisha, Ltd., [1962] 2 Q.B. 26; [1962] 1 All E.R. 474	59, 60, 61, 94, 195
Hood v. West End Motor Car Packing Co., [1917] 2 K.B. 38	100
Household Fire Insurance Co. v. Grant (1879), 4 Ex.D. 216	14
Howard v. Pickford Tool Co., [1951] 1 K.B. 417	193
Howatson v. Webb, [1908] 1 Ch 1	81
Hughes v. Liverpool, etc., Friendly Society, [1916] 2 K.B. 482; [1916–17] All E.R. Rep. 819	130
Humble v. Hunter (1848), 12 Q.B. 310	180
Hutton v. Warren (1836), 1 M. & W. 466	49
Hyde v. Wrench (1840), 3 Beav. 334	9, 19

I

Imperial Loan Co. v. Stone, [1892] 1 Q.B. 599; [1891–4] All E.R. Rep. 412	119
Inche Noriah v. Shaik Alli Bin Omar, [1929] A.C. 127; [1928] All E.R. Rep. 189	106, 107
Ingram v. Little, [1961] 1 Q.B. 31; [1960] 3 All E.R. 332	73, 74, 75, 76, 77
Ionides v. Pender (1874), L.R. 9 Q.B. 531	100
Ireland v. Livingstone, (1872), L.R. 5 H.L. 395	81

J

Jarvis v. Swan Tours, Ltd., [1973] 3 W.L.R. 945; [1973] 1 All E.R. 71	215
Jocelyne v. Nissen, [1970] 1 All E.R. 1213	86
Jones v. Padavatton, [1969] 1 W.L.R. 328; [1969] 2 All E.R. 616	23

TABLE OF CASES

PAGE

Jordan v. Norton (1838), 7 L.J. Ex. 281 19
Joseph Constantine S.S. Line, Ltd. v. Imperial Smelting Corporation, Ltd., [1942] A.C. 154; [1941] 2 All E.R. 165 . . *198*

K

Karsales (Harrow), Ltd. v. Wallis, [1956] 2 All E.R. 866 . *45, 46*
Kaufman v. Gerson, [1904] 1 K.B. 591; [1904–7] All E.R. Rep. 896 *104*
Kearley v. Thomson (1890), 24 Q.B.D. 742; [1886–90] All E.R.
   Rep. 1055 . . . . *128, 129*
Keighley, Maxsted & Co. v. Durant, [1901] A.C. 240; [1900–3] All
   E.R. Rep. 40 180
Kenyon, Son & Craven v. Baxter Hoare, [1971] 2 All E.R. 708 . 46
Keppel v. Wheeler, [1927] 1 K.B. 577; [1926] All E.R. Rep. 207. 181
Kier & Co., Ltd. v. Whitehead Iron and Steel Co., Ltd., [1938] 1
   All E.R. 591 12
King's Norton Metal Co. v. Eldridge, Merrett & Co. (1897), 14
   T.L.R. 98 77
Knox v. Gye (1872), L.R. 5 H.L. 656 227
Koufos v. Czarnikow, [1967] 2 Lloyd's Rep. 457; [1967] 2 All E.R.
   686 . . . . *213*
Krell v. Henry, [1903] 2 K.B. 740; [1900–3] All E.R. Rep. 20 200, *201*

L

Lagunas Nitrate Co., Ltd. v. Lagunas Syndicate, Ltd., [1899] 2
   Ch. 392 . . . . *96, 97*
Lamb v. Evans, [1893] 1 Ch. 218 181
Lancashire Loans, Ltd. v. Black, [1934] 1 K.B. 380; [1933] All
   E.R. Rep. 201 . . . . *107*
Lancaster v. Walsh (1838), 4 M. & W. 16 . . . . . *14*
Larner v. L.C.C., [1949] 2 K.B. 683; [1949] 1 All E.R. 964 . *233*
Leaf v. International Galleries, [1950] 2 K.B. 86; [1950] 1 All
   E.R. 693 . . . . *96*, 97, 227
Lee v. Showmen's Guild, [1952] 2 Q.B. 329; [1952] 1 All E.R. 1175 137
Lemprière v. Lange (1879), 12 Ch. D 675 113
Leslie v. Sheill, [1914] 3 K.B. 607; [1914–15] All E.R. Rep.
   511 . . . . *110, 111*, 113
L'Estrange v. Graucob, Ltd., [1934] 2 K.B. 394; [1943] All E.R.
   Rep. 16 . . . . *42, 44*, 78
Lewis v. Averay, [1972] 1 Q.B. 198; [1971] 3 All E.R. 907 *75, 76*
Locker and Woolf, Ltd. v. Western Australian Insurance Co., Ltd.,
   [1936] 1 K.B. 408 100
Lord Strathcona S.S. Co. v. Dominion Coal Co., [1926] A.C. 108 166
Lumley v. Wagner (1852), 21 L.J.Ch. 898 . . . 223, 224
Luxor (Eastbourne), Ltd. v. Cooper, [1941] A.C. 108; [1941] 1
   All E.R. 33 51

M

M'Kinnell v. Robinson (1838), 3 M. & W. 434 136
McCutcheon v. MacBrayne, Ltd., [1964] 1 All E.R. 430 . *42, 43*, 44
Macpherson Train & Co., Ltd. v. Howard Ross & Co., Ltd., [1955]
   2 All E. R. 455 . . . . *53*

TABLE OF CASES

McRae v. Commonwealth Disposals Commission, [1951] 84 C.L.R. 377 . . . . 71, 72
Maredelanto Compania Naviera v. Bergbau-Handel G.m.b.H., [1970] 3 All E.R. 125 . . . . . 160, 207, 212
Maritime National Fish, Ltd. v. Ocean Trawlers, Ltd., [1935] A.C. 524; [1935] All E.R. Rep. 86 198
Martin v. Gale (1876), 4 Ch.D. 428 117
Mason v. Provident Clothing and Supply Co., [1913] A.C. 724; [1911–13] All E.R. Rep. 400 139
Mercantile Union Guarantee Corporation, Ltd. v. Ball, [1937] 2 K.B. 498; [1937] 2 All E.R. 1 117
Mihalis Angelos, *see* Maredelanto Compania, etc.
Miller's Agreement, *Re*, Uniacke v. A.-G., [1947] Ch. 417; [1947] 2 All E.R. 78 164
Milner & Son v. Bilton, Ltd., [1966] 2 All E.R. 894 . . 22
Moorcock, The (1889), 14 P.D. 64 . . . . . 50, 51
Moore & Co. and Landauer & Co., *Re*, [1921] 2 K.B. 519; [1921] All E.R. Rep. 466 53
Morris, Ltd. v. Saxelby, [1916] 1 A.C. 688; [1916–17] All E.R. Rep. 305 . . . . 139, 140
Muskham Finance, Ltd. v. Howard, [1963] 1 All E.R. 81 . 80

N

Napier v. National Business Agency, Ltd., [1951] 2 All E.R. 264 125, 128
Nash v. Inman, [1908] 2 K.B. 1; [1908–10] All E.R. Rep. 317 116, 117
National Savings Bank Association, *Re* (1867), L.R. 4 Eq. 9 . 17
Nelson v. Larholt, [1948] 1 K.B. 232
Nicolene, Ltd. v. Simmonds, [1953] 1 Q.B. 543; [1953] 1 All E.R. 822 40
Nordenfelt v. Maxim Nordenfelt Co., Ltd., [1894] A.C. 535; [1891–4] All E.R. Rep. 1 . . . . . . 138, 142
Northcote v. Doughty (1879), 4 C.P.D. 385 118

O

Olley v. Marlborough Court Hotel, Ltd., [1949] 1 K.B. 532; [1949] 1 All E.R. 127 . . . . 41, 44
Overstone, Ltd. v. Shipway, [1962] 1 All E.R. 52 . . 219, 220

P

Paradine v. Jane (1648), Aleyn 26 197
Parker v. S.E. Railway Co. (1877), 2 C.P.D. 416 . . . 41
Parkinson v. College of Ambulance, Ltd., [1925] 2 K.B. 1; [1924] All E.R. Rep. 325 . . . . 128, 129
Payne v. Cave (1789), 3 T.R. 148 17
Pearce v. Brain, [1929] 2 K.B. 310; [1929] All E.R. Rep. 627 . 111
Pearce v. Brooks (1866), L.R. 1 Ex. 213 . . . 127, 128, 130
Percival, Ltd. v. L.C.C. (1918), 87 L.J.K.B. 677 . . . 12
Peters v. Fleming (1840), 6 M. & W. 42 115
Pharmaceutical Society of G.B. v. Boots Cash Chemists, Ltd., [1953] 1 Q.B. 401; [1953] 1 All E.R. 482 . . . 6, 50

TABLE OF CASES

	PAGE
Phillips v. Brooks, Ltd., [1919] 2 K.B. 243; [1918–19] All E.R. Rep. 246	74, 75, 76, 77
Phonographic Equipment, Ltd. v. Muslu, [1961] 3 All E.R. 626	218
Pinnel's Case (1602), 5 Co. Rep. 117a	32, 190
Planché v. Colburn (1831), 8 Bing. 14	221
Pollard v. Clayton (1855), 1 K. & J. 462	228
Poussard v. Spiers and Pond (1876), 1 Q.B.D. 410	59
Powell v. Lee (1908), 99 L.T. 284	8
Prager v. Blatspiel, Stamp and Heacock, Ltd., [1924] 1 K.B. 566; [1924] All E.R. Rep. 524	177
Prenn v. Simmonds, [1971] 3 All E.R. 237	2, 38
Price v. Easton (1833), 4 B. & Ad. 433	29
Priest v. Last, [1903] 2 K.B. 148	54
Pym v. Campbell (1856), 6 E. & B. 370	192

Q

Quenerduaine v. Cole (1883), 32 W.R. 185	15

R

Raffles v. Wichelhaus (1864), 2 H. & C. 906	73
Ramsgate Victoria Hotel Co. v. Montefiore (1866), L.R. 1 Ex. 109	18
Rawlinson v. Ames, [1925] 1 Ch. 96	158
Robb v. Green, [1895] 2 Q.B. 315	139
Roberts v. Gray, [1913] 1 K.B. 520; [1911–13] All E.R. Rep. 870	117
Robinson v. Davison (1871), L.R. 6 Ex. 269	200, 201
Robinson, Re, McLaren v. Public Trustee, [1911] 1 Ch. 502; [1911–13] All E.R. Rep. 296	227
Robson and Sharpe v. Drummond (1831), 2 B. & Ad. 303	171, 172
Roscorla v. Thomas (1842), 3 Q.B. 234	30
Rose and Frank Co. v. Crompton Bros., Ltd., [1925] A.C. 445; [1924] All E.R. Rep. 245	22
Routledge v. Mckay, [1954] 1 All E.R. 855	38, 92
Rowland v. Divall, [1923] 2 K.B. 500; [1923] All E.R. Rep. 270	52

S

St. John Shipping Corporation v. Joseph Rank Ltd., [1956] 3 All E.R. 683	131
Sajan Singh v. Sadara Ali, [1960] 1 All E.R. 269	130
Samuels v. Davis, [1943] 2 All E.R. 3	58
Saunders v. Anglia Building Society, [1971] A.C. 1004; [1970] 3 All E.R. 961	78, 79, 81, 82
Scammell and Nephew v. Ouston, [1941] A.C. 251; [1941] 1 All E.R. 14	5, 31, 39
Schuler v Wickman Machine Tool Sales, Ltd., [1973] 2 All E.R. 39	58
Schweppes, Ltd.'s Agreement, Re, [1965] 1 All E.R. 195	146
Scotson v. Pegg (1861), 6 H. & N. 295	28
Scriven v. Hindley, [1913] 3 K.B. 564	73
Scruttons, Ltd. v. Midland Silicones, Ltd., [1962] A.C. 446; [1962] 1 All E.R. 1	161

TABLE OF CASES

	PAGE
Seddon v. N.E. Salt Co., Ltd., [1905] 1 Ch. 326	95
Shadwell v. Shadwell (1860), 9 C.B. (N.S.) 159	28
Silver v. Ocean Steamship Co., [1930] 1 K.B. 416; [1929] All E.R. Rep. 611	97, 98
Simpkins v. Pays, [1955] 3 All E.R. 10	23
Sinclair's Life Policy, Re, [1938] Ch. 799: [1938] 3 All E.R. 124	164
Snelling v. John G. Snelling, Ltd. [1972] 1 All E.R. 79	162
Solle v. Butcher, [1950] 1 K.B. 671; [1949] 2 All E.R. 1107	70, 83
Spiro v. Lintern, [1973] 1 W.L.R. 1002	176
Springer v. Great Western Railway, [1921] 1 K.B. 257; [1920] All E.R. Rep. 361	177
Spurling, Ltd. v. Bradshaw,]1956] 2 All E.R. 121	42, 44
Starkey v Bank of England, [1903] A.C. 114	182
Steinberg v. Scala (Leeds), Ltd., [1923] 2 Ch. 452; [1923] All E.R. Rep. 239	115
Steven & Co. v. Bromley & Son, [1919] 2 K.B. 722	220, 221
Stevenson v. McLean (1880), 5 Q.B.D. 346	9, 19
Stilk v. Myrick (1809), 2 Camp. 317.	27
Stocks v. Wilson, [1913] 2 K.B. 235	111, 113
Strathcona Case, see Lord Strathcona S.S. Co. v. Dominion Coal Co.	
Strickland v. Turner (1852), 7 Exch. 208	73
Suisse Atlantique Société v. N.V.R. Kolen Centrale, [1966] 2 All E.R. 61	44, 45, 46, 47, 48
Sumpter v. Hedges, [1898] 1 Q.B. 673	186, 221

T

Tamplin v. James (1880), 15 Ch.D. 215	84
Tate v. Williamson (1866), 2 Ch.App. 55	101
Taylor v. Caldwell (1863), 3 B. & S. 826	199, 200
Taylor v. Laird (1856), 25 L.J.Ex. 329	7
Thomas v. Brown (1876), 1 Q.B.D. 714	157
Thoroughgood's Case (1584), 2 Co. Rep. 9	80
Tool Metal Manufacturing Co., Ltd. v. Tungsten Electric Co., Ltd., [1955] 2 All E.R. 657	33
Torkington v. Magee, [1903] 1 K.B. 644; [1900–3] All E.R. Rep. 991	168
Trollope & Colls, Ltd. v. N.W. Regional Hospital Bd., [1973] 2 All E.R. 260	49
Trueman v. Loder (1840), 9 L.J.Q.B. 165	176, 177, 184
Tsakiroglou & Co., Ltd. v. Noblee Thorl, G.m.b.H., [1962] A.C. 93; [1961] 2 All E.R. 179	198
Tweddle v. Atkinson (1861), 1 B. & S. 393	161, 164

U

U.G.S. Finance, Ltd. v. National Mortgage Bank of Greece and National Bank of Greece, S.A., [1964] 1 Lloyd's Rep. 446	45
Universal Steam Navigation Co. v. McKelvie, [1923] A.C. 492	179
Upton R.D.C. v. Powell, [1942] 1 All E.R. 220	220

TABLE OF CASES

V
PAGE

Valentini v. Canali (1889), 24 Q.B.D. 166 . . 111, *112*, 113
Victoria Laundry, Ltd. v. Newman Industries, Ltd., [1949] 2 K.B.
   528; [1949] 1 All E.R. 997 . . . . *210, 211, 212, 213*

W

Ward v. Byham, [1956] 2 All E.R. 318 . . . . *28*
Warner Bros. Pictures Inc. v. Nelson, [1937] 1 K.B. 209; [1936]
   3 All E.R. 160 . . . . *225*
Webster v. Cecil (1861), 3 Beav. 62 . . . . *84*
West London Commerical Bank v. Kitson (1884), 13 Q.B.D. 360   91
Whelan, *Re*, (1897), 1 I.R. 575 . . . . . *19*
White v. Bluett (1853), L.J.Ex. 36 . . . . *5, 31*
White v. Garden (1851), 10 C.B. 919 . . . . *96*
White and Carter, Ltd. v. McGregor, [1962] A.C. 413; [1961] 3 All
   E.R. 1178 . . . . . *193*, 194, 207, 216
Whittington v. Seale-Hayne (1900), 82 L.T. 49 . . *94, 95*, 96
Wilensko Slaski, etc. v. Fenwick & Co., Ltd., [1938] 3 All E.R.
   429 . . . . *53*, 188
Wilkinson v. Lloyd (1845), 7 Q.B. 27 . . . . *233*
William Lacey, Ltd. v. Davis, [1957] 2 All E.R. 712 . . *234*
William Robinson & Co., Ltd. v. Heuer, [1898] 2 Ch. 451 . *225*
Williams v. Bayley (1866), L.R. 1 H.L. 200 . . . *107*
Williams v. Carwardine (1833), 4 B. & Ad. 621 . . *8*
Williams v. Greatrex, [1956] 3 All E.R. 705 . . . *228*
Wilson v. Rickett Cockerell & Co., Ltd., [1954] 1 Q.B. 598; [1954]
   1 All E.R. 868 . . . . *54*
With v. O'Flanagan, [1936] 1 Ch. 575; [1936] 1 All E.R. 727 . *99*
Wren v. Holt, [1903] 1 K.B. 610 . . . . . *54*

Y

Yeoman Credit, Ltd. v. Latter, [1961] 2 All E.R. 294 . *111, 112*
Yeoman Credit, Ltd. v. Waragowski, [1961] 3 All E.R. 145 . *219*
Yonge v. Toynbee, [1910] 1 K.B. 215; [1908–10] All E.R. Rep. 204 *182*
Young & Marten v. McManus Childs, Ltd., [1968] 2 All E.R. 1169   *57*

CHAPTER I

INTRODUCTORY

1. Simple contracts. A contract is made where parties have reached agreement, or where they are deemed to have reached agreement, and the law recognises rights and obligations arising from the agreement. Almost all contracts are simple contracts, as distinguished from specialty contracts, *i.e.* contracts made under seal. Any general study of the law of contract must be concerned almost entirely with simple contracts.

2. Essential elements. There are three fundamental elements in any simple contract. They are:

(a) *Agreement:* the parties must have reached, or be deemed to have reached, agreement.
(b) *Intention:* the parties must have intended, or be deemed to have intended, to create legal relations.
(c) *Consideration:* according to the terms of the agreement, some advantage moves from one party to the other. The giving of mutual advantages by the parties is the essence of a bargain. Any advantage or benefit moving from one party to another is known as consideration.

In any transaction where one of these elements is missing there is no contract.

3. Manner of agreement. An agreement may be made in any manner whatsoever, provided the parties are in communication. An agreement may be made

(a) in writing, or
(b) by word of mouth, or
(c) by inference from the conduct of the parties and the circumstances of the case, or
(d) by any combination of the above modes.

4. The test of agreement. Adequate tests are necessary to enable the court to decide cases involving dispute:

1

(a) as to whether agreement was reached at all, or
(b) as to the extent of the agreement, *i.e.* the terms of the agreement.

In both issues the intention of the parties is paramount. The function of contract law is, largely, to develop principles which may be used towards the settlement of such disputes.

5. Intention and agreement. The intention of the parties is gathered from the express terms of contract. Also, where necessary, the conduct of the parties is taken into account, for much can be inferred from conduct. The court is not concerned with the inward mental intent of the parties, but rather, with what a reasonable man would say was the intention of the parties, having regard to all the circumstances. Wherever necessary, the court will infer terms to give effect to the presumed intentions of the parties. Notice that the presumed intention may or may not be the same as the actual intention. It must follow that when we speak of "agreement" in contract, we include the notional agreement which the parties may be deemed to have reached.

It has been held by the House of Lords that in construing the written terms of a contract, evidence of the preceding negotiations is not admissible, nor is evidence of the parties' intentions during negotiations: *Prenn* v. *Simmonds* (1971).

6. Offer and acceptance. In order to discover whether agreement was reached between the parties, it is usual to analyse the negotiations into offer and acceptance. Many negotiations are too complicated to lend themselves to an easy analysis of this kind, but the courts will try to discover whether, at any time, one party can be said to have accepted the firm offer of the other.

7. Rights and obligations. Where parties have made a binding contract, they have created rights and obligations between themselves. The contractual rights and obligations are correlative, *e.g.* X agrees with Y to sell his car for £500 to Y. In this example, the following rights and obligations have been created:

(a) X is under an obligation to deliver his car to Y: Y has a correlative right to receive the car.

I. INTRODUCTORY 3

(b) Y is under an obligation to pay £500 to X: X has a correlative right to receive the £500.

8. Breach of contract. Where a party neglects or refuses to honour a contractual obligation, there is a breach of contract. A breach by one party causes a right of action to accrue to the other party.

The usual remedy for breach of contract is damages, *i.e.* the award of a sum of money to put the aggrieved party in the position he would have enjoyed had the contract not been broken. The sum is paid, of course, by the contract-breaker following the award of the court. In certain special circumstances, the court may order the contract-breaker to carry out his contractual promise specifically. This is known as the equitable remedy of *specific performance*. Specific performance is never awarded where damages will suffice.

9. Specialty contracts. The terms of some contracts are embodied in a document which is then signed, sealed and delivered by the parties. This is the most solemn formality of contract-making known to English law. The most important practical difference between simple contracts and specialty contracts is that the period of limitation is six years and twelve years respectively. The period of limitation is the period of time in which an action for breach of contract may be brought. The *Limitation Act*, 1939, provides that an action upon a specialty contract cannot be brought after the expiration of twelve years from the date on which the cause of action accrued, *i.e.* the date of the breach of contract (*see* XVIII, 28). A promise given under seal does not need to be supported by consideration.

PROGRESS TEST 1

1. What are the three fundamental elements of a valid simple contract?
2. "An agreement may be made in any manner whatsoever, provided the parties are in communication." Explain this statement.
3. How do the courts discover the "intention" of the parties?
4. Do you think it possible that contracting parties might be deemed to have reached an agreement which is different from the one they thought they reached?

4 THE LAW OF CONTRACT

5. Make up an example to illustrate the correlative nature of rights and obligations arising from a contract.

6. What do you understand by the expression "breach of contract"?

7. A and B make an agreement to the effect that A shall pay the sum of £50 to B by way of gift, payment to be made one month after the date of the agreement. A now refuses to pay anything to B. Has B a right of action against A? Would your answer be different if the agreement had been made under seal?

8. Distinguish between simple contracts and specialties.

CHAPTER II

OFFER AND ACCEPTANCE

THE OFFER MUST BE DEFINITE

1. The terms must be certain. The offer is an undertaking by the offeror to be contractually bound in the event of a proper acceptance being made. The offer must, therefore, be clear, complete, and final.

White v. *Bluett* (1853): a father promised to release his son from an obligation to pay on a promissory note if the son would cease from complaining. HELD: there was no enforceable contract because the son's promise was too vague.

Guthing v. *Lynn* (1831): L bought a horse from G on the terms that "if the horse was lucky to him he would give five pounds more." HELD: too vague to be binding.

Scammell v. *Ouston* (1941): O ordered a motor van from S "on the understanding that the balance of the purchase price can be had on hire purchase terms over a period of two years." HELD by the House of Lords: the order (*i.e.* the offer) was so vague that it had no definite meaning. Further negotiations would be required before agreement could be reached.

2. Bilateral and unilateral contracts. An offer may be regarded as a proposal to make a contract. There are two kinds of offer. First, the proposal may call for an acceptance in the form of an unqualified promise to perform according to the terms contained in the offer. The acceptance of this kind of offer leads to the most usual kind of contract, generally known as the bilateral contract. Secondly, the offeror's proposal may be in terms which call for an act to be performed, *e.g.* the return of specific lost property. A unilateral contract is made upon performance according to the terms of the offer. See *Carlill* v. *Carbolic Smoke Ball Co.* (1892); *Errington* v. *Errington and Woods* (1952).

3. An invitation to treat is not an offer. An offer must be distinguished from a mere invitation to treat. An invitation to treat is a first step in negotiations which may, or may not, be a prelude to a firm offer by one of the parties.

Harris v. *Nickerson* (1873): N, an auctioneer, advertised that he would sell certain goods, including office furniture, on a specified date. H attended the sale with the intention of buying some office furniture. N withdrew the office furniture from the sale. H claimed damages for breach of contract, contending that the advertisement was an offer which he had accepted by attending the sale. HELD: the advertisement was a mere statement of intention amounting to an invitation to treat.

Fisher v. *Bell* (1960), an appeal by way of case stated: B displayed in his shop window a flick-knife behind which was a ticket bearing the words, "Ejector knife—4s." He was charged with offering for sale a flick-knife, contrary to the provisions of the *Restriction of Offensive Weapons Act*, 1959. HELD: the displaying of the flick-knife was merely an invitation to treat.

Pharmaceutical Society etc. v. *Boots etc.* (1953): the B company operated a self-service shop in which certain drugs specified under the *Pharmacy and Poisons Act*, 1933, were displayed with prices attached. The P society contended that the sales of the listed poisons took place when the customers took the goods from the shelves and put them in the wire baskets provided, and that, accordingly, the sales took place otherwise than "under the supervision of a registered pharmacist" as required by the *Pharmacy and Poisons Act*. HELD by the Court of Appeal: the display of goods on the shelves was an invitation to treat. An offer was made by the customer when he presented the goods at the cash desk. The customer's offer could be accepted or rejected by the pharmacist whose duty it was to supervise transactions at the cash desk.

4. A mere statement of price is not an offer. A mere statement of price will not be construed as an offer to sell.

Harvey v. *Facey* (1893): the following telegraph messages passed between the parties:
H: "Will you sell us Bumper Hall Pen? Telegraph lowest cash price."
F: "Lowest cash price for Bumper Hall Pen £900."
H: "We agree to buy Bumper Hall Pen for £900 asked by you."
There was no reply to the last message. H claimed that there was a contract. HELD by the Privy Council: "Lowest cash price for Bumper Hall Pen £900" was not an offer: it was merely a statement of the lowest price in the event of a decision to sell. The last message could not, therefore, be regarded as an acceptance.

II. OFFER AND ACCEPTANCE

Although an agreement on price alone does not constitute an agreement for sale and purchase, nevertheless, such an agreement may constitute an element in a contract subsequently to be concluded.

Bigg v. *Boyd Gibbins, Ltd.* (1971) C.A.: the parties were negotiating for the sale of certain freehold property. During the course of dealings the plaintiffs wrote to the defendants saying, "As you are aware that I paid £25,000 for this property, your offer of £20,000 would appear to be at least a little optimistic. For a quick sale I would accept £26,000 . . ." The defendants replied, "I accept your offer." In their reply, the defendants asked the plaintiffs to contact their (the defendants') solicitors. The plaintiffs then wrote: "I am putting the matter in the hands of my solicitors. My wife and I are both pleased that you are purchasing the property." On the question whether a contract had been formed, HELD: the plaintiffs' first letter constituted an offer which was accepted by the defendants, thus making a binding contract.

COMMUNICATION OF THE OFFER

5. Manner of communication. An offer may be communicated in any manner whatsoever. Express words may be used, orally or in writing, or an offer may be implied from conduct. An offer may be partly expressed and partly implied.

6. Necessity of communication. An offer has no validity unless and until it is communicated to the offeree so as to give the opportunity to accept or reject.

Taylor v. *Laird* (1856): T threw up the command of L's ship during the course of a voyage. T then helped to work the ship home. He claimed to be paid for this work. HELD: since T had not communicated his offer to do the work so as to give L the opportunity to accept or reject the offer, there was no contract.

7. Communication may be particular or general. An offer may be communicated to a particular person or group of persons; or it may be communicated generally to the whole world.

(*a*) Where an offer is made to a particular person or group of persons, no valid acceptance may be made by a person who is not an offeree.

Boulton v. *Jones* (1857): the plaintiff had been manager for one Brocklehurst, with whom the defendant had a running account. The plaintiff bought and paid for Brocklehurst's business and, immediately afterwards, a written order was received from the defendant, addressed to Brocklehurst. The goods were supplied to the defendant and the plaintiff's book-keeper struck out Brocklehurst's name on the order, inserting the plaintiff's. When the plaintiff sent an invoice to the defendant, he said that he knew nothing of him and refused to pay him. The plaintiff brought this action for the price of goods sold. HELD: there was no contract because the offer made by the defendant was not addressed to the plaintiff who, therefore, could not accept it. *Per* Pollock, C.B.: "The point raised is, whether the facts proved did not show an intention on the part of the defendants to deal with Brocklehurst. The plaintiff, who succeeded Brocklehurst in business, executed the order without any intimation of the change that had taken place, and brought this action to recover the price of the goods supplied. It is a rule of law, that if a person intends to contract with A, B cannot give himself any right under it. Here the order in writing was given to Brocklehurst. Possibly Brocklehurst might have adopted the act of the plaintiff in supplying the goods, and maintained an action for their price. But since the plaintiff has chosen to sue, the only course the defendants could take was to plead that there was no contract with him."

Powell v. *Lee* (1908): P had applied to a committee of school managers for the post of headmaster of a school. The committee decided to appoint P, but did not inform him of the decision. One of their number, without authorisation, informed P that he had been selected. The committee then had a change of mind and selected another person. P contended that there was a breach of contract. HELD: there was no contract because the committee had not accepted P's offer. The purported acceptance made without authority was not binding on the committee.

(*b*) Where an offer is made generally to the world at large, a valid acceptance may be made by any person with notice of the offer: *Carlill* v. *Carbolic Smoke Ball Co.* (1892). It seems that an acceptance is valid even though made for a motive which is quite unconnected with the terms of the offer: *Williams* v. *Carwardine*. But it is essential that the person accepting the offer had notice of the offer.

II. OFFER AND ACCEPTANCE

ACCEPTANCE MUST BE UNQUALIFIED

8. Unreserved assent. Acceptance must be unqualified and must correspond exactly with the terms of the offer. Not all transactions lend themselves to an easy analysis into "offer" and "acceptance," yet the court will always examine the communications between the parties to discover whether, at any time, one party may be deemed to have assented to all the terms, express and implied, of a firm offer by the other party. An assent which is qualified in any way does not take effect as an acceptance. For example, where goods are offered at a certain price, an assent coupled with a promise to pay by instalments is not an acceptance.

9. A counter-offer operates as a rejection. Where an offeree makes a counter-offer, the original offer is deemed to have been rejected and cannot be subsequently accepted.

Hyde v. *Wrench* (1840): On 6th June, W offered H a farm for £1000: H made a counter-offer of £950. On 27th June, W rejected the counter-offer. On 29th June, H made a purported acceptance of the offer of 6th June. HELD: the counter-offer operated as a rejection of the original offer. No contract.

NOTE: a mere request for further information must be distinguished from a counter-offer. Such a request does not operate as a rejection of an offer: *Stevenson* v. *McLean* (1880).

Where a counter-offer is accepted, then its terms, and not the terms of the original offer, become the terms of the contract.

Davies & Co. v. *William Old* (1969): in April 1964 the defendants entered into a building contract with employers (not parties to this action) in the R.I.B.A. standard form of contract. In May 1965 the architect as agent for the employers, invited the plaintiffs to tender for certain sub-contract works and the plaintiffs tendered. The architect, as agent for the employers, gave written instructions to the defendants to enter into a sub-contract with the nominated sub-contractors, *i.e.* the plaintiffs for the shopfitting work. The defendants thereupon sent to the plaintiffs their own standard form of order, instructing them to carry out the sub-contract works according to their tender. At the bottom of the order form, it was stated that the order was subject to the conditions overleaf. On the other side of the form were certain conditions, number 8 of which provided that the contractor (*i.e.* the defendants) should from time to time apply under the main contract for certificates of payment to include the amount for the sub-contract work, but that the main contractor would be under no liability to pay the sub-contractor for his work until it had been approved and paid for by the employer under the main contract. The plaintiffs accepted the order by letter dated 15th June and work was done for which the plaintiff received payments. On 2nd November the architect certified £307 8s. to be due but the defendant failed to pay this sum to the plaintiffs. The plaintiffs brought this action against the main contractor contending that the failure to pay the sum certified was a breach of the sub-contract. HELD: the conditions on the back of the order form were binding and the main contractor was under no liability to pay the sub-contractor until he (the main contractor) was paid by the employers. *Per* Blain, J.: "The problem is to define the sub-contract itself. The architect was not the agent of the defendant in nominating the sub-contractors. The tender when received by the architect constituted an offer by the plaintiffs. The defendants had done what was reasonable to bring the conditions or the existence of the conditions to the notice of the plaintiffs. The general principle is that in case of doubt and where words of a contract are in conflict, greater force is to be given to words selected by the parties to express their intent than to general words of a *pro forma* nature, but for that doctrine to apply the words selected by the parties had to be selected to show a mutual intent. The conditions in the order varied or modified the terms of the tender, and so the order was not an unqualified acceptance of the offer comprised in the tender but was a counter-offer. That was accepted by the plaintiffs' letter dated 15th June either by itself or together with the carrying out of the work. The conditions were incorporated in the sub-contract, and since the defendants had not received from the employer the sums claimed, they were not liable to pay them to the plaintiffs."

10. Tentative assent. Acceptance "subject to contract" is not binding. In sale of land, it is usual to express tentative preliminary agreements to be "subject to contract," so as to give the parties an opportunity to reflect or to seek legal or other advice before entering a binding contract. The expression "subject to contract" and similar expressions have received judicial recognition, and have become a safe formula for this purpose. But if any other form of wording is used, care must be taken to show clearly that assent is qualified. There is a difference between a tentative agreement (not binding) and a provisional agreement, which may be binding: *Branca* v. *Cobarro* (1947).

Chillingworth v. *Esche* (1924): the parties agreed on the sale of certain property "subject to a proper contract to be prepared by the vendor's solicitors." HELD: there was no contract between the parties.

Eccles v. *Bryant* (1948): the parties agreed on the sale of certain property "subject to contract." The contract was drawn up and counterparts prepared for each party. The purchaser signed his counterpart and posted it to the vendor, but the vendor did not sign his counterpart. HELD: there was no contract between the parties.

Branca v. *Cobarro* (1947): the parties signed an agreement by which B was to buy the lease and goodwill of C's mushroom farm. The agreement ended with the words, "This is a provisional agreement until a fully legalised agreement drawn up by a solicitor embodying all the conditions herewith stated is signed." B paid a deposit, but subsequently changed his mind over the transaction. B sued for the return of his deposit, contending that the agreement was not binding. HELD: the wording of the agreement showed that the parties intended it to be binding, and that it would remain in force until its provisions were embodied in a formally drawn up document.

ACCEPTANCE OF A TENDER

11. Categories of tender. A tender may be either

(a) a definite offer to supply specified goods or services, or

(b) a standing offer, or

(c) not an offer at all, *e.g.* if made subject to contract.

12. Tender as a definite offer. Where tenders are invited for the supply of specified goods or services, and each tender submitted is an offer, the party inviting the tenders can accept any tender he chooses, and thus bring about a binding contract. For example if X, who requires a million bricks, invites tenders to supply this quantity, and X in due course accepts Y's tender, there is a contract between X and Y: the terms of the contract are that Y shall supply, and that X shall accept and pay for, one million bricks.

13. Tender as a standing offer. Where tenders are invited to supply goods or services as and when demanded, a trader who submits a tender is making a standing offer. "Acceptance" of a standing offer has not the same effect as acceptance of a definite offer. Where a standing offer has been made, there is a separate acceptance each time an order is placed with the person who submitted the tender and, accordingly, a distinct contract is made on each occasion. It also follows that the standing offer can be revoked at any time, except as to goods or services actually ordered, unless there is a binding undertaking to keep the standing offer open for a stipulated period: *i.e.* the standing offer must be under seal or consideration must be given for it, otherwise it can be revoked at any time.

Great Northern Railway v. *Witham* (1873): the G. N. Railway invited tenders for the supply of certain goods for a period of 12 months. W submitted a tender to supply for 12 months "such quantities . . . as the Company may order from time to time." G.N.R. accepted W's tender and several orders were given and executed. Before the period of 12 months had expired, G.N.R. gave an order and W refused to execute it. HELD: the tender was a standing offer which resulted in a contract each time an order was given by G.N.R. W was contractually bound to execute the orders already given by G.N.R. (It was suggested that W was free to revoke the agreement except as to orders already given.)

NOTE: where a tender to supply goods as and when demanded is accepted, and the agreement includes an estimate of the quantities required, there is no obligation on the buyer to order any particular quantity or, indeed, anything at all: *Percival* v. *L.C.C.* (1918). But where the buyer has undertaken to buy *all* his requirements of specified goods from the person whose tender has been accepted, there is a breach of contract if he buys such goods elsewhere: *Kier* v. *Whitehead Iron Co.* (1938).

THE COMMUNICATION OF ACCEPTANCE

14. Acceptance must be communicated. The general rule is that acceptance must be communicated to the offeror. Acceptance speaks from the moment it is communicated. Where the offeree merely intended to accept, but did not communicate his intention to the offeror, there is no contract, *i.e.* mere mental acceptance is not sufficient. Moreover, the offeror may not stipulate that he will take silence to be acceptance, and thus bind the offeree.

II. OFFER AND ACCEPTANCE

Felthouse v. *Bindley* (1863): F offered to buy his nephew's horse for £30 15s. In the letter containing the offer, F wrote, "If I hear no more about him, I consider the horse mine at £30 15s." The nephew did not reply to this letter. Six weeks later, when the nephew was about to sell his farming stock, he instructed B, an auctioneer, to keep the horse out of the sale as he was already sold. B inadvertently sold the horse. F sued B for conversion. (To succeed in conversion, F would have to show that he had a right to immediate possession of the horse, *i.e.* that there was a contract between himself and his nephew.) HELD: the nephew had not communicated his intention to sell the horse to F, therefore there was no contract, and no property in the horse had ever vested in F.

15. Where acceptance need not be communicated. There are two important exceptions to the rule that a contract is not made until acceptance is actually communicated to the offeror:

(*a*) Where performance constitutes acceptance.
(*b*) Where acceptance is duly made by post.

16. Where performance constitutes acceptance. In the case of the unilateral contract the offeror is deemed to have included in his offer a term providing that performance by the offeree shall be a sufficient acceptance and communication is not necessary. The offeror is bound when the offeree performs whatever act is required of him according to the terms of the offer.

Carlill v. *Carbolic Smoke Ball Co*. (1893): the following advertisement appeared in newspapers: "£100 reward will be paid by the Carbolic Smoke Ball Company to any person who contracts the increasing epidemic influenza, colds, or any other disease caused by taking cold, after having used the ball three times daily for two weeks according to the printed directions supplied with each ball. £1000 is deposited with the Alliance Bank, Regent Street, showing our good faith in the matter." C, in reliance on this advertisement, bought a smoke ball and used it according to the directions but nevertheless suffered an attack of influenza. She claimed £100 from the company. HELD: (i) the deposit of £1000 showed that the company intended to create legal relations, (ii) the advertisement was an offer made to all the world, and a contract was made with that limited portion of the public who came forward and performed the condition on the faith of the advertisement, (iii) the offer contained an intimation that performance of the condition was sufficient acceptance and that there was no need for notification of acceptance to be given to the offeror.

NOTE: the third part of the judgment in the *Smoke Ball Case* should be carefully distinguished from the rule in *Felthouse* v. *Bindley*, in which there was no performance required of the offeree.

In cases where a reward has been offered in return for a specific piece of information, or the finding of a specific thing, acceptance can be made once only, even though the offer was made to the public.

Lancaster v. *Walsh* (1838): an offer was made to pay £20 reward to any person who came forward with information leading to the conviction of the thief of certain property. The second person to give the information claimed £20 reward. HELD: acceptance was made by the first person to give the information, and no further acceptance was possible.

17. Acceptance by post. Where post is deemed to be the proper means of communicating acceptance, the acceptance takes effect from the moment the letter of acceptance is properly posted. This rule applies even where the acceptance is delayed or lost in the post.

Henthorn v. *Fraser* (1892): F, representing a building society, offered in writing to sell certain houses to H, the offer to remain open for 14 days. H received the offer in person. Next day the following events took place: mid-day: the society posted a letter to H revoking the offer. 3.50 p.m.: H posted a letter to the society accepting the offer. 5.00 p.m.: H received the society's revocation. HELD: a contract was made at 3.50 p.m., when H posted his letter of acceptance. *Per* Lord Herschell: "Where the circumstances are such that it must have been within the contemplation of the parties that, according to the ordinary usages of mankind, the post might be used as a means of communicating the acceptance of an offer, the acceptance is complete as soon as it is posted."

Household Fire Insurance Co. v. *Grant* (1879): G applied for shares in the plaintiff company. The company sent a letter of allotment by post, but it never reached G. The company went into liquidation and the liquidator, on behalf of the company, sued for the balance outstanding on the shares. G contended that he was not bound to pay, since he had not received a reply to his offer to buy the shares. HELD: a contract was made at the moment the letter of allotment (*i.e.* the acceptance) was posted.

18. Place of contracting. In cases with an international element, it is sometimes necessary to establish *where* a contract was made. Where agreement is reached between parties present in a particular country, the contract is obviously made in that country. But where the parties are in different countries and they use the post as the means of communicating, the contract is made in the country where the acceptance is posted. Similarly, where acceptance is made by cable, the contract is made in the country from which the acceptance was sent: *Benaim* v. *Debono* (1924). If, however, the communication is instantaneous, for example by telex, the contract is made at the place where the acceptance is received: *Entores* v. *Miles Far East Corporation* (1955).

19. Manner of acceptance. Acceptance may be communicated in any manner whatsoever. Generally, the offeree may decide for himself the manner of acceptance: but if the offeror prescribes, expressly or by implication, the mode of acceptance, it seems that communication of acceptance in any other manner will not suffice.

Compagnie de Commerce et Commission S.A.R.L. v. *Parkinson Stove Co., Ltd.* (1953): P made an offer to C with the stipulation that acceptance should be made on a particular form and that no other manner of acceptance would be valid. C accepted by letter. HELD by the Court of Appeal: no valid acceptance had been made.

Quenerduaine v. *Cole* (1883): Q made an offer to C by post. C made a counter-offer by telegraph. Q immediately posted a letter accepting the counter-offer, but by the time it reached C he no longer wished to enter the contract. Q claimed that a contract had been made. HELD: the fact that the counter-offer was made by telegraph indicated an implied condition that prompt acceptance was required. The purported acceptance by letter reached C after the counter-offer had lapsed. No contract was made.

Holwell Securities v. *Hughes* (1973): An agreement was made on 19th October, 1971, in which an option was granted to X to purchase certain land. The agreement provided that "The said option shall be exercisable by notice in writing to [the offeror] at any time within six months from the date hereof." On 14th April, 1972, X posted a properly stamped and addressed letter to the offeror giving notice of the exercise of the option. This letter went astray in the post and was never delivered to the offeror. The offeror refused to sell the land and X brought this action for specific performance, contending that the option had been validly exercised by the mere posting of the letter. HELD by the Court of Appeal: since the agreement prescribed the manner in which the option was to be exercised, it could only be exercised in that way, *i.e.*, by actually serving notice on the offeror. The mere posting of the notice which went astray did not constitute a valid exercise of the option.

There remains the following question to be considered: where acceptance has been made in a manner other than that prescribed, may the offeror waive his stipulation and treat the acceptance as valid and binding on the offeree? There is no clear authority on this point, but it was suggested *obiter* in the *Parkinson Stove Case* that such a waiver would be valid.

When a unilateral contract is made it seems that the offeror is bound from the time when the offeree began his performance of what was required of him by the offer.

Errington v. *Errington and Woods* (1952): X promised to give his house to his son and daughter-in-law provided they paid off the building society mortgage loan. The couple thereafter made regular payments to the building society on account of the mortgage. X died leaving all his property to his widow. The son then left his wife and went to live with his widowed mother, leaving his wife (X's daughter-in-law) in the house in question. She continued to make the regular payments to the building society. X's widow later sought to recover possession of the house. HELD: X's promise had led to a unilateral contract —a promise of the house in return for their act of paying the instalments. X's promise could not be revoked after the couple had started to pay the instalments.

20. Cross offers. Consider the following: A makes an offer to B, and, by coincidence, B makes an offer to A in identical terms, and the two offers cross in the post. Is there a contract? There are no cases exactly on the point, but arguing from general principles, it appears that there has been no agreement between A and B in the manner required by the law, *i.e.* there has been no acceptance of an offer.

REVOCATION

21. Termination of an offer. An offer may come to an end by revocation, lapse, or rejection. In any case, the offer loses its legal effect and becomes incapable of acceptance.

II. OFFER AND ACCEPTANCE

22. When revocation is possible. The offeror may withdraw (*i.e.* revoke) his offer at any time before acceptance: but once a valid acceptance has been made, he is bound by the terms of his offer. An offer cannot be revoked after acceptance.

Payne v. *Cave* (1789): C made the highest bid for P's goods at an auction sale, but he withdrew his bid before the fall of the hammer. P contended that C was bound by the sale. HELD: C's bid was an offer and could be revoked before acceptance, *i.e.* before the fall of the hammer. There was an effective revocation by C.

Re National Savings Bank Association (1867): an application for shares in a company was withdrawn before delivery of the letter of allotment. HELD: no contract to take the shares.

23. Options. Where the offeror gives an undertaking to keep the offer open for a stipulated period he is not bound by his undertaking unless the offeree gave consideration in return for it. Where the offeree gives consideration to keep the offer open for a period there is a separate binding contract known as an *option*, and revocation within the period will be in breach of contract. (*See Dickinson* v. *Dodds* (1876) in **26** below.)

24. Companies Act, 1948, s. 50 (5). An offer to buy shares in or debentures of a company made in pursuance of a prospectus issued generally shall not be revocable until after the expiration of the third day after the time of the opening of the subscription lists.

25. Communication essential. Revocation is effective only upon actual notice of it reaching the offeree. Where revocation is communicated by post, it takes effect from the moment it is received by the offeree, and not from the time of posting.

Byrne v. *Van Tienhoven* (1880): the following communications passed between the parties:

1st Oct: T posted an offer in Cardiff to B in New York.
8th Oct: T posted a revocation of the offer.
11th Oct: B sent a telegram accepting the offer of 1st Oct.
15th Oct: B sent a letter confirming the acceptance.
20th Oct: B received the revocation dated 8th Oct.

HELD: T's revocation was inoperative because it did not reach B until after acceptance had been made. A contract was made on 11th October, when B accepted the offer.

26. Indirect communication of revocation.
Provided the offeror has shown, by words or conduct, a clear intention to revoke, and notice has reached the offeree, the revocation is effective. The means of communication do not matter.

Dickinson v. *Dodds* (1876): on 10th June P received from D an offer to sell a house, the offer "to be left over until Friday, 9 o'clock a.m., June 12th." On 11th June P was informed by X that D had offered or agreed to sell the houses to Y. P then delivered an acceptance of D's offer. D had, in fact, sold the houses to Y on 11th June. P contended that D was contractually bound to sell the houses to him. HELD: D's undertaking to keep the offer open for a certain time was not binding, for the plaintiff had given no consideration for it. There was no need for an express withdrawal of the offer. It was sufficient that P knew that D had changed his mind and had offered the property to another. Effective revocation had taken place before the purported acceptance, and there was no contract between the parties.

LAPSE

27. Lapse of an offer.
An offer may lapse, and thus become incapable of acceptance,

  (a) by passage of time, or
  (b) by the death of one of the parties, or
  (c) the non-fulfilment of a condition precedent, *see* XVII, **8**.

28. Passage of time.
An offer will lapse through passage of time in the following circumstances:

(a) Where acceptance is not made within the period prescribed by the offeror.

(b) Where no period is prescribed, and acceptance is not made within a reasonable time. (What is reasonable depends upon the circumstances of the case.)

Ramsgate Victoria Hotel Co., Ltd. v. *Montefiore* (1866): in June, M offered to buy shares from the company. In November, the company allotted shares to M, who refused to take them, contending that his offer had lapsed. HELD: the offer had lapsed through passage of itme: acceptance had not been made within a reasonable period.

II. OFFER AND ACCEPTANCE

29. Death of a party. The death of the offeror or offeree sometimes causes the offer to lapse. The position is not free from doubt, and may be summarised as follows:

(a) The offer lapses when the offeree hears of the death of the offeror: *re Whelan*, (1897). But whether an acceptance made in ignorance of the offeror's death is effective, is a matter of doubt: *Bradbury* v. *Morgan* (1862).

(b) It seems that the death of the offeree will cause the offer to lapse.

Duff's Executors' Case (1886): D received an offer of some shares in return for certain shares held by D. D died without accepting, but his executors purported to accept. HELD: the offer had lapsed on D's death.

REJECTION

30. Rejection: express and implied. An offeree who has rejected an offer cannot subsequently accept it. Rejection may be express or implied.

31. Express rejection. Express rejection is effective when notice of it has reached the offeror. But where rejection is made by post it is not clear whether it operates from the moment of posting the letter, or from the moment the letter reaches the offeror. For example, if X posts an offer to Y, and Y posts a letter rejecting the offer, but soon afterwards changes his mind and sends a telegram accepting the offer, what is the position if X receives the telegram before the letter?

It is suggested that a contract is made when X receives the telegram, and that Y's letter has no legal effect.

32. Implied rejection. Rejection is implied by law.

(a) where the offeree makes a counter-offer: *Hyde* v. *Wrench* (1840).

(b) where the offeree makes a conditional acceptance: *Jordan* v. *Norton* (1838).

NOTE: there is no implied rejection of the offer where the offeree makes a request for further information: *Stevenson* v. *McLean* (1880).

PROGRESS TEST 2

1. Is it necessary for the offeror to express all the terms of his offer?

2. What is an invitation to treat? Give examples.

3. Has an offer any validity before it is communicated to the offeree?

4. "The communication of an offer may be particular or general." Comment on this statement.

5. "Acceptance must be unqualified and must correspond exactly with the terms of the offer." Would it, therefore, be true to say that the terms of the offer become the binding contractual terms after acceptance has taken place?

6. What is the effect of a counter-offer?

7. Distinguish between a tentative agreement and a provisional agreement.

8. Explain the legal effect of (a) a tender which is a definite offer to supply specified goods or services, and (b) a tender which is a standing offer.

9. Are there any exceptions to the rule that a contract is not made until acceptance is actually communicated to the offeror?

10. May the offeror stipulate the manner in which acceptance is to be made?

11. May an offeror always revoke before acceptance has taken place?

12. Explain how an offer may lapse (a) by passage of time, (b) by death, and (c) by the non-fulfilment of a condition.

13. In what circumstances will rejection of an offer be implied?

14. A borrowed £10 from B, saying that he would pay him back the following week, together with an extra £5 if business was good during the week. A has repaid the £10 and B wishes to know whether he can claim the £5. Advise him.

15. C sees a rare book in a bookshop window. It is labelled "First Edition—£5." C goes into the shop and puts a £5 note on the counter and asks for the book. The bookseller tells C that it was marked at £5 by mistake, and that its real price is £12. Is the bookseller bound to sell the book to C for £5? Give reasons for your answer.

16. D goes into a self-service store, takes up a wire basket from the stack provided, and then fills the basket with goods from the shelves. He is about to leave the store, when he remembers that he has forgotten to bring money with him: so he starts to replace the goods on the shelves. The store manager stops him, saying that he has bought these goods and must pay for them. Advise the manager.

17. E says to F, "How much would you sell your car for?"

II. OFFER AND ACCEPTANCE

F replies, "A hundred and fifty pounds." Is there a contract between the parties?

18. G's lawn is infested with weeds, and his neighbour, H, treats the lawn with weed killer. G knows nothing of this until H presents him with a bill for £2.50, the price of the weed killer. Is G bound to pay H?

19. J applied for a post as a legal assistant in the secretary's department of XYZ Ltd. The company's appointments committee decided to appoint J. A committee member happened to meet J at his club and told him that he had been appointed. On the strength of this information, J immediately resigned from his present post, and ordered four new suits from his tailor. In the meantime, the committee decided to appoint K instead of J to the post. Two days later, J received a letter from XYZ Ltd., signed by the chairman of the appointments committee, thanking J for his application, but regretting that he had not been successful, and that the post had gone to K. J, who now has no job, and cannot pay his tailor's bill, seeks your advice as to whether he has an action for breach of contract against XYZ Ltd.

20. L offered to sell his motor cycle to M for £80. M replied, "I'll give you £75 for it." L then shook his head. M then produced £80 from his pocket saying, "Here you are then, eighty pounds." L replies that he has changed his mind, and that he does not want to sell the motor cycle. Is he within his legal rights? State your reasons for your answer fully.

21. N and O entered into a written agreement containing a clause "this is a provisional agreement until a proper agreement containing these terms is drawn up by a solicitor and signed." Are the parties bound by this agreement? Would the result have been the same if the term was expressed "this agreement is subject to a contract to be prepared by a solicitor"?

22. The P Company Ltd. invited tenders for the supply of certain goods "in such quantities as the company may order from time to time." Q's tender was accepted by the company. The company have placed no orders with Q, who has discovered that the company is buying goods of the type specified from R. Advise Q whether he has a right of action against the P Company, Ltd. (a) on the footing that his agreement with the company included an estimate of the quantities required by the company over a twelve-month period, and (b) on the footing that the agreement included an undertaking by the company to buy all their requirements of the specified goods from Q.

23. After prolonged and unfriendly negotiations between S and T for the sale of S's vintage car, T wrote to S offering to pay £850 for it. The letter went on to say, "If I do not hear from you within a week, I shall assume that the car is mine at that price." Three weeks later, S sells the car to U for £860. T asks you to advise him whether he can make any claim against S.

CHAPTER III

INTENTION TO CREATE LEGAL RELATIONS

1. Intention to be bound is essential. The intention to create legal relations is an essential element in contract. Where no intention to be bound can be attributed to the parties, there is no contract. The test of intention is objective. The courts seek to give effect to the presumed intentions of the parties.

2. Commercial and business agreements. In commercial and business agreements, there is a rebuttable presumption that the parties intended to create legal relations. To rebut the presumption, it must be shown that the parties did not intend to be bound. The parties are not contractually bound where the agreement is expressed to be binding in honour only, or where it is expressed to be subject to contract. *See* II, **10.**

Rose and Frank Co. v. *Crompton Bros.* (1925): an agreement was expressed to be "not subject to legal jurisdiction in the law courts." HELD by the House of Lords: no binding contract.

Appleson v. *Littlewood Ltd.* (1939) by the Court of Appeal: A sent in a football pools coupon containing a condition that it "shall not be attended by or give rise to any legal relationship, rights, duties, consequences." HELD by the Court of Appeal: the condition was valid and the agreement was not binding.

J. H. Milner & Son v. *Percy Bilton, Ltd.* (1966): in negotiations between solicitors and their clients, a letter was written stating, "May we please take this opportunity of placing on record the understanding that all legal work of and incidental to the completion of the development and the grant of leases shall be carried out by us." HELD: no contract.

3. Social and domestic agreements. In agreements of a social or domestic nature, there is a presumption that the parties did not intend legal relations to arise. But this presumption is rebuttable by evidence to the contrary.

Balfour v. *Balfour* (1919): a husband agreed to send his wife £30 a month for her support while he was working abroad. HELD by the Court of Appeal: no contract.

III. INTENTION TO CREATE LEGAL RELATIONS

Simpkins v. *Pays* (1955): a lodger and the members of the family with whom he lived agreed to go shares in a newspaper competition. They sent in a winning entry. HELD: there was an intention to be bound. The prize money should be shared according to the agreement.

Jones v. *Padavatton* (1969): in this action the plaintiff and defendant were mother and daughter respectively. There was an agreement between the parties to the effect that if the daughter gave up her very satisfactory pensionable job in the U.S.A. and came to London to read for the Bar with the intention of practising law in Trinidad (where the mother lived), the mother would pay an allowance of 200 dollars a month to maintain the daughter and her small son while in England. According to this agreement, the daughter began her legal studies in November 1962, continuing up to the time this action was brought. At the time of the agreement, the mother meant 200 West Indian dollars a month and the daughter understood it to be 200 U.S. dollars. But once arrived, the daughter accepted the allowance in West Indian dollars without dispute. In 1964, because the daughter was finding it difficult to live on her allowance, a house was found and the purchase price of £6000 was provided by the mother, to whom the property was conveyed. The varied arrangement was that the daughter should live in part of the house and let the rest furnished, using the rent to cover expenses and the daughter's maintenance in place of the 200 dollars a month. In 1967 the parties quarrelled and the mother, complaining that she could not get any accounts, brought this action for possession of the house, on the grounds that the agreement between the parties was not made with the intention to create legal relations. HELD: the arrangement of 1964 by which the daughter had the use of the house was lacking in contractual intent. The mother was entitled to possession.

4. Collective agreements. Before the *Industrial Relations Act*, 1971, came into force, the vast majority of collective agreements were regarded as unenforceable: *see Ford Motor Co. Ltd.* v. *A.E.E.F.U. & T.G.W.U.* (1969). The Act provides that a written collective agreement is enforceable against the parties to it provided it does not contain an express provision to the effect that it is not enforceable. "Enforceability" in this connection does not mean enforceability in the High Court. It means enforceable by the Industrial Court, which has exclusive jurisdiction over collective agreements. A breach of a collective agreement constitutes an unfair industrial practice—a new category of civil wrong introduced by the 1971 Act.

NOTE: "collective agreement" is defined in the 1971 Act as any agreement or arrangement which is for the time being in force and

(i) is an agreement or arrangement made (in whatever way and whatever form by or on behalf of one or more organisations of workers and either one or more employers, one or more organisations of employers, and

(ii) is either an arrangement or arrangement prescribing (wholly or in part) the terms and conditions of employment of workers of one or more descriptions, or a procedure agreement or both. (A procedure agreement is a collective agreement relating to procedural machinery for the regulation of the relationship between employer and employees.)

5. Jurisdiction cannot be ousted. Although it is possible for parties to make an agreement which does not give rise to contractual rights and obligations, it is not possible to make an agreement which ousts the jurisdiction of the courts. The question as to whether the parties intended to create legal relations is always a question for the court to decide (*see* XII, **10**).

PROGRESS TEST 3

1. "The intention to create legal relations is an essential element in a binding contract." Explain this statement.

2. Where the parties do not expressly state whether or not they intend to be legally bound by their agreement, how do the courts discover their intention in this respect?

3. Consider the legal effect of the two following stipulations:

   (*a*) "This agreement is binding in honour only and is not to give rise to legal rights and obligations."
   (*b*) "This agreement is outside the jurisdiction of the courts, and the parties hereby agree not to bring any action in the courts on any question arising from this agreement."

4. A invited B to his (A's) home for dinner, and B accepted the invitation. In an attempt to impress B, A arranged for a sumptuous and expensive meal to be prepared. B forgot about the invitation and did not arrive. The food was wasted. A now wishes to know whether he has any claim against B. Advise him.

III. INTENTION TO CREATE LEGAL RELATIONS

5. C, D, and E have agreed to form a syndicate for the purpose of making a weekly entry in a football pools competition. C and D, who know nothing about football, agree to give E a sum of money weekly, and to leave it to him to fill in the forms and send them off in his own name. Seven weeks after the start of this arrangement, E sends off an entry which wins £18,000, which he now refuses to share with C and D. Advise C and D.

CHAPTER IV

CONSIDERATION

THE NATURE OF CONSIDERATION

1. A bare promise is not binding. In an action on a simple contract, the plaintiff must show that the defendant's promise was *part of a bargain* between the parties. The plaintiff must show that he gave, or promised to give, some advantage to the defendant in return for his promise. This advantage moving from the plaintiff to the defendant is known as valuable consideration.

It is a complete defence for the defendant to show that no consideration was given. A bare promise is not binding, *e.g.* if A promises to make a gift of £5 to B, and subsequently changes his mind, B cannot succeed against A for breach of contract.

2. Definition. A valuable consideration "may consist either in some right, interest, profit, or benefit accruing to the one party, or some forbearance, detriment, loss, or responsibility given, suffered, or undertaken by the other": *Currie* v. *Misa* (1875).

3. Executory and executed consideration. Valuable consideration may be something promised or something done. Regarding a simple contract as a transaction which is essentially a bargain, consideration may be a price promised, or a price paid. ("Price" is used here in the widest sense.)

(*a*) *Executory consideration* is the price *promised* by one party in return for the other party's promise.

(*b*) *Executed consideration* is the price *paid* by one party in return for the other party's promise.

NOTE: The party alleging the breach of contract must show that he gave consideration: generally, this is the plaintiff, but where a defendant brings a counter-claim for breach of contract,—*i.e.* where he alleges that the plaintiff was in breach of

IV. CONSIDERATION

contract—then he must show that he, the defendant, gave consideration.

4. Rules governing consideration. The following rules govern consideration:

(a) Consideration must be real (or sufficient).
(b) Consideration need not be adequate.
(c) Consideration must move from the promisee.
(d) Consideration must not be past.
(e) Consideration must not be illegal.
(f) Consideration must not be vague.
(g) Consideration must be possible of performance.

Rules (a) to (d) above are fundamental to the nature of consideration. Rules (e) to (g) may be regarded as auxiliary.

5. Consideration must be real. Consideration must have some value. It matters not how small that value is, so long as it is worth something. Indeed, the word "value" is sometimes used to mean consideration. It follows that where a party performs an act which is merely a discharge of a pre-existing obligation, there is no consideration: but where a party does more than he was already bound to do, there may be consideration.

Stilk v. *Myrick* (1809): the captain of a ship promised his crew that, if they shared between them the work of two seamen who had deserted, the wages of the deserters would be shared out between them. HELD: the promise was not binding because the seamen gave no consideration: they were already contractually bound to do any extra work to complete the voyage.

Hartley v. *Ponsonby* (1857): a ship's crew had been seriously depleted by a number of desertions. The captain promised the remaining crew members £40 extra pay if they would complete the voyage. HELD: the promise was binding. It was dangerous to put to sea in a ship so under-manned. The seamen were not obliged to do this under their contracts of service and were, therefore, free to enter into a fresh contract for the remaining part of the voyage.

Glasbrook Brothers, Ltd. v. *Glamorgan County Council* (1925): at the time of a strike at a colliery, the managers asked for police protection of the colliery property. The superintendent of police thought that a mobile patrol would be sufficient, but he agreed to supply a standing guard on payment by the colliery. It was claimed that the promise to pay was not binding as the police were under a duty to protect property, and there was, therefore, no consideration. HELD by the House of Lords: the promise was binding because the police had done more than they were bound to do under their public duty.

Ward v. *Byham* (1956): the father of an illegitimate daughter promised the mother £1 a week provided "that she will be well looked after and happy." HELD by the Court of Appeal: the promise was binding because the woman's undertaking amounted to more than her bare legal obligations to the child.

In the above cases the test was: *"Did the party claiming to have given consideration do any more than he was already bound to do either under the public law or under a previous contract with the other party?"* There is also authority for the proposition that performance of an existing contractual obligation *to a third party* may amount to consideration.

Shadwell v. *Shadwell* (1860): after becoming engaged to marry, the plaintiff received a letter from his uncle stating that he was glad to hear of the intended marriage and that he would make an annual payment of £150 yearly to assist the plaintiff in starting his career as a barrister. The plaintiff did marry. At the time of the uncle's death the promised payments were not all made and the plaintiff brought this action against the personal representatives for their recovery. The defendants contended that the plaintiff had given no consideration to support the uncle's promise because he was already contractually bound to marry his fiancée at the time the uncle made the promise. HELD: the plaintiff's marriage was "an object of interest" to the uncle and was, therefore, sufficient consideration to support the promise of the annual payments.

Scotson v. *Pegg* (1861): by a previous contract with X, the plaintiffs had undertaken to deliver a cargo of coal to X or to the order of X. X then directed the plaintiffs to deliver to the defendants. The defendants promised the plaintiffs that they would unload the cargo at a stated rate. The plaintiff sued for breach of this promise. The defendants contended that the promise was not binding for lack of consideration. It was argued that the plaintiffs were already bound under the previous contract with X to deliver the cargo and that, therefore, no consideration moved from the plaintiff to the defendant. HELD: the delivery of the coal was a benefit to the defendants and was, therefore, consideration. The defendants' promise was binding.

6. Consideration need not be adequate. According to the doctrine of freedom of contract, the courts will not interfere with a bargain freely reached by the parties. It is no part of the court's duty to assess the relative value of each party's contribution to the bargain. Once it is established that a bargain was freely reached, it will be presumed that each party stipulated according to his wishes and intentions at the time. There is no reason, for example, why a party should not be bound by a promise to sell a new Rolls Royce motor car for one penny. If the agreement was freely reached, the inadequacy of the price is immaterial to the existence of a binding contract.

7. Consideration must move from the promisee. No stranger to the consideration may by himself sue on a contract. Any action for breach of contract must be brought by a party who gave consideration. This rule is related to, but must be distinguished from, the doctrine of privity of contract. In *Dunlop* v. *Selfridge* (1915), Lord Haldane said that the two principles were fundamental.

Price v. *Easton* (1833): X and the defendant agreed that if X did specified work for him, he, the defendant, would pay £19 to P. X did the work but the defendant did not pay the money to P. P sued for the money. HELD: the plaintiff could not succeed because no consideration had passed from him to the defendant.

Consider the following situations:

(a) X, Y, and Z enter into an agreement under which X promises to do certain work for Y if Y will pay £10 to Z. If X does the work, he can sue Y on his promise: but Z cannot sue by himself, for he gave no consideration to Y.

(b) X and Y enter into an agreement under which X promises to do certain work for Y if Y will pay £10 to Z. If X does the work, he can sue Y on his promise: but Z cannot sue by himself, for he gave no consideration to Y, nor is he a party to the contract. *See* XIV.

8. Consideration must not be past. Where one party has performed an act before the other party's promise was made, that act cannot be consideration to support the promise.

Thus A offers to drive B from London to Cambridge in his motor car. On arrival at Cambridge, B promises A to pay fifty pence towards the cost of the petrol. B's promise is not binding because the "consideration" for which it was given was past.

Roscorla v. *Thomas* (1842): at T's request, R bought T's horse for £30. After the sale, T promised R that the horse was sound and free from vice. The horse proved to be vicious. HELD: there was no consideration to support T's promise and he was not bound. The sale itself could not be valuable consideration, for it was completed at the time the promise was given.

9. Bills of Exchange Act, 1882, s. 27 (1). Section 27 (1) of the *Bills of Exchange Act*, 1882, provides an exception to the rule that past consideration is no consideration.

s. 27 (1). "Valuable consideration for a bill may be constituted by:

(*a*) Any consideration sufficient to support a simple contract;

(*b*) An antecedent debt or liability. Such debt or liability is deemed valuable consideration whether the bill is payable on demand or at a future time."

10. Apparent exceptions to the rule of past consideration. Section 27 of the *Bills of Exchange Act*, 1882, provides the only real exception to the rule of past consideration. There are, however, two circumstances which are often quoted as apparent exceptions:

(*a*) Where the plaintiff performs a service at the request of the defendant and the defendant subsequently makes a promise to pay, an action is allowed on the defendant's promise. In *re Casey's Patents*, Bowen, L.J., said, "The fact of a past service raises an implication that at the time it was rendered it was to be paid for, and, if it was a service which was to be paid for, when you get in a subsequent document a promise to pay, that promise may be treated as an admission which evidences or as a positive bargain which fixes the amount of that reasonable remuneration on the faith of which the service was originally rendered."

(*b*) Where a right of action to recover a debt or other liquidated claim is barred by the *Limitation Act*, 1939, *s.* 2, and the person liable acknowledges the claim or makes any payment in respect thereof, the right shall be deemed to have accrued on and not before the date of the acknowledgment or the last payment: *Limitation Act*, 1939, *s.* 23 (4).

IV. CONSIDERATION 31

This means that a promise by a debtor to pay a statute-barred debt is actionable. Notice that *s.* 23 provides for a fresh accrual of a *right of action*: the section concerns procedural rights and not the accrual of substantive contractual rights. Thus, the section provides only an apparent exception to the rule that past consideration is no consideration.

11. Consideration must not be illegal. Where the consideration is either contrary to a rule of law or immoral, the courts will not usually allow an action on the contract: the rule is *ex turpi causa non oritur actio* (no action arises from a base cause). See XI.

12. Consideration must not be vague. The general rule is that the promise by a contracting party must be clear and definite. A vague promise is not binding unless the vagueness can be cured by the implication of terms: *Scammell* v. *Ouston* (1941); *Hillas* v. *Arcos* (1932); *White* v. *Bluett* (1853). See II, **1** and V, **14.**

13. Consideration must be possible of performance. A promise to do something which is impossible cannot be binding. Such a promise cannot constitute consideration. Promises to do what is obviously impossible may be regarded as lacking the essential intention to create legal relations.

Thus, A promises B that he will swim the Atlantic Ocean from Brighton to New York. No consideration moves from A to B.

WAIVER MUST BE SUPPORTED BY CONSIDERATION

14. Waiver of a contractual right. Where a contracting party waives his rights under the contract, wholly or in part, the waiver is not binding unless consideration is given for it. For example, if X owes Y £100, and Y tells X that he will take £90 in full satisfaction of the debt, X will not be discharged from his obligation to pay the £100. If X pays £90 to Y, he will remain liable to the extent of £10.

15. Consideration makes a waiver binding. Where a debtor gives consideration in return for the waiver, there is accord and satisfaction, and the waiver becomes a part of a new binding contract between the parties (*see* XVII, **7**).

16. Where payment of a lesser sum discharges an obligation to pay a greater sum.

Where a debtor pays a lesser sum to his creditor than that which is due, the debtor is not discharged from his obligation to pay the balance. At common law the debtor remains liable even where the creditor has agreed to release him from further liability, for the creditor's promise is not supported by any consideration moving from the debtor: *Foakes* v. *Beer* (1884). But if, at the creditor's request, some new element is introduced, such as payment at a different place, or at a different time, compliance with this request will amount to consideration for the waiver.

Thus if D is under a contractual obligation to pay C the sum of £1000 in London on 28th June, and he (C) requests D to pay £800 in London on 2nd June, saying that he will take the lesser sum in full discharge of the greater, C will have no further claim against D if he complies.

NOTE: there must be some new element introduced at the request of the creditor. But see *D. & C. Builders* v. *Rees* (1965).

Pinnel's Case (1602): Pinnel sued Cole for a debt of £8 10s. due on 11th November. Cole pleaded that, at Pinnel's request, he had paid £5 2s. 6d. on 1st October, and that this had been accepted by Pinnel in full satisfaction. The court found for the plaintiff Pinnel, on a technical point of pleading, but it was made clear in the judgment that, but for this flaw, the court would have found for the defendant, Cole, because the payment of the lesser sum had been made on an earlier date and at the plaintiff's request.

Where a third party enters into an agreement with a creditor by which the creditor accepts payment of a lesser sum than the debt in full satisfaction of the debtor's obligation, the creditor cannot sue the debtor for the difference: *Hirachand Punamchand* v. *Temple* (1911).

THE DOCTRINE OF EQUITABLE ESTOPPEL

17. The doctrine as a defence.

Where a party has waived his contractual rights against another, and that other party has changed his position in reliance on the waiver, it would be unjust to allow an action against him on the original contract to succeed. In equity, the party who waived his rights may

IV. CONSIDERATION 33

be estopped from denying that he intended the waiver to be binding.

18. What the defendant must prove. In order to raise the defence of equitable (or promissory) estoppel, the following conditions must be satisfied:

(a) There must have been an original agreement between the parties out of which the defendant owed an obligation to the plaintiff.

(b) The plaintiff must have waived, partly or wholly, his rights against the defendant.

(c) The defendant must have given no consideration for the waiver so as to make it binding at law.

(d) The defendant must have altered his position in reliance on the waiver, so that it would be inequitable to allow the plaintiff to insist on the terms of the original agreement.

19. A shield and not a sword. It is important to notice that *the doctrine does not create a cause of action*. The doctrine does not relieve a plaintiff from the need to show that he gave consideration for the defendant's promise. In the language of counsel in *Combe* v. *Combe* (1951), the doctrine is a shield and not a sword. Equitable estoppel was explained in the *High Trees Case* (1947), and in *Combe* v. *Combe* (1951). It was applied by the House of Lords in *Tool Metal Manufacturing Co. Ltd.* v. *Tungsten Electric Co., Ltd.* (1955). In the *Tool Metal* case, Viscount Simonds emphasised that the gist of the equitable right lies in the fact that one party has by his conduct led the other to alter his position. He indicated that mere acts of indulgence in commercial transactions are not likely to create rights and that the statement of principle in *Combe* v. *Combe* may well be far too widely stated.

Central London Property Trust, Ltd. v. *High Trees House, Ltd.* (1947): the property company let a block of flats to High Trees House Ltd., the tenants, at a ground rent of £2500 p.a. in 1937. Owing to war conditions prevailing in London, few of the flats could be let off by the tenants, and they consequently found it difficult to pay £2500 p.a. ground rent. Accordingly, the landlords agreed in writing to reduce the rent to £1250 p.a. *There was no consideration given for this reduction.* By 1945 the tenants found no difficulty in letting off the flats. The whole block became full. The landlords brought this action to recover the balance of rent for the last two quarters of 1945 at the original contract rate. HELD: (i) the landlord's promise to reduce the rent was intended to be legally binding and to be acted on, and having been acted on by the tenants, the landlords would not be permitted to act in a manner inconsistent with it, but (ii) the promise to reduce the rent was a temporary measure and was to be effective only so long as war conditions prevented the tenants from letting the full block. Since the block was fully let early in 1945, the landlords were entitled to the full rent with effect from the quarter ending September 1945.

Combe v. *Combe* (1951): in 1943 a wife obtained a decree nisi against her husband, and immediately afterwards her solicitors wrote to her husband's solicitors asking whether the husband was prepared to make an allowance of £100 a year to the wife. The husband's solicitors replied that the husband agreed. The husband never paid the allowance. In 1950, the wife brought this action, claiming arrears of payment under the husband's promise. At first instance, the judge found for the wife. He held that, although the agreement was not supported by consideration, the husband's promise was enforceable because it was an absolute acceptance of liability, which was intended to be binding and acted on, and was in fact acted on by the wife. The husband appealed, contending that the judge had misapplied the High Trees principle, which could be used "as a shield and not as a sword." HELD by the Court of Appeal: the wife had given no consideration for the husband's promise, therefore she could not succeed in an action on it. Lord Denning said, "It [the High Trees principle] does not create new causes of action where none existed before. It only prevents a party from insisting on his strict legal rights when it would be unjust to allow him to do so, having regard to the dealings which have taken place between the parties. Thus a creditor is not allowed to enforce a debt which he has deliberately agreed to waive if the debtor has carried on some business or in some other way changed his position in reliance on the waiver."

PROGRESS TEST 4

1. "A bare promise is not binding." Explain this statement.
2. How was consideration defined in *Currie* v. *Misa*?
3. Distinguish between executory consideration and executed consideration.
4. State the rules governing consideration. Comment on the exceptions, real and apparent, to the rule that past consideration is no consideration.

IV. CONSIDERATION

5. "Where a party performs an act which is merely a discharge of a pre-existing obligation, there is no consideration: but where a party does more than he was already bound to do, there may be consideration." Explain this statement, using decided cases to illustrate your explanation.

6. Are the courts concerned with the adequacy of consideration?

7. From whom must consideration move?

8. Explain the difference between past consideration and executed consideration.

9. Where a party waives a contractual right, is he bound by the waiver?

10. Does payment of a lesser sum ever discharge an obligation to pay a greater sum? Give full reasons for your answer.

11. What do you understand by the statement, "The High Trees principle does not create new causes of action where none existed before"?

12. Explain fully the circumstances in which a party may benefit from the doctrine of equitable estoppel.

13. A is under a contractual obligation to pay £1000 to B. According to the agreement, the sum is payable in Paris on 4th November. Six weeks before the money is due, B asks A if he will pay the debt into his (B's) New York bank account on 4th October. B tells A that if he complies with this request, £900 will be taken as full discharge of the debt of £1000. A agrees to do this and, in fact, pays £900 into B's New York account. On 15th November B writes to A demanding the balance of £100, which he claims is still outstanding. Advise A.

14. C is a teacher in a state primary school, and D, aged 10, is one of her pupils. E, D's father, promises C that he will pay her £10 if she will give private tuition to D on the four Saturday mornings preceding a scholarship examination for which D has been entered. C agrees, and gives D private tuition accordingly. E now refuses to pay the agreed £10 to C, contending that C was obliged to teach D in any case, and that there was, therefore, no consideration. Advise C. Would it affect your answer if (*a*) D took the examination and failed; (*b*) D was unable to take the examination due to sickness?

15. F's motor car has broken down on a lonely country road. F asks G, who is passing that way in his Land Rover, if he will tow the car to the nearest garage. G agrees and tows the car 20 miles to the nearest garage. On arrival at the garage, F promises to send G £5 as payment for his services. Is F bound by his promise to pay, or is the consideration for it past?

16. H, a tailor, agrees to make a suit for J at a price of £35. Shortly afterwards, H loses his job and he tells H that he cannot now afford to pay £35 for the suit. H then promises orally that he will reduce the price to £25.

(a) If H delivers the suit to J, and J pays £25 for it, can H subsequently claim the original contract price of £35? Would it make any difference to your answer if J had obtained a highly paid job before the suit was finished?

(b) If H sells the suit to another customer for £30, can J bring an action against H for breach of contract? Give your answer on the footing that J is not able or willing to pay more than £25.

CHAPTER V

THE TERMS OF A CONTRACT

1. Terms. The terms of a contract are its contents, and these determine the extent to which the parties are in agreement. Accordingly, the terms of the contract define the rights and obligations arising from the contract. Contractual terms may be expressed or implied:

(a) *Express terms* are express statements made by the parties and by which they intended to be bound.

(b) *Implied terms* are those which have been implied by the law either (i) according to the provisions of a statute, or (ii) to give effect to the presumed intentions of the parties.

EXPRESS TERMS

2. Statements made during negotiations. Material statements made by the parties during negotiations leading up to a contract can be divided into two groups:

(a) Statements by which the parties intended to be bound. These are terms of the contract and may be warranties or conditions.

(b) Statements made, but which the parties did not intend to be binding terms. These statements are mere representations if they helped to induce the making of the contract.

Thus, the parties are bound by statements by which they intended to be bound: where there is no such intention, the parties are not bound. In this connection, the court discovers intention by the application of an objective test. The test question is: *"What would a reasonable man understand to be the intention of the parties, having regard to all the circumstances?"* In applying this test, the court will take notice of all the circumstances of the negotiations between the parties. Where a statement is made during negotiations for the purpose of inducing the other party to enter the contract, there is prima facie ground for inferring that the statement was intended to be a binding term of contract: but the inference can be rebutted if the party making the statement can show that it would not be reasonable to hold him bound by it: *Dick Bentley* v. *Harold Smith* (1965).

In construing the written terms of a contract, evidence of the preceding negotiations is not receivable in proceedings: nor is evidence of the parties' intentions during negotiations. However, evidence of the factual background known to the parties at or before the date of the contract is receivable: *Prenn* v. *Simmonds* (1971) H.L.

Couchman v. *Hill* (1947): C bought a heifer at an auction sale. The heifer was described in the sale catalogue as "unserved." The printed conditions of sale contained the following stipulation: "The lots are sold with all faults, imperfections, and errors of description, the auctioneers not being responsible for the correct description, genuineness, or authenticity of, or any fault or defect in, any lot, and giving no warranty whatever". Before he bid for the heifer, C asked the auctioneer and H, the owner, "Can you confirm heifer unserved?" Both answered in the affirmative. The heifer died two months later as a result of a miscarriage. C sued H for breach of contract. HELD by the Court of Appeal: the substance of the conversation between the parties before the sale amounted to a contractual term over-riding the stultifying exemptions clause in the printed conditions.

Routledge v. *McKay* (1954): B bought a motor cycle from S by private sale. A week before the sale S told B in good faith that it was a 1941 or 1942 model. The written memorandum of the sale did not mention the year of the model. The motor cycle was a 1930 model and B sued S for breach of contract. HELD by the Court of Appeal: the oral statement as to the year of the model was a mere representation and not a term of the contract. (N.B. The statement was made (i) a full week before the sale, and (ii) it was not included in the written memorandum.)

Heilbut, Symons & Co. v. *Buckleton* (1913): the defendants underwrote a large number of shares in Filisola Rubber and Produce Estates, Ltd. The defendants instructed one Johnston, their Liverpool manager, to obtain applications for shares. The plaintiff telephoned Johnston, saying, "I understand that you are bringing out a rubber company." To which Johnston replied "We are." The plaintiff than asked Johnston whether he had any prospectuses, and he replied that he had not. The plaintiff then asked "if it was all right," to which Johnston replied,

"We are bringing it out." The plaintiff then said, "That is good enough for me." As a result of this telephone conversation a large number of shares were allotted to the plaintiff. At this time, there was a rubber boom and the Filisola shares were at a premium. Shortly afterwards, the shares fell in value. The plaintiff brought this action for fraudulent misrepresentation by the defendants through their agent Johnston, and, alternatively, damages for breach of warranty that the Filisola company was a rubber company whose main object was to produce rubber. At Liverpool Assizes before Lush, J., and a special jury, the jury found that there was no fraud: but that the company could not properly be described as a rubber company and that the defendants or Johnston or both had warranted that the company was a rubber company. The jury based its findings as to warranty on the telephone conversation, there being no other evidence. The defendants appealed without success to the Court of Appeal. The defendants then appealed to the House of Lords. HELD, by the House of Lords: Johnston's telephone statements did not amount to a warranty. There was, accordingly no breach of contract.

Dick Bentley Productions, Ltd. v. *Harold Smith (Motors) Ltd.* (1965): The second plaintiff, Mr Bentley, told Mr Smith of the defendant company that he was on the look-out for a well-vetted Bentley car. Mr Smith subsequently obtained a Bentley car and Mr Bentley went to see it. Mr Smith told Mr Bentley that the car had done twenty thousand miles only since the fitting of a new engine and gearbox. (The mileometer showed twenty thousand miles.) Later that day Mr Bentley took his wife to see the car and Mr Smith repeated his statement. Mr Bentley took the car out for a run and then bought it for £1850, paying by cheque. The car was a disappointment to Mr Bentley and it soon became clear that the car had done more than twenty thousand miles since the change of engine and gearbox. The action for £400 damages was brought against the defendant company in the county court, the plaintiffs alleging fraud. The defendants counterclaimed for £190 for works carried out on the car. His Honour Judge Herbert held that there was no fraud, but that there was a breach of warranty, awarding £400 damages to the plaintiffs and £77 to the defendants on their counterclaim. The defendants appealed, contending that their representation did not amount to a warranty. HELD: the representation was a warranty.

3. Certainty of terms. The parties should make their contracts in terms which are certain or the contract may fail: *Scammell* v. *Ouston* (1941). Meaningless terms will be ignored and the contract will operate without them: *Nicolene* v. *Simmonds* (1953). A contract couched in uncertain or vague terms may be saved if the contract contains a term which will resolve the uncertainty: *Foley* v. *Classique Coaches* (1934). Moreover, the law will, in certain circumstances, infer a term to give effect to the presumed intentions of the parties.

4. Construction of a contract. The court will construe a contract as follows:

(*a*) Words are presumed to have their ordinary literal meaning; but legal terms are presumed to have their technical meaning.

(*b*) Where a contract is ambiguous so that it may have either a legal or an illegal meaning, the legal meaning will be preferred.

(*c*) Where the meaning of words used is not clear, or where two terms cannot be reconciled, the intention of the parties will prevail: indeed, an oral term may thus prevail over a contradictory written term as in *Couchman* v. *Hill*. Where a contract is made up of a standard printed form together with specially prepared documents which conflict with the standard form, the Court will generally take the view that the intention of the parties should be gathered from the specially prepared documents, and that the conflicting provision in the standard form should be disregarded.

(*d*) The contract will be construed most strongly against the party who drew it up. Thus, where there is an ambiguous passage in a contract so that the words will bear two different meanings the court will choose that meaning which is against the interest of the party who drew up the document, to the benefit of the other party. This is known as the *contra proferentem* rule, and is most important in connection with exemption clauses.

EXEMPTION CLAUSES AND FUNDAMENTAL BREACH

5. Exemption clauses. An exemption clause is a contractual stipulation purporting to limit or exclude the liability of one of the parties in contract or in tort. Where a standard form contract is used, it is not unusual for the party who drew it up

V. THE TERMS OF A CONTRACT

to take advantage of his dominant position by including an exemption clause. Where a case turns on whether an exemption clause is binding, the ordinary rules are followed: *e.g.* the existence of the clause must be communicated to the other party; the circumstances must show an intention to be bound; the clause will be construed most strongly against the party seeking to take advantage of it. (The courts tend to lean against exemption clauses, following the *contra proferentem* rule.)

Parker v. *S.E. Railway Co.* (1877): P deposited a bag in the defendants' cloakroom. He paid two pence and was given a ticket on the face of which was printed "See Back." On the back of the ticket was a printed notice saying that the company would not be responsible for any item whose value was more than £10. P's bag, which was worth more than £10, was lost and he brought this action for damages from the company. P had not read the notice on the back of the ticket. HELD: P had notice of the condition on the back of the ticket, the condition was part of a counter-offer by the defendant company which was accepted by P. The printed notice was, therefore, part of the contract and the company could rely on it in their defence.

Chapelton v. *Barry U.D.C.* (1940): the Council hired out deck chairs and by the stack of chairs was a notice containing the terms of hire. C hired two chairs, paid his money, and received two tickets which he put in his pocket. When C sat in one of the chairs, it broke and caused him injury. The chair was not fit for use. C sued the Council for negligence and was met with the defence that the words printed on the back of his ticket included "The Council will not be liable for any accident or damage arising from hire of chair." HELD by the Court of Appeal: the terms of the contract of hire were contained in the notice by the stack of chairs. The ticket issued was a mere receipt, therefore the writing on the back of it could not be included in the contract. The Council could not rely on the exemption clause.

Olley v. *Marlborough Court Hotel, Ltd.* (1949): O locked the door of her hotel room and deposited the key at the reception desk, and then left the hotel for a few hours. On returning, she found that her key was missing from the reception desk and some of her belongings had been stolen from her room. O sued the hotel company for negligence and was met with the defence that she was contractually bound by the terms of a notice in her room providing that, "The proprietors will not hold themselves responsible for articles lost or stolen unless handed to the manageress for safe custody." HELD by the Court of Appeal:

(i) the company was negligent; (ii) the notice was not a term in O's contract with the company, for she did not see it before the contract was made, nor was she aware of its existence then. (But NOTE the effect of previous dealings between the parties, in which case a party may be fixed with notice of an exemption clause communicated on previous occasions: *Spurling* v. *Bradshaw* (1956).)

L'Estrange v. *Graucob, Ltd.* (1934): E signed a printed contract of sale of a slot machine without reading it. The machine proved unsatisfactory and E claimed damages for breach of the implied condition as to fitness for purpose under the *Sale of Goods Act*, *s.* 14 (1). She was met with the defence that one of the printed terms excluded the implied conditions. HELD: the printed condition excluded the implied condition under the Act. Since E had signed the contract, it was irrelevant that she had not read it.

Curtis v. *Chemical Cleaning and Dyeing Co., Ltd.* (1951): C took a wedding dress to the cleaning company for cleaning and was asked to sign a document which contained a clause that the garment is "accepted on condition that the company is not liable for any damage." C asked why she had to sign it and was told that the company would not accept liability for damage done to the beads and sequins on the dress. C signed the document. The dress was stained badly while being cleaned and C brought this action for damages. The company raised the exemption clause in their defence. HELD by the Court of Appeal: the clause gave no protection to the company because of the misrepresentation as to its extent.

McCutcheon v. *MacBrayne, Ltd.* (1964): the appellant asked his brother-in-law, one McSporran, to have his car sent by the respondents from the isle of Islay to the Scottish mainland. McSporran went to the respondents' office where he was quoted the freight for the return journey of the car. He paid the money, for which he was given a receipt, and he delivered the car. The car was shipped on a vessel which subsequently sank owing to the negligent navigation of the respondents' servants. The car was lost and the appellant sued in negligence for the value of it. The respondents' practice was to require consignors to sign risk notes which included their elaborate printed conditions, one of which excluded liability for negligence. On the occasion in question, McSporran was not asked to sign a risk note. McSporran had previously consigned goods to the mainland and had sometimes signed a risk note and sometimes not. He had never read the risk notes on those occasions when he had signed them. He did not know that, by the conditions on the risk note, the consignor agreed to send the goods at owner's risk. The appellant

V. THE TERMS OF A CONTRACT

had consigned goods on four previous occasions and each time he had signed a risk note, but he had never read the conditions and did not know what they meant. The respondents contended that the appellant was bound by the conditions in the risk note by reason of the knowledge gained by the appellant and his agent in previous transactions. The conditions were also displayed in the respondents' office and in the respondents' ship, but neither the appellant nor McSporran had read them. On the question whether the exemption clause in the conditions was part of the contract, HELD by the House of Lords: the contract was an oral contract and the printed conditions were not part of it because the respondents had not discharged the burden of showing the appellant had knowledge of the printed conditions—accordingly, the liability of the appellants in negligence was not excluded.

Per Lord Devlin: "In my opinion, the bare fact that there have been previous dealings between the parties does not assist the respondents at all. The fact that a man has made a contract in the same form ninety-nine times (let alone the three or four times which are here alleged) will not of itself affect the hundredth contract, in which the form is not used. Previous dealings are relevant only if they prove knowledge of the terms, actual and not constructive, and assent to them."

6. Exclusion of liability for misrepresentation.

The *Misrepresentation Act*, 1967, *s*. 3, provides that if any agreement contains a provision which would exclude or restrict

(*a*) any liability to which a party to a contract may be subject by reason of any misrepresentation made by him before the contract was made; or

(*b*) any remedy available to another party to the contract by reason of such a misrepresentation;

that provision shall be of no effect except to the extent (if any) that, in any proceedings arising out of the contract, the court or arbitrator may allow reliance on it as being fair and reasonable in the circumstances of the case.

The Act applies only to exemption clauses which are designed to protect a party from liability for misrepresentations made during negotiations leading to a contract. Notice that such exemption clauses remain unaffected by the Act if reliance on them is fair and reasonable in the circumstances of the case.

7. Validity of exemption clauses. The courts will lean against exemption clauses and will not enforce them unless they are clearly intended to be binding terms. Note:

(a) An exemption clause will not be binding if it was not brought to the attention of the other party before the contract was made: *Olley* v. *Marlborough Court* (1949); *Chapelton* v. *Barry U.D.C.* (1940); *F.M.C. (Meat)* v. *Fairfield Cold Stores* (1971).

(b) An exemption clause written on a receipt and nowhere else has no validity: *Chapelton* v. *Barry U.D.C.* (1940).

(c) Where the clause was brought to the notice of the other party during previous dealings it may be implied to give effect to the presumed intentions of the parties: *Spurling* v. *Bradshaw* (1956). But even where there have been previous dealings, the party seeking to uphold the exemption clause must discharge the burden of showing knowledge of the clause on the part of the other party, otherwise the exemption clause will not be binding; *McCutcheon* v. *MacBrayne* (1964).

(d) Where a party signs a document containing an exemption clause, it is binding even though it may not have been read by that party: *L'Estrange* v. *Graucob* (1934).

(e) Where the party seeking to rely on an exemption clause has misrepresented the extent of the clause, the clause will not be binding: *Curtis* v. *Chemical Cleaning Co.* (1951).

(f) Where there has been a fundamental breach of contract or breach of a fundamental term, it is a question of construction of the contract whether an exemption clause was intended to give protection from the consequences of the breach: *Suisse Atlantique Société* case (1966).

(g) In a contract for the sale of goods, an exemption clause purporting to exempt the implied warranties as to title under *s.* 12 of the *Sale of Goods Act* will be void. See V, **17**.

(h) In the case of a consumer sale, any exemption clause purporting to exclude liability for breach of the implied terms under *ss.* 13, 14 or 15 of the *Sale of Goods Act* will be void. See V, **22**.

(i) In the case of a business sale, any exemption clause purporting to exclude liability for breach of the implied terms under *ss.* 13, 14 or 15 of the *Sale of Goods Act* will not be enforceable to the extent that it would not be fair or reasonable to allow reliance on it. *See* V, 22.

8. Basis of fundamental breach. The doctrine of "fundamental breach" or "breach of a fundamental term" has appeared largely as a result of the court's policy to lean against exemption clauses. This doctrine implies that there is a "fundamental term" as distinct from a "condition." This distinction lies in the fact that it may be possible for a party to rely on the protection of an exemption clause in the event of a breach of condition, but there may be no protection at all where there has been a fundamental breach. This was the principle enunciated by the Court of Appeal in *Karsales* v. *Wallis* (1956), but the decision of the House of Lords in the *Suisse Atlantique* case (1966) makes it clear that the principle is not one of law, but a matter of construction to be decided by looking at the entire contract. In the *Suisse Atlantique* case, Viscount Dilhorne, L.C., cited with approval the following passage from the judgment of Pearson, L.J., in *U.G.S. Finance, Ltd.* v. *National Mortgage Bank of Greece and National Bank of Greece* (1964): "As to the question of 'fundamental breach,' I think there is a rule of construction that normally an exception or exclusion clause or similar provision in a contract should be construed as not applying to a situation created by a fundamental breach of contract. This is not an independent rule of law imposed by the court on the parties willy-nilly in disregard of their contractual intention. On the contrary it is a rule of construction based on the presumed intention of the contracting parties. It involves the implication of a term to give to the contract that business efficacy which the parties as reasonable men must have intended it to have. This rule of construction is not new in principle but it has become prominent in recent years in consequence of the tendency to have standard forms of contract containing exceptions clauses drawn in extravagantly wide terms, which would produce absurd results if applied literally."

Karsales (Harrow), Ltd., v. *Wallis* (1956): W entered into a contract of hire-purchase of a motor car which he had inspected and found to be in excellent condition. The contract contained a clause: "No condition or warranty that the vehicle is roadworthy, or as to its age, condition, or fitness for any purpose is given by the owner or implied herein." The car was shortly afterwards delivered by night. Next morning, when W came to inspect it, he found it to be in a deplorable condition. Many of the original parts had been removed and the car would not go. HELD by the Court of Appeal: the car delivered was not the thing contracted for. There was a fundamental breach of contract and, in consequence, the exemption clause could not be relied upon.

9. Two types of fundamental breach. A helpful distinction was drawn by Lord Wilberforce in *Suisse Atlantique* when he explained that the expression "fundamental breach" of contract denotes either (i) a performance totally different from that which the contract contemplates or (ii) a breach of contract more serious than one which would entitle the other party merely to damages and which would entitle him at least to refuse performance or further performance. Lord Wilberforce went on to say: "There is in fact no necessary coincidence between the two kinds of (so-called fundamental) breach. For, though it may be true generally, if the contract contains a wide exceptions clause, that a breach sufficiently serious to take the case outside that clause will also give the other party the right to refuse further performance, it is not the case, necessarily, that a breach of the latter character has the former consequence. An act which, apart from the exceptions clause, might be a breach sufficiently serious to justify refusal of further performance, may be reduced in effect or made not a breach at all, by the terms of the clause." It would seem to follow that only in cases where the fundamental breach takes the form of a totally different performance from that which was contemplated by the contract will the exemption clause be invalidated regardless of its wording. See *Kenyon, Son & Craven* v. *Baxter Hoare* (1971). Where, on the other hand, the question is whether a serious breach of contract affects the validity of an exemption clause, it is a matter of construction of that exemption clause.

10. Effects of fundamental breach. *Suisse Atlantique* and *Harbutt's Plasticine* may be regarded as heading a long line of cases affirming that where one party has committed a fundamental breach of contract and the other party accepts it, or if the contract is brought to an end anyway by reason of the breach, then the contract-breaker cannot rely on an

V. THE TERMS OF A CONTRACT

exemption or limitation clause to escape liability for the breach.

If the innocent party, on becoming aware of the breach, does not accept it—preferring to keep the contract alive—then it is a matter of construction whether the guilty party can rely on the exemption clause. In construing an exemption clause in these circumstances, the courts will reject it if it would lead to an absurdity or if it would defeat the main object of the contract. And so it follows that a widely-drawn exemption clause will not generally be construed so as to exclude or reduce liability for the consequences of a fundamental breach. In other words, the courts may allow a party to avail himself of an exemption clause if he is carrying out his contract in substance, but not if he is in breach going to the very root of the contract.

Suisse Atlantique Soc. D'Armament Maritime v. *Rotterdamsche Kolen Centrale* (1966): the plaintiffs agreed by a charterparty dated December 1956 to charter their ship to the defendants for carrying coal from the U.S.A. to Europe. The charter was expressed to remain in force for two years' consecutive voyages between U.S.A. and Europe. By the charter, if the vessel was delayed beyond the agreed loading time, the defendants were to pay $1000 a day demurrage. Similarly, demurrage was payable if the vessel was delayed beyond the agreed unloading time. In September 1957 the plaintiffs regarded themselves as being entitled to treat the charterparty as repudiated by reason of the defendants' delays in loading and unloading the vessel. The defendants did not accept this contention, and it was agreed (without prejudice to this dispute) that the charterparty should be continued. From October 1957 the vessel made eight round voyages under the charter. It was contended by the plaintiffs that each round voyage ought reasonably to have been completed in thirty to thirty-seven days, including loading and unloading. On this basis, the eight voyages which took 511 days should have been completed in 240 or 296 days. From this the plaintiffs argued that they had lost the freights which they would have earned on nine or, alternatively, six voyages. The plaintiffs claimed damages of $773,000 or alternatively, $476,000. The basis of the plaintiffs' contention was that the charterparty gave them a contractual right to the number of voyages which would be made in the event of both parties carrying out their contractual obligations, and that their claim was not limited to their entitlement to demurrage. The plaintiffs (who had failed before Mocatta, J., and before the Court of

Appeal) appealed to the House of Lords. An argument, not advanced in the courts below, was put forward, namely that if the delays were such as to entitle the appellants to treat the charterparty as repudiated, the demurrage clauses did not apply, and that the appellants would then be entitled to recover their full loss on the basis they claimed. HELD by the House of Lords: the appellants, having elected in 1957 to affirm the charterparty, were bound by its provisions, including the demurrage clauses, which operated as agreed damages. The appellants were not entitled to damages for loss of freight, nor would they be so entitled if the respondent's breaches were deliberate.

Harbutt's Plasticine Ltd. v. *Wayne Tank and Pump Co. Ltd.* (1970) C.A: the plaintiffs were manufacturers of plasticine and the defendants were designers and manufacturers of pumping equipment. The defendants agreed to design and install equipment at the plaintiffs' factory for the storing and dispensing of molten stearine. The contract contained a clause designed to limit the liability of the defendants for accidents and damage done during the course of carrying out the work. It was part of the design specification that the temperature of the stearine be kept between 120°F. and 160°F. The defendants used a form of plastic piping known as durapipe. The temperature was to be controlled by a thermostat connected to electrical tapes wound round the piping. Durapipe was, in fact, entirely unsuitable for the purpose of this design owing to its liability to distort at temperatures above 180°F. and its thermal conductivity was low. When the installation was completed an employee of the defendants switched on the heating tapes and left the installation unattended. During that night a fire broke out owing to the distortion of the durapipe under heat and the escape of molten stearine. This fire destroyed the plaintiffs' factory. It was held at first instance that the defendants were in fundamental breach of contract by designing and supplying a system which was totally unsuitable for its purpose. In calculating damages, the trial judge made a deduction in respect of betterment resulting from the more convenient lay-out of the new factory as compared with the old factory which was burnt down. The defendants appealed. HELD: (i) in deciding whether a breach of contract is one which causes the innocent party to be relieved of further performance of his obligations it is necessary to look not only at the breach but also at the results of it. (ii) The consequences of the breach was an event which would have frustrated the contract had it occurred without the fault of either party and was therefore a fundamental breach, the plaintiffs having no alternative but to accept the breach as a repudiation of the contract and must therefore be treated as having accepted the breach. (iii) The defendants were not entitled to rely on the clause purporting to limit their liability. (iv) The measure of damages must include the full cost of rebuilding the factory with no deduction under the heading of betterment on account of the new factory being more modern and convenient than the one that was burnt down. (v) Insurance moneys received by the plaintiffs to be taken into account in the defendants' favour.

IMPLIED TERMS

11. Unexpressed terms. There is a general presumption that the parties have expressed, orally or in writing, every material term which they intend should govern their contract. But there are circumstances where terms which have not been expressed by the parties are inferred by the law. An implied term is binding to the same extent as an express term. The courts will infer a term

(a) to give effect to the presumed intentions of the parties; or

(b) on the grounds of a statute.

12. Implied terms and presumed intentions. In order to discover the unexpressed intention of the parties, the courts may take notice of trade customs, the conduct of the parties, or the need to give "business efficacy" to a contract.

It must be emphasised that, where the parties have made an unambiguous express provision in their contract, the Court will not imply a term to the contrary: *see Trollope & Colls* v. *N.W. Regional Hospital Board* (1973), a House of Lords decision.

13. Trade or professional customs. In *Hutton* v. *Warren* (1836), Baron Parke said, "It has long been settled that in commercial transactions extrinsic evidence of custom and usage is admissible to annex incidents to written contracts in matters with respect to which they are silent. The same rule has also been applied to contracts in other transactions in life in which known usages have been established and prevailed; and this has been done upon the principle of presumption that, in such transactions, the parties did not mean to express in writing the whole of the contract by which they intended to be bound, but to contract with reference to those known usages."

Although Baron Parke spoke only of terms implied in written contracts, the same principle applies to oral contracts.

Where a term is implied on the grounds of a custom, the implication is based on the assumption that it was the intention of the parties to be bound by the custom. A custom can, of course, be excluded from an agreement by an express term to that effect.

An example of a term implied by custom occurs in contracts of marine insurance, where there is an implied undertaking by the broker that agreed premiums will be paid, *i.e.* he is deemed to promise the insurer that he will be liable for payment of premiums in the event of default on the part of the assured.

14. Conduct of the parties. A term may be implied by reason of the conduct of the parties. For example, when a customer selects goods from the shelves of a self-service store and presents them at the cashier's desk, and the cashier rings up the price, which the customer immediately pays, there is a contract. There is an express term as to price, *i.e.* the sum of the prices on the labels of the selected items, the remaining terms being implied by the conduct of the parties: *Pharmaceutical Society* v. *Boots* (1953).

Hillas & Co. v. *Arcos Ltd.* (1932): there was an agreement between the parties for the supply of 22,000 standards of timber during 1931, the agreement containing an option clause allowing the buyers to take 100,000 standards during 1932. The agreement was vague as to the kind of timber, the terms of shipment, and other important details usually expressed in commercial contracts: however, the parties managed to get through the part of the agreement relating to the 22,000 standards in 1931. In 1932 the sellers claimed that they were not bound to deliver the 100,000 standards: they contended that the clause was vague and was merely a basis for further negotiations. HELD by the House of Lords: the option clause was not specific as to details, but it was couched in the same language as the agreement to supply timber in 1931. The unexpressed details of the option clause could, therefore, be inferred from the course of dealing between the parties during 1931.

15. "Business efficacy." A term may be implied to give to a contract what has become known as "business efficacy." Bowen, L.J., said in *The Moorcock* (1889), "The implication

V. THE TERMS OF A CONTRACT

which the law draws from what must obviously have been the intention of the parties, the law draws with the object of giving efficacy to the transaction and preventing such a failure of consideration as cannot have been within the contemplation of either side. . . . In business transactions . . . what the law desires to effect by the implication is to give such business efficacy to the transaction as must have been intended at all events by both parties who are business men. . . ." As a result of the decision in this case, the courts were often asked to imply a term on vague or uncertain grounds.

In 1941, however, the rule in *The Moorcock* was given some precision by the House of Lords in *Luxor* v. *Cooper*. In this case, Lord Wright said, "It is agreed on all sides that the presumption is against the adding to contracts of terms which the parties have not expressed. The general presumption is that the parties have expressed every material term which they intended should govern their agreement, whether oral or in writing. It is well recognised, however, that there may be cases where obviously some term must be implied if the intention of the parties is not to be defeated, some term of which it can be predicated that 'it goes without saying,' some term not expressed, but necessary to give the transaction such business efficacy as the parties must have intended. . . . The implication must arise inevitably to give effect to the intention of the parties."

The Moorcock (1889): there was a contract between the defendants, who owned a Thameside wharf and jetty and the plaintiffs that the plaintiffs' vessel *Moorcock* should be unloaded and reloaded at the defendants' wharf. The *Moorcock* was, accordingly, moored alongside the wharf but, as the tide fell, she took to the ground and sustained damage on account of the unevenness of the river bed at that place. The plaintiffs brought this action for damages for breach of contract. HELD: there was an implied term in the contract that the defendants would take reasonable care to see that the berth was safe: both parties must have known at the time of the agreement that if the ground were not safe the ship would be endangered when the tide ebbed: there was a breach of the implied term.

It is important to notice that no term will be implied to give the contract efficacy unless the implication must arise inevitably. In order to imply a term it is necessary to say not merely that it would be a businesslike arrangement to make, but that any other arrangement would be so unbusinesslike that sensible people could not be supposed to have entered into it: *see Brown & Davis, Ltd.* v. *Galbraith* (1972), C.A.

16. Terms implied on the grounds of a statute. Certain statutes provide for the implication of terms in contracts. Statutory implied terms will operate irrespective of the intention of the parties, unless there is a valid exclusion clause. Examples of statutory implied terms are to be found in *ss.* 12–15 of the *Sale of Goods Act*, 1893, as amended by the *Supply of Goods (Implied Terms) Act*, 1973. These Acts provide for the implication of certain very important undertakings by the seller in contracts of sale of goods. It is necessary now to consider the implied terms separately (**17–21** below) and then to consider the restrictions on the seller's power to contract out of the implied undertakings (**22**).

All references are to the *Sale of Goods Act*, 1893, as amended by the *Supply of Goods (Implied Terms) Act*, 1973.

17. Implied terms as to title (s. 12). The 1893 Act provides for the implication of three terms as to title to the goods, namely,

(*a*) a condition that the seller has the right to sell the goods, and

(*b*) a warranty that the buyer will enjoy quiet possession, and

(*c*) a warranty that the goods will be free from any undisclosed encumbrance.

Any term purporting to exempt from any of these implied terms in any contract of sale of goods will be void: *s.* 55 (3).

Rowland v. *Divall* (1923): after a buyer had used a motor car for four months, the police took it away because it had been stolen before it had come into the seller's possession. The buyer sought to recover the full price on the ground that the consideration had wholly failed. HELD by the Court of Appeal: there was a breach of the implied condition arising under *s.* 12 of the *Sale of Goods Act*. The seller had no title and the buyer, therefore, received nothing from him. There was a complete failure of consideration and the full purchase price was recoverable. The fact that the buyer had enjoyed the use of the car for four months was not a benefit conferred by the seller under the contract.

V. THE TERMS OF A CONTRACT

18. Correspondence with description (s. 13). Where there is a contract for the sale of goods by description, there is an implied condition that the goods will correspond with the description. A sale of goods will not be prevented from being a sale by description by reason only that, being exposed for sale (as, *e.g.*, in a self-service store) they are selected by the buyer.

Where a sale is by sample as well as by description, it is not sufficient that the bulk of the goods corresponds with the sample if the goods do not also correspond with the description.

The following cases indicate the strictness with which the Court has applied *s*. 13.

Wilensko Slaski, etc. v. *Fenwick & Co. Ltd.* (1938): there was a contract for the sale of a quantity of pit props of specified lengths. The buyer undertook that he would "not reject the goods . . . or any part of them." One per cent of the goods delivered did not comply with the specification and the buyer claimed to be able to reject them. HELD: notwithstanding his undertaking, the buyer was entitled to reject the goods because the seller was in breach of the implied condition in *s*. 13.

Re Moore & Co. and Landauer & Co. (1921): the terms of a contract for the sale of tinned pears provided that the goods were to be packed in cases of 30 tins each. When the buyers inspected the tendered consignment they found that about half the cases contained 24 tins each, the remainder containing 30 tins each. The buyers rejected all the cases. HELD by the Court of Appeal: it was part of the contract description of the goods that there should be 30 tins to the case and that, accordingly, the sellers were in breach of the implied condition in *s*. 13. Further, by *s*. 30 (3), the buyer was entitled to reject the entire consignment.

Macpherson Train & Co. Ltd. v. *Howard Ross & Co. Ltd.* (1955): there was a contract for the sale of 5,064 cases of cans of peaches. The contract included a clause which provided as follows: "Shipment and destination: afloat per S.S. *Morton Bay* due London approximately June 8th." The *Morton Bay* did not arrive in London until June 21st. The buyers refused to accept the goods, contending that there was a breach of condition, as "afloat per S.S. *Morton Bay* due London approximately June 8th" was part of the description of the goods. The sellers contended that June 8th was not intended to be the delivery date. HELD: the clause was part of the description of the goods, and the sellers were in breach of the implied condition in *s*. 13. The buyers were entitled to refuse to accept the goods.

19. Merchantable quality (s. 14 (2)).

Where the seller sells goods in the course of a business, there is an implied condition that the goods supplied under the contract are of merchantable quality (*i.e.* without defects). But there is no such condition as regards defects specifically drawn to the buyer's attention before the contract was made, or, if the buyer examines the goods before the contract is made, as regards defects which that examination ought to reveal. Nor where the sale is not in the course of a business.

Wilson v. *Rickett, Cockerell & Co.* (1954): W bought from the defendant coal merchants "a ton of Coalite." When part of the consignment was being burnt in the grate, there was an explosion which caused damage to W's goods in the room. The explosive substance was not Coalite, but some foreign matter which had got mixed with the Coalite. W claimed damages under *s*. 14. HELD by the Court of Appeal: there was a breach of the implied condition of merchantable quality under *s*. 14.

Wren v. *Holt* (1903): the buyer bought a glass of beer in a public house and later became ill because the beer was contaminated with arsenic. HELD: there was a breach of the implied condition as to merchantable quality under *s*. 14.

20. Fitness for purpose (s. 14 (3)).

Where the seller sells goods in the course of a business and the buyer, expressly or by implication, makes known to the seller any particular purpose for which the goods are being bought, there is an implied condition that the goods supplied under the contract are reasonably fit for that purpose. The implied condition arises whether or not the purpose is one for which such goods are commonly supplied. There is, however, no implied condition as to fitness for purpose where the circumstances show that the buyer does not rely, or that it is unreasonable for him to rely, on the seller's skill or judgment. Nor where the sale is private, *i.e.* not in the course of a business.

Where goods have a self-evident purpose, *e.g.* a hot-water bottle or a pair of underpants, the purpose for which the goods are being bought is made known to the seller by implication.

Priest v. *Last* (1903): there was a retail sale of a hot-water bottle. The bottle burst and injured the buyer's wife. The buyer brought this action to recover damages for the medical expenses incurred. HELD: the seller was in breach of the implied condition as to fitness for purpose, the purpose being self-evident in the case of goods of this kind.

Ashington Piggeries v. *Christopher Hill* (1971): the defendants were two mink companies concerned with the breeding of mink and with the supply of equipment and foodstuffs to other mink breeders. The plaintiffs, who manufactured compounds for animal feeding, entered into an agreement with the defendants for the manufacture of a mink food to be called King Size. The formula was supplied by the defendants, and the plaintiffs had made it clear that they knew nothing about the nutritional requirements of mink. The plaintiff did, however, suggest as a variation in the formula, the substitution of herring meal for fishmeal. For about a year, King Size was used by about 100 mink farms without complaint. But in March 1961 the plaintiffs bought a large consignment of herring meal which had been contaminated by a chemical known as D.M.N.A., toxic to mink but harmless to other animals. The inclusion of contaminated herring meal in the manufacture of King Size resulted in serious losses on some mink farms.

The defendant buyers refused to pay for a consignment of King Size containing contaminated meal and the plaintiff sellers brought this action for payment. The defendants counterclaimed for breach of contract. HELD by the House of Lords: (*i*) there was a breach of the implied condition in *s*. 14 that the goods were reasonably fit for purpose, the buyers having relied on the skill and judgment of the sellers; (*ii*) the sellers were also in breach of the implied condition that the goods were of merchantable quality.

21. Sale by sample (s. 15). In the case of a contract of sale by sample there are the following further implied conditions:

(*a*) that the bulk will correspond with the sample in quality, and

(*b*) that the buyer will have a reasonable opportunity of comparing the bulk with the sample, and

(*c*) that the goods will be free from any defect, rendering them unmerchantable, which would not be apparent on reasonable examination of the sample.

22. Contracting out of the implied terms (s. 55). Before the 1973 amendments to the *Sale of Goods Act*, 1893, any or all of the implied undertakings on the part of the seller could be excluded by an express term to that effect. But the 1973 Act provides for important restrictions on the right of the parties to exclude the implied terms. These restrictions are contained in *s.* 55 as amended.

By *s.* 55 (2), any term purporting to exclude the implied terms as to title under *s.* 12 will be void. There remain the implied terms under *ss.* 13–15 to be considered, for which it is necessary to distinguish between consumer sales and other sales, *i.e.* business sales. "Consumer sale" is defined as a sale of goods (other than a sale by auction or by competitive tender) by a seller in the course of a business where the goods—

(*a*) are of a type ordinarily bought for private use or consumption; and

(*b*) are sold to a person who does not buy or hold himself out as buying them in the course of a business.

Consumer sales and ss. 13–15: Any term purporting to exempt from all or any of the provisions of *ss.* 13, 14 or 15 will be *void* in the case of a consumer sale: *s.* 55 (4). Thus the 1973 amendment to the *Sale of Goods Act* gives an important new protection to the consumer-buyer.

Sales other than consumer sales and ss. 13–15: In the case of a contract of sale of goods other than a consumer sale, any term exempting from all or any of the provisions of *ss.* 13, 14 or 15 will not be enforceable to the extent that it is shown that it would not be fair or reasonable to allow reliance on the term: *s.* 55 (4). In other words, the validity of an exemption clause seeking to excuse the seller from the implied undertakings in *ss.* 13–15 will depend on whether the clause is "fair or reasonable" in the circumstances. Section 55 (5) gives some assistance in the problem of deciding what should be regarded as "fair or reasonable" in any case: it provides that, in determining whether or not it would be fair and reasonable to allow the seller to rely on an exemption clause, regard must be had to all the circumstances of the case and, in particular, to the following matters:

(*a*) the strength of the bargaining positions of the seller and buyer relative to each other, taking into account the availability of suitable alternative products and sources of supply;

(*b*) whether the buyer received an inducement to agree to the exemption clause or in accepting it had an opportunity

V. THE TERMS OF A CONTRACT

of buying the goods or suitable alternatives without it from any source of supply;

(c) whether the buyer knew or ought reasonably to have known of the existence and extent of the exemption clause;

(d) where the clause exempts from all or any of the provisions of ss. 13, 14 or 15 if some condition is not complied with, whether it was reasonable at the time of the contract to expect that compliance with that condition would be practicable;

(e) whether the goods were manufactured, processed or adapted to the special order of the buyer.

The provisions of s. 55 (5)—set out above—do not affect the ordinary rules of contract law which might be applicable to determine the question whether an exemption clause is part of the contract. Section 55 (6) provides that these provisions will not prevent the court from holding, in accordance with any rule of law, that a term which purports to exclude or restrict any of the provisions of ss. 13, 14 or 15 is not a term of the contract.

23. Contracts for work and materials. Where a contract requires a party to provide materials and to do work involving the incorporation of those materials the Court will imply terms as to quality and fitness analagous to those contained in the *Sale of Goods Act*. The Act does not apply to such contracts because there is more than a mere sale involved. The most obvious contracts in this category are building and civil engineering contracts. In these contracts the contractor undertakes to provide the materials and to do the construction work described in the contract. The House of Lords explained the implied terms applicable to the materials provided by the contractor in *Young & Marten* v. *McManus Childs, Ltd.* (1968). According to this decision, in every contract for work and materials there is an implied term that the materials are of good quality, *i.e.* that there are no latent defects. This term is implied even where the materials are specified by the employer of the contractor. There is also an implied term as to fitness for purpose where the materials are not specified by the employer, but are selected by the contractor.

There is, however, no hard and fast dividing line between contracts for sale of goods and contracts for work and materials. Difficulties arise, for example, in contracts to make a chattel, such as a chair, or a set of false teeth. In *Samuels* v. *Davis* (1943), a dentist contracted to make a set of false teeth for the defendant's wife. The teeth proved to be so uncomfortable that they could not be worn. It was held by the Court of Appeal that the question whether the contract was for sale of goods or for work and materials was irrelevant, because in either case the same term as to fitness would apply.

CONDITIONS AND WARRANTIES

24. Conditions and warranties. The traditional view is that each term of a contract, express or implied, is either a condition or a warranty, depending upon its importance with regard to the purpose of the contract. Broadly, a term which goes to the essence of the contract is a condition, and any other term is a warranty. The question whether a term is a condition or a warranty becomes significant in case of breach of contract.

According to the traditional approach, the difference between a condition and a warranty is as follows. If a promisor breaks a *condition* in *any* respect, however slight, the other party has a right to elect to treat himself as discharged from future obligations under the contract and to sue for damages immediately. If he did not exercise the right to elect to treat the contract as at an end he would remain bound by the contract, but could sue for damages with respect to the other party's breach. If, on the other hand, a promisor breaks a warranty in any respect the only remedy available to the other party is to sue for damages, *i.e.* there is no right to treat the contract as at an end.

Where the parties describe a term as a condition it is open to the Court to hold that the term is, nevertheless, a mere warranty: *Schuler* v. *Wickman Machine Tool Sales, Ltd.* (1973).

The traditional division was adopted in the drafting of the *Sale of Goods Act*, 1893, where a condition is defined in s. 11 as a term "the breach of which may give rise to a right to treat the contract as repudiated": a warranty is defined as a term "the breach of which may give rise to a claim for damages but not a right to reject the goods and treat the contract as repudiated." The Act provides by s. 62 that a warranty is "collateral to the main purpose of the contract."

V. THE TERMS OF A CONTRACT

Since there is, usually, a stronger remedy available for breach of condition than for breach of warranty, it is not unusual for the parties to be in dispute as to whether a term is a condition or a warranty. The difference is conveniently illustrated by the following cases.

Poussard v. *Spiers* (1876): an actress was under a contractual obligation to play in an operetta as from the beginning of its London run. The producers were forced to use a substitute for her as she was ill until a week after the show had opened. HELD: the obligation to perform as from the first night was a condition and the breach of it entitled the other party to repudiate the contract.

Bettini v. *Gye* (1876): a singer was under contractual obligation to sing in a series of concerts and to take part in six days of rehearsals before the first performance. He arrived three days late, thus leaving only three days for rehearsals. HELD: the undertaking to take part in the rehearsals for six days was a warranty and not a condition. The breach entitled the other party to damages but not to repudiate the contract.

There is now some doubt as to whether every contractual term may be categorised as either a condition or a warranty. In the *Hong Kong Fir* case (1962), the charterers of a ship sought to treat the charterparty as repudiated by the owners on the grounds that there was a breach of the owners' undertaking that the ship was "in every way fitted for ordinary cargo service." The ship had broken down on a number of occasions due to the incompetence of the engine room crew. It was held by the Court of Appeal that in these circumstances there was no breach of condition and, therefore, no right to treat the contract as repudiated. In this case, Upjohn, L.J., said, "the question to be answered is, does the breach of the stipulation go so much to the root of the contract that it makes further commercial performance impossible, or, in other words, is the whole contract frustrated? If yea, the innocent party may treat the contract as at an end. If nay, his claim sounds in damages only." In the same case, Diplock, L.J., expressed the view that many contractual undertakings cannot be categorised as being "conditions" or "warranties," and that of such undertakings, "all that can be predicated is that some breaches will, and others will not, give rise to an event which will deprive the party not in default of substantially the whole benefit which it was intended that he should obtain from the contract; and the legal consequences of such an undertaking, unless provided for expressly in the contract, depend on the nature of the event to which the breach gives rise and do not follow automatically from a prior classification of the undertaking as a 'condition' or a 'warranty.'"

In the *Hong Kong Fir* case (*see* XVII, **10**) the Court of Appeal took the view that the legal consequences of a breach of contract depends on the consequences of the breach—or, to use the words of Diplock, L.J., "the nature of the event to which the breach gives rise." This is quite different from the traditional approach based on the distinction between minor terms (warranties) and important terms (conditions)—the distinction resting on the intention of the parties at the time they made their contract. In *Behn* v. *Burness* (1863), Williams, J., said that a term "is more or less important in proportion as the object of the contract more or less depends upon it."

The distinction was once more before the Court of Appeal in the *Mihalis Angelos* (1970): *see* XVIII, **3**. In this case the approach was different from that taken in *Hong Kong Fir*. The term in question was an "expected readiness" clause in a charterparty. The Court was concerned with the standing of the clause in the light of the expectations or intentions of the parties rather than with the events consequent upon the breach of the clause. In holding that the "expected readiness" clause was a condition, Lord Denning said that the clause was "an assurance by the owner that he honestly expects that the vessel will be ready to load on that date and that his expectation is based on reasonable grounds." Edmund Davies, L.J., held that the "expected readiness" clause was a condition, "particularly having regard to the importance to the charterer of the ability to be able to rely on the owner giving no assurance as to expected readiness save on grounds both honest and reasonable." Megaw, L.J., took the same view on grounds, *inter alia*, "that it would only be in the rarest case, if ever, that a ship-owner could legitimately feel that he had suffered an injustice by reason of the law having given to a charterer the right to put an end to the contract because of the breach by the ship-owner of a clause such as this. If a ship-owner has chosen to assert contractually, but dishonestly or without reasonable grounds, that he expects his vessel to be ready to load on such and such a date, wherein does the grievance lie?"

V. THE TERMS OF A CONTRACT

25. Time of performance—the common law position. At common law the rule is that, where there is an express stipulation as to the time of performance, the contract must be performed accordingly. Similarly, where there is an implied term that performance shall take place within a reasonable time, the contract must be performed within the reasonable time. Whether a stipulation as to time of performance is of the essence of the contract will depend on the intention of the parties as gathered from the terms, express and implied, of the contract.

26. Time of performance—in equity. In equity, if a stipulation as to time is regarded by the court as non-essential, a breach of it will not cost a party his rights under the contract: he may still be awarded specific performance, provided that no injustice is thereby caused to the other party.

Thus if a vendor of land fails to complete the conveyance within the specified time, equity will not allow the purchaser to treat the contract as repudiated, but may award specific performance at the suit of the vendor.

27. Time of performance—present position. Section 41 of the *Law of Property Act*, 1925, provides that, "Stipulations in a contract, as to time or otherwise, which according to rules of equity are not deemed to be or to have become of the essence of the contract, are also construed and have effect at law in accordance with the same rules." The effect of this provision is that time is not of the essence where the contract is specifically enforceable, but otherwise, time *is* of the essence.

NOTE: Section 41 of the *L.P.A.*, 1925, re-enacts the provisions of *s.* 25 of the *Judicature Act*, 1873.

28. Criticisms. There have been serious criticisms of the use of the words "condition" and "warranty" to mean the two kinds of contractual term. In particular:

(*a*) The question for the court may not be "*Is the broken term a condition or a warranty?*" but rather "*What is the effect of the breach on the innocent party?*" *Hong Kong Fir case.*

(*b*) The word "condition" is also used in a different sense in the expressions "condition precedent" and "condition subsequent." This can lead to confusion. (Where an agreement contains a condition precedent, no rights or obligations arise until its fulfilment. Where an agreement contains a condition subsequent, its fulfilment releases all parties from obligations under the agreement.) *See* XVII, **8**.

(c) In commercial usage, the word "warranty" often denotes a major term of the contract. Also, in some instances, the parties may have described a minor term as a condition. It matters not whether the parties have called any particular term a condition or a warranty—in the event of a breach, the court will decide according to the intention of the parties.

COLLATERAL CONTRACTS

29. Express collateral contracts. There is no reason why the consideration given by a party to a contract should not be to enter, or to promise to enter, another contract. Where two or more contracts bear this kind of relationship, they may be described as collateral to one another.

EXAMPLES:

(a) Where G guarantees D's debt to C, there are at least two express collateral contracts:

(i) *As between C and D:* The debt which is guaranteed arises out of this contract.

(ii) *As between G and C:* This is the contract of guarantee. In effect, G promises C that if C will enter the contract with D, then he (G) will honour D's obligation in the event of default by D.

(iii) *As between G and D:* There may be an express contract of indemnity. In effect, D promises G that in consideration for G's acting as guarantor, D will repay G if G is forced to pay C. (If this indemnity is not express, it will be implied by law.)

(b) X makes a promise to Y, the promise being conditional on Y's entering a specified contract with X. If Y then enters this specified contract, X becomes bound by the original promise.

City and Westminster Properties, Ltd. v. *Mudd* (1958): the landlords offered to M a renewal of his lease, the draft renewal containing a covenant for M "to use the demised premises as and for showrooms, workrooms, and offices only." The landlords informed M that if he signed the lease they would not object to his continuing to reside on the premises. M entered the lease. Later, the landlords claimed that the lease was

V. THE TERMS OF A CONTRACT 63

forfeit because M had continued to live on the premises in breach of his covenant. HELD: the claim to forfeit the lease failed because M signed it in reliance on the promise not to enforce the covenant. This promise was part of a contract, separate from, but collateral to, the lease.

30. Implied collateral contracts. In proper circumstances, the court will imply a collateral contract so as to give effect to the presumed intentions of the parties. The rules governing the discovery of intention will be applied. Thus, where A enters a contract with B on the faith of an express or implied promise by C, there is a collateral contract between A and C. This principle is of general application, but it is of special significance with respect to the relationship between a guarantor and the principal debtor, and to the relationship between dealer and hirer in contracts of hire-purchase.

NOTE: in hire-purchase transactions the relationships of the parties are often as follows: dealer and customer arrange the transaction and the dealer then sells the article to a finance company which lets the goods on hire-purchase to the customer. Thus the *express* contract of hire-purchase is between the customer and the finance company, but the courts now recognise there may be an *implied collateral contract* between the dealer and the customer: see *Andrews* v. *Hopkinson*, below.

Clarke v. *Dunraven* (1897): C and D, who were competitors in a yacht regatta, each gave an undertaking to X to abide by certain rules. HELD by the House of Lords: a contract had been created between C and D. It was presumed that, by entering the competition, each had given to the other an undertaking to abide by the rules.

Andrews v. *Hopkinson* (1956): H, a car dealer, induced A to enter a hire-purchase agreement with a finance company by praising a second-hand car which he wished to supply to A. H said, "It's a good little bus. I would stake my life on it." A week later the car was wrecked and A was injured in an accident caused by the faulty steering mechanism of the car. HELD: there was a contract between A and H, collateral to the hire-purchase contract. H was in breach of this collateral contract.

31. Hire-Purchase Act, 1965. Section 16 of the *Hire-Purchase Act*, 1965, provides that in any hire-purchase agreement governed by the Act, any representations made by the dealer to the customer with respect to the goods shall be deemed to have been made by him as agent of the owner (*i.e.* the finance company). The word "representations" is used here to mean any statement whether a condition or a warranty or not.

This provision leaves unaffected the dealer's personal liability at common law under the rule in *Andrews* v. *Hopkinson*.

PROGRESS TEST 5

1. "Contractual terms may be express or implied." Explain.
2. How does the Court decide whether a particular statement is contained as a term of a contract?
3. "The court discovers intention by the application of an objective test." Explain and illustrate.
4. What rules do the Courts follow in construing the express terms of a contract?
5. What is the general purpose of exemption clauses in contracts? It is said that the Courts lean against exemption clauses: explain this.
6. In what circumstances are terms, which are not expressed by the parties, nevertheless implied by law?
7. What implied conditions are imported into contracts governed by the *Sale of Goods Act*, 1893?
8. Distinguish between "conditions" and "warranties." Do you consider the distinction satisfactory?
9. When is time of the essence of a contract?
10. Explain what is meant by the "doctrine of fundamental breach."
11. What are collateral contracts? In what kinds of transaction are they of special significance?
12. At an auction sale a picture, described in the sale catalogue as a Picasso, was up for sale. Before the bidding started, A asked the auctioneer whether he could confirm that it was a genuine Picasso. The auctioneer replied, "It is definitely a Picasso." The picture was knocked down to A for £750. Seven months later he discovered that it was by an unknown artist, and was almost worthless. Advise A. How would it affect your advice if the printed conditions of sale contained a clause to the effect that the auctioneer would not be liable for errors of description?
13. B bought a motor car from C by private sale. C had described the car as being a 1961 model. Three months after the sale, B discovered that it was a 1956 model. Advise B.
14. D took his girl friend, E, for a ride in the "Tunnel of Love" at a fairground. He paid the fare for two and put the tickets into his pocket without looking at them. During the ride, their vehicle overturned due to a defect in its construction. D and E

V. THE TERMS OF A CONTRACT

were both seriously injured. Advise them, (*a*) on the footing that there was a large notice at the entrance saying that "All passengers ride at their own risk," and (*b*) that on the back of the tickets were the words, "The proprietor is not to be held liable for injuries to riders in the Tunnel of Love, no matter how caused."

15. When F stayed in London he always had a room at the Fritz Hotel. On the last occasion, his room key was taken from the reception desk by a thief, who then stole F's diamond tiepin from his room. In the room, there was a notice to the effect that the management of the hotel did not accept liability for theft, and advised guests to deposit valuables with the manager for safe keeping. F's solicitor has told the hotel manager that F intends to sue him for negligence. Advise the manager.

16. G, a ship owner, had bought coal from H for the past three years. Although there was never an express stipulation as to delivery, H had always delivered the consignments into G's ships. H has ordered 10 tons of coal for his ship *Sylvester*, now lying in dock. H has accepted the order, but refuses to deliver it to the *Sylvester*, saying that he never promised to do this. H has told G that the 10 tons of coal is ready for collection at H's yard. Is G bound to arrange for the collection of the consignment?

17. J, a farmer, hired a threshing machine from K. When the machine arrived at J's farm, it was found that the engine was worn out and would not work at all. J had to wait a fortnight before K could replace the engine. J was unable to hire another machine at that time and, in consequence, much of his wheat crop was spoiled. Advise J.

18. L bought an electric blanket from M, a dealer in electrical goods. When L used the blanket for the first time, it set the bed alight, and L's wife was seriously burnt. L wishes to know whether he had any remedy against M.

19. N ordered a "Snip" lawnmower from O, who promised to deliver it to N's house on the following Friday. The mower was not delivered as promised, and on the day following, N, who was worried because his lawn looked unkempt, bought a "Snip" mower from P, who delivered it immediately. Three days later, O delivered a "Snip" mower to N, who refused to accept it. Advise O.

20. Q contracted to buy a new car from R. In the printed standard form contract there was a clause, "All conditions, express or implied, are hereby excluded." After taking delivery of the car, Q discovered that it was not new. It has been used for demonstration purposes. R refuses to take the car back. Advise Q.

21. R is considering taking a 10 year lease of certain property from a landlord, S. One of the lessee's covenants in the lease

states that "All outside woodwork shall be painted every two years." S tells R that if he signs the lease, he will be satisfied if the woodwork is painted at the end of the ten year period. R is thus induced to sign the lease. Is he bound by his covenant to have the woodwork painted every two years?

22. T, a television set dealer, induced U to enter a hire-purchase agreement with the XYZ Finance Company, by describing a second-hand television set as being "Good for a year. You'll have no trouble from this one." After U had used the set for a month, the tube failed and the set was useless. Has U a right of action against T? If so, on what grounds?

CHAPTER VI

MATTERS AFFECTING THE VALIDITY OF A CONTRACT

1. Vitiating factors. The validity of a contract may be impaired in any of the following circumstances:

(a) Where the element of agreement is impaired by

(i) *mistake*, *i.e.* where one party, or both parties, entered the contract under a misapprehension; or,

(ii) *misrepresentation*, *i.e.* where one party was induced to enter the agreement partly by a false representation of the other party, the false representation not being a term of the contract; or,

(iii) *duress or undue influence*, *i.e.* direct or subtle coercion brought to bear on a contracting party.

(b) Where one or more of the contracting parties has not full contractual capacity.

(c) Where the contract is illegal.

(d) Where the contract is partly or wholly void under a statute.

(e) Where a contract is partly or wholly void at common law as being against public policy.

(f) Where the contract is of a class requiring formalities, and these are absent.

2. The impaired contract. Where any vitiating factor is present in a contract, the legal consequences will vary according to the circumstances. The problems involved are considered in the next seven chapters. It will be seen that a contract may be:

(a) *Void*, *i.e.* an absolute nullity.

(b) *Voidable*, *i.e.* a contract which gives rise to legal consequences, but may be set aside, or rescinded.

(c) *Illegal*, *i.e.* one upon which no action may be taken except in very special circumstances.

(d) *Unenforceable*, *i.e.* a good contract, but one upon which a plaintiff may not bring an action at law because of the absence of written evidence where this is required, or because of some defect in the contractual capacity of the defendant.

PROGRESS TEST 6

1. Agreement is an essential element in the formation of a simple contract. Explain, very briefly, how agreement, reached by offer and acceptance, may, nevertheless, contain a vitiating element.

2. Mention all the ways you know in which the validity of a contract may be impaired.

3. Distinguish, in outline only, between the following:

(a) Void contracts;
(b) Voidable contracts;
(c) Illegal contracts;
(d) Unenforceable contracts.

CHAPTER VII

MISTAKE

MISTAKE—ITS EFFECT UPON AGREEMENT

1. Agreement affected in two ways. Where there was some kind of misapprehension or misunderstanding as to a material fact at the time of reaching agreement, the factual circumstances will fall into one of the two following classes:

(a) Where agreement has been reached on the basis of a mistake common to both parties.
(b) Where there was a mere appearance of agreement because of mutual or unilateral mistake.

2. Common mistake. Common mistake occurs where both parties to an agreement are suffering from the same misapprehension. Where this kind of mistake occurs, offer and acceptance correspond, *i.e.* there has been agreement between the parties. It is necessary to consider whether the underlying common mistake affects the validity of the contract. An example of common mistake would be where X agrees to sell certain goods to Y, and at the time of the agreement, the goods have perished unknown to both parties.

3. Mutual and unilateral mistake.

(a) *Mutual mistake* occurs where the parties have negotiated at cross-purposes, *e.g.* where A agrees to sell a horse to B, and A intended to sell his white horse, while B thought he was agreeing to buy A's grey horse.

(b) *Unilateral mistake* occurs where one party only is mistaken and the other party knows, or is deemed to know, of the mistake. An example would be where C makes an offer to D only and it is accepted by X, who knows that the offer was made to D only: C thinks, mistakenly, that acceptance was made by D.

Where mutual or unilateral mistake has occurred, the acceptance may not correspond with the offer, and there is, consequently, doubt as to the validity of the agreement.

4. Mistake at law and mistake in equity. Lord Denning said in *Solle* v. *Butcher*, "... mistake is of two kinds: first, mistake which renders the contract void, that is, a nullity from the beginning, which is the kind of mistake which was dealt with by the courts of common law, and secondly, mistake which renders the contract not void, but voidable, that is, liable to be set aside on such terms as the court thinks fit, which is the kind of mistake which was dealt with by the courts of equity." Since 1875 the court has had the power to give equitable relief or legal relief for mistake, according to the circumstances of the case, and according to the kind of relief asked for by the parties.

Mistake at law and mistake in equity need not be confused. They should be considered separately. It should be noticed that where the court has declared a contract void for operative mistake, no question of equitable mistake can arise: the contract is void *ab initio*. The rules relating to mistake in equity can apply only in cases where the court has not found operative mistake at law.

MISTAKE AT COMMON LAW

5. Operative mistake. Where there is a mistake of fact which prevents the formation of any contract at all, the court will declare the contract void. This kind of mistake is known as operative mistake: any other kind of mistake does not affect the contract in the eyes of the common law, *e.g.*,

Harrison & Jones, Ltd. v. *Bunton & Lancaster, Ltd.* (1953): there was a contract for the sale of a quantity of Calcutta Kapok "Sree" brand. Buyer and seller thought this to be tree kapok, whereas, in fact, it contained an admixture of bush cotton. The true nature of "Sree" brand kapok was generally known in the trade. HELD: goods answering the contract description had been supplied and there was no operative mistake.

Operative mistake is an exceptional occurrence. It is exceptional to the general rule of contract that parties are bound by the terms of their agreement and must rely on their contractual stipulations for protection from the effect of facts unknown to them.

6. Examples of operative mistake. Operative mistake may be common, mutual, or unilateral. It must be of such a nature that it cannot be deemed that there was any contract at all.

The circumstances in which operative mistake can occur are as follows:

(a) Common mistake as to the existence of the subject-matter of the contract.
(b) Common mistake as to a fact fundamental to the entire agreement.
(c) Mutual mistake as to the identity of the subject-matter of the contract.
(d) Unilateral mistake as to the identity of the person with whom the contract is made.
(e) Unilateral mistake by the offeror in expressing his intention, the mistake being known to the offeree.
(f) Unilateral mistake as to the nature of a document signed or sealed.

NOTE: in all these cases, the mistake is operative only where the mistake prevented the formation of any real agreement between the parties. If any party is under some misapprehension at the time of making the contract, and the mistake is not operative, then the contract is valid at common law in spite of the mistake. The mistaken party is then bound by the contract unless there is fraud or illegality, or some relief for the mistake in equity.

7. Common mistake as to the existence of the subject-matter. Where both parties believe the subject-matter of the contract to be in existence, but in fact it is not in existence at the time of making the contract, there is operative mistake and the contract is void. Section 6 of the *Sale of Goods Act*, 1893, provides that: "Where there is a contract for the sale of specific goods, and the goods without the knowledge of the seller have perished at the time when the contract is made, the contract is void." But where the circumstances are such that the seller is deemed to have warranted the existence of the goods, the seller is probably liable to the buyer for breach of contract if the goods are non-existent: *McRae* v. *Commonwealth*

Disposals Commission (1951), a case before the High Court of Australia.

8. Common mistake as to a fact or quality fundamental to the agreement.

Where the parties have made a contract based on a common misapprehension relating to the fundamental subject-matter of the contract, there is operative mistake. In *Bell* v. *Lever Brothers* (1932), Lord Atkin suggested that the test should be: "Does the state of the new facts destroy the identity of the subject-matter as it was in the original state of the facts?" But this kind of mistake is not operative unless it is the common mistake of the parties as to the existence of a fact or quality which makes the subject-matter of the contract essentially different from what they believed it to be.

Bell v. *Lever Bros.* (1931): B was under a contract of service with Lever Bros. as chairman of a subsidiary company in Africa. Lever Bros. entered into a contract with B by which it was agreed that B should resign from his post before the expiry of the contract of employment and that, in return, he would be paid a specified sum as compensation. After Lever Bros. had paid the agreed sum to B they discovered that B had previously engaged in private trading contrary to the terms of the contract of service. Had they known of this before the completion of the compensation agreement, they could have treated the contract of service as repudiated and there would have been no need to negotiate the compensation agreement. But B had always been under the impression that his private trading activities were not such as to entitle Lever Bros. to have the service contract set aside, and that the contract could be prematurely terminated only by agreement. Lever Bros. claimed the return of the compensation on the grounds that the compensation agreement was not binding because of the mistake of the parties. HELD by the House of Lords: the common mistake that the service contract was not determinable except by agreement merely related to the quality of the subject matter and was not sufficiently fundamental to constitute an assumption without which the parties would not have entered the compensation agreement. An agreement to terminate a broken contract is not fundamentally different from an agreement to terminate an unbroken contract. The mistake was not operative and the compensation agreement was binding.

Galloway v. *Galloway* (1914): the parties, believing themselves to be married, entered into a separation agreement under seal by which the man undertook to make money payments to the woman. It was later discovered that they were not, in fact, married. The woman claimed the promised payments. HELD: the deed was void on the ground of the parties' mistake.

Strickland v. *Turner* (1852): there was a contract of sale of an annuity and, unknown to the parties, the annuitant was already dead. HELD: the purchaser was entitled to the return of his money. The contract was void for total failure of consideration.

(NOTE: there was a failure of consideration because of the mistake of fact relating to that consideration.)

9. Mutual mistake as to the identity of the subject-matter.
Where the parties have negotiated completely at cross-purposes, it cannot be said that they were ever in agreement.

Raffles v. *Wichelhaus* (1864): there was a contract for the sale of 125 bales of cotton "to arrive ex *Peerless* from Bombay." It happened that there were two ships named *Peerless* leaving Bombay at about the same time: the buyer meant one and the seller meant the other. HELD: the contract was void for mistake.

Scriven v. *Hindley* (1913): in an auction sale, the auctioneer was selling tow. X bid for a lot, thinking that he was buying hemp. HELD: no contract.

10. Unilateral mistake as to identity of the person contracted with.
Where an offer is made to a particular offeree and to no one else, a purported acceptance by any other person will not be valid. In *Boulton* v. *Jones* (1857), X purported to accept an offer which was made by Y and addressed to Z. Y, for a very good reason, intended to deal with Z, and Z only. There was, therefore, no contract between X and Y. Note that the identity of the offeree was a material element in the offer.

The courts have sometimes held that mistake as to the identity of the person with whom the contract is made may operate to nullify the contract where

(*a*) the identity is of material importance to the contract, and

(*b*) the mistake is known to the other person, *i.e.* he knows that it is not intended that he should become a party to the contract.

Ingram v. *Little* (1960): three ladies, the joint owners of a car, advertised for its sale. A swindler called at their home and agreed to buy the car for £717. He offered a cheque in payment and this was refused. The swindler then attempted to convince the ladies that he was a Mr Hutchinson of Stanstead Road, Caterham. One of the ladies checked this name and address in the telephone directory. The ladies then decided to accept the cheque in payment. The cheque was dishonoured and the swindler disappeared (he was not Mr Hutchinson). The swindler had sold the car to L, who bought it in good faith. The ladies sought to recover possession of the car from L. HELD by the Court of Appeal: the offer to sell, with payment to be made by cheque, was made to Hutchinson only. As the swindler knew this, the offer was not one which he could accept. Therefore, there was no contract for the sale of the car, and the plaintiffs were entitled to its return.

Notice that, since the contract between the swindler and the ladies was void for mistake, the swindler got no title to the car, and he could not, therefore, pass a good title, even to a purchaser in good faith. The general rule is *nemo dat quod non habet* (no one can give a better title than he has).

Phillips v. *Brooks* (1919): the plaintiff was a jeweller. One North entered his shop and asked to see some jewellery. He chose a pearl necklace, price £2550, and a ring, price £450. He then took out his cheque-book and wrote out a cheque for £3000. As he signed the cheque, he said, "You see who I am, I am Sir George Bullough," and gave a London address, which the jeweller checked in a directory. The jeweller then asked whether he would like to take the articles with him, to which North replied that he would like to take the ring. North promptly pledged the ring with the defendant, a pawnbroker, for £350. The cheque was dishonoured and the jeweller claimed to recover the ring from the pawnbroker. HELD: the jeweller intended to contract with the person present in front of him, whoever he was, *i.e.* the mistake as to identity of the man North did not affect the formation of the contract. North got a voidable title to the ring, and since it was not avoided at the time of pledging it, the pawnbroker got a good title.

In this case, North's title to the ring was voidable because of the fraudulent misrepresentation, but at the time of the pledge, his title was still good, since by then the jeweller had done nothing to avoid his title. In connection with sale under a voidable title, the *Sale of Goods Act*, *s.* 23, provides that: "When the seller of goods has a voidable title thereto, but his title has not been avoided at the time of the sale, the buyer

VII. MISTAKE

acquires a good title to the goods, provided he buys them in good faith and without notice of the seller's defect in title."

Cundy v. *Lindsay* (1878): Alfred Blenkarn ordered certain goods from Lindsay & Co., signing the order in such a way as to make it appear to have come from Blenkiron & Co., a respectable firm. The goods were delivered to Blenkarn but he did not pay for them. Blenkarn sold the goods to Cundys. Lindsays claimed the recovery of the goods, or their value from Cundys. HELD by the House of Lords: the contract between Blenkarn and Lindsays was void for mistake, therefore no property passed to Cundys. Cundys were liable to Lindsays for the value of the goods.

The line between *Ingram* v. *Little* and *Phillips* v. *Brooks* is a very difficult one to draw, and it seems unfair that the title of the ultimate innocent purchaser should depend on so fine a distinction.

Lewis v. *Averay* (1972): the plaintiff put an advertisement in a newspaper, offering to sell his car for £450. In reply to the advertisement, a man (who turned out to be a rogue) telephoned and asked if he could see the car. That evening, he came to see the car, tested it and said that he liked it. The rogue and the plaintiff then went to the flat of the plaintiff's fiancée, where the rogue introduced himself as Richard Greene, making the plaintiff and his fiancée believe that he was the well-known film actor of that name. The rogue wrote a cheque for the agreed sum of £450, but the plaintiff was, at first, not prepared to let him take the car until the cheque was cleared. When the rogue pressed to be allowed to take the car with him, the plaintiff asked: "Have you anything to prove that you are Mr Richard Greene?" Whereupon, the rogue produced a special pass of admission to Pinewood Studios, bearing the name of Richard A. Greene and a photograph, which was clearly of the man claiming to be Richard Greene. The plaintiff was satisfied that the man was really Mr Richard Greene, the film actor. He let the rogue take the car in return for the cheque. A few days later, the plaintiff discovered that the cheque was from a stolen book and that it was worthless. In the meantime, the rogue sold the car to the defendant, who paid £200 for it in entire good faith. The rogue then disappeared. The plaintiff brought this action against the defendant, claiming damages for conversion. The County Court judge found in favour of the plaintiff. The defendant appealed. On the essential question whether there was a contract of sale by which property in the car passed from the plaintiff to the rogue, HELD, by the Court of Appeal: the fraud rendered the contract between the plaintiff and the rogue voidable (and not void) and, accordingly, the defendant obtained good title since he bought in good faith and without notice of the fraud, the plaintiff having failed to avoid the contract in time.

In *Lewis* v. *Averay* Lord Denning said:

"There are two cases in our books which cannot, to my mind, be reconciled the one with the other. One of them is *Phillips* v. *Brooks*, where a jeweller had a ring for sale. The other is *Ingram* v. *Little* where two ladies had a car for sale. In each case the story is very similar to the present. A plausible rogue comes along. The rogue says that he likes the ring, or the car, as the case may be. He asks the price. The seller names it. The rogue says that he is prepared to buy it at that price. He pulls out a cheque book. He writes, or prepares to write, a cheque for the price. The seller hesitates. He has never met this man before. He does not want to hand over the ring or the car not knowing whether the cheque will be met. The rogue notices the seller's hesitation. He is quick with his next move. He says to the jeweller, in *Phillips* v. *Brooks*: 'I am Sir George Bullough of 11 St James' Square'; or to the ladies in *Ingram* v. *Little*: 'I am P. G. M. Hutchinson of Stanstead House, Stanstead Road, Caterham'; or to Mr Lewis in the present case: 'I am Richard Greene, the film actor of the Robin Hood series.' Each seller checks up the information. The jeweller looks up the directory and finds there is a Sir George Bullough at 11 St James' Square. The ladies check up too. They look up the telephone directory and find there is a 'P. G. M. Hutchinson of Stanstead House, Stanstead Road, Caterham.' Mr Lewis checks up too. He examines the official pass to the Pinewood Studios and finds that it is a pass for a 'Richard A. Greene' to the Pinewood Studios with this man's photograph on it. In each case the seller feels that this is sufficient confirmation of the man's identity. So he accepts the cheque signed by the rogue and lets him have the ring, in the one case, and the car and log book in the other two cases. The rogue goes off and sells the goods to a third person who buys them in entire good faith and pays the price to the rogue. The rogue disappears. The original seller presents the cheque. It is dishonoured. Who is entitled to the goods? The original seller or the ultimate buyer? The courts have given different answers. In *Phillips* v. *Brooks* the ultimate buyer was held to be entitled to the ring. In *Ingram* v. *Little* the original seller was held to be entitled to the car. In the present case the deputy county court judge has held the original seller entitled. It seems to me that the material facts in each case are quite indistinguishable the one from the other. In each case there was, to all outward appearance, a contract; but there was a mistake by the seller as to the identity of the buyer. This mistake was fundamental. In each case it has led to the handing over of the goods. Without it the seller would not have parted with them. This case therefore raises the question: What is the effect of a mistake by one party as to the identity of the other? It has sometimes been said that, if a party makes a mistake as to the identity of the person with whom he is contracting, there is no contract, or, if there is a contract, it is a nullity and void, so that no property can pass under it. This has been supported by a reference to the French jurist Pothier; but I have said before, and I repeat now, his statement is no part of English law.... But the statement by Pothier has given rise to such refinements that it is time it was dead and buried altogether.... As I listened to the argument in this case, I felt it wrong that an innocent purchaser (who knew nothing of what passed between the seller and the rogue) should have his title depend on such refinements. After all, he has acted with complete circumspection and in entire good faith; whereas it was the seller who let the rogue have the goods and thus enabled him to commit the fraud. I do not, therefore, accept the theory that mistake as to identity renders a contract void. I think the true principle is that which underlies the decision of this court in *King's Norton Metal Co.* v. *Eldridge* and of Horridge, J., in *Phillips* v. *Brooks*, which has stood for these last 50 years. It is this: when two parties have come to a contract—or rather what appears, on the face of it, to be a contract—the fact that one party is mistaken as to the identity of the other does not mean that there is no contract, or that the contract is a nullity and void from the beginning. It only means that the contract is voidable, that is, liable to be set aside at the instance of the mistaken person, so long as he does so before third parties have in good faith acquired a right under it."

11. Unilateral mistake as to the expression of intention. Where the offeror makes a material mistake in expressing his intention, and the other party knows, or is deemed to know, of the error, the mistake may be operative.

Hartog v. *Colin & Shields* (1939): H claimed damages for breach of contract, alleging that C had agreed to sell him 30,000 Argentinian hare skins and had failed to deliver them. C contended that the offer contained a material mistake and that H was well aware of this mistake when he accepted the offer. The mistake alleged by C was that the skins were offered at certain prices *per pound* instead of *per piece*. In the negotiations preceding the agreement, reference had always been made to prices *per piece*, moreover, this was the custom of the trade. C contended (i) that the contract was void for mistake, and (ii) if there was a contract, rescission should be allowed. HELD: the contract was void for mistake. H could not reasonably have supposed that the offer expressed C's real intention: H must have known that it was made under a mistake.

Note that, in this case, the defendants asked for a declaration that the contract was void for mistake at common law and, in the alternative, for the equitable remedy of rescission. Since the court declared the contract void, there was no need to consider the question of rescission.

12. Unilateral mistake as to the nature of the document signed. The general rule is that a person is bound by the terms of any instrument which he signs or seals even though he did not read it, or did not understand its contents: see *L'Estrange* v. *Graucob* (1934), and *Blay* v. *Pollard and Morris* (1930). An exception to this general rule arises where a person signs or seals a document under a mistaken belief as to the nature of the document and the mistake was due to either

(*a*) the blindness, illiteracy, or senility of the person signing, or
(*b*) a trick or fraudulent misrepresentation as to the nature of the document, provided that person took all reasonable precautions before signing.

Where a person signs a document or executes a deed in these circumstances, he may raise the ancient defence of *non est factum* (it is not his deed). Until the decision of the House of Lords in *Saunders* v. *Anglia Building Society* (1971) it was thought that the defence was available even where there had been negligence, unless the instrument signed was negotiable. In the *Saunders* case, Lord Reid said: "The plea of *non est factum* obviously applies when the person sought to be held liable did not in fact sign the document. But at least since the sixteenth century it has also been held to apply in certain cases so as to enable a person who in fact signed a document to say that it is not his deed. Obviously any such extension must be kept within narrow limits if it is not to shake the confidence of those who habitually and rightly rely on signatures when there is no obvious reason to doubt their validity. Originally this extension appears to have been made in favour of those who were unable to read owing to blindness or illiteracy and who therefore had to trust someone to tell them what they were signing. I think that it must also apply in favour of those who are permanently or temporarily unable through no fault of their own to have without explanation any real understanding of the purport of a particular document, whether that be from defective education, illness or innate incapacity.

But that does not excuse them from taking such precautions as they reasonably can. The matter generally arises where an innocent third party has relied on a signed document in ignorance of the circumstances in which it was signed, and where he will suffer loss if the maker of the document is allowed to have it declared a nullity. So there must be a heavy burden of proof on the person who seeks to invoke this remedy. He must prove all the circumstances necessary to justify its being granted to him, and that necessarily involves him proving that he took all reasonable precautions in the circumstances. I do not say that the remedy can never be available to a man of full capacity. But that could only be in very exceptional circumstances; certainly not where his reason for not scrutinising the document before signing it was that he was too busy or too lazy. In general I do not think that he can be heard to say that he signed in reliance on someone he trusted. But particularly when he was led to believe that the document which he signed was not one which affected his legal rights, there may be cases where this plea can properly be applied in favour of a man of full capacity.

The plea cannot be available to anyone who was content to sign without taking the trouble to try to find out at least the general effect of the document. Many people do frequently sign documents put before them for signature by their solicitor or other trusted advisors without making any enquiry as to their purpose or effect. But the essence of the plea *non est factum* is that the person signing believed that the document he signed had one character or one effect whereas in fact its character or effect was quite different. He could not have such a belief unless he had taken steps or been given information which gave him some grounds for his belief. The amount of information he must have and the sufficiency of the particularity of his belief must depend on the circumstances of each case. Further the plea cannot be available to a person whose mistake was really a mistake as to the legal effect of the document, whether that was his own mistake or that of his advisor."

Thoroughgood's Case (1584): an illiterate woman was induced to execute a deed in the belief that it was concerned with arrears of rent. In fact, the document was a deed releasing another from claims which the woman had against him. HELD: the deed was a nullity.

Foster v. *Mackinnon* (1869): a senile gentleman was induced to sign a bill of exchange in the belief that it was a guarantee. HELD: no liability was incurred by the signature.

Carlisle and Cumberland Banking Co. v. *Bragg* (1911): B was fraudulently induced to sign a guarantee in the belief that it was a document concerning insurance. HELD: the guarantee was not binding.

Muskham Finance, Ltd. v. *Howard* (1963): K, who had entered a hire-purchase agreement with the finance company, obtained the company's permission to sell the car which was the subject-matter of the agreement. At this time, K still owed the company £197. K arranged for T to sell the car for him. T then arranged for H to enter into a hire-purchase agreement with the company. The company required T to have an indemnity form signed by a person willing to indemnify them with respect to their agreement with H. T asked K to sign this form, saying, "Could you sign this paper, which is a release note?" The heading "Indemnity Form" was hidden by papers on the desk, and T pointed to the document and said, "Just sign there and that will clear you with the vehicle." K thereupon signed. H subsequently defaulted on his payments to the company, who then brought this action against H and K to enforce the indemnity. K pleaded *non est factum*. HELD by the Court of Appeal: the document signed by K was different in class and character from that which he thought he was signing. The mistake was induced by a trick. The indemnity was not enforceable against K.

VII. MISTAKE

Howatson v. *Webb* (1908): W, who held certain land as nominee only, was asked to sign documents which he was told were "deeds for transferring the Edmonton property." When the mortgagee sued W for sums due, he pleaded *non est factum*. HELD by the Court of Appeal: the plea must fail because W was misled only as to the contents of the documents and not as to their character and class. He knew that they concerned the property held by him as nominee.

Saunders v. *Anglia Building Society* (1971): the plaintiff was an elderly widow who had made a will leaving all her possessions to her nephew, Walter Parkin. Her house was leasehold with more than 900 years to go. She gave the deeds of the house to Parkin because she had left it to him in her will and she knew that he wanted to raise money on it. She was content to allow him to do this provided she was able to remain in the house during her lifetime. When Parkin told his friend, the first defendant, that the plaintiff had left the house to him in her will, they came to an arrangement by which the first defendant, who was heavily in debt, could raise some money. According to the arrangement, a document was drawn up by solicitors by which the plaintiff was to sell the house to the first defendant for £3000. The understanding between Parkin and the first defendant was that after signature by the plaintiff, no purchase price would be paid over, and the first defendant would then mortgage the property to raise money. The first defendant took the document to the plaintiff, who at that time was seventy-eight years old, to get her signature. She did not read the document because she had broken her spectacles. She asked him what it was for, and he replied, "It is a deed of gift for Wally (Parkin) for the house." She thought at the time that Parkin was going to borrow money on the deeds and that the first defendant was arranging this for him. After the plaintiff had signed the document no money was paid to her, although the document provided that she acknowledged receipt of £3000 paid by the first defendant. The first defendant then obtained a loan of £2000 from the second defendant, a building society, on the security of the deeds. For this purpose, Parkin gave a reference to the building society, falsely stating that he was a reliable person. Subsequently the first defendant defaulted in the instalment payments to the building society, which then sought to recover possession of the house. The plaintiff then brought this action, contending that she was not bound by the assignment on the grounds that it was not her deed. Stamp, J., held that the assignment was not her deed and ordered the building society to deliver up the title deed to the plaintiff. (It is noteworthy that, had matters been allowed to rest at this decision, the only person to benefit would be Parkin, for the building society had given an undertaking to allow the plaintiff to remain in the house for the rest of her life.) The building society appealed to the Court of Appeal. It was held by the Court of Appeal that the plea of *non est factum* could not be supported and that the appeal must be allowed. The executrix of the plaintiff's estate appealed to the House of Lords. HELD, by the House of Lords: the plaintiff fell very short of making the clear and satisfactory case which is required of those who seek to have a legal act declared void and of establishing a sufficient discrepancy between her intentions and her act. The plea of *non est factum* failed.

MISTAKE IN EQUITY

13. Equitable relief for mistake. Where a person has entered a contract under a misapprehension, and the contract is good at common law, (*i.e.* the court has not declared it void for operative mistake), the mistaken party may, in proper circumstances, obtain equitable relief from his contractual obligations. The relief afforded by equity is of three kinds:

(*a*) Rescission on terms.
(*b*) Refusal of specific performance.
(*c*) Rectification.

14. Rescission on terms. In order to get rescission on terms, the claimant must show the court that it would be against good conscience for the other party to take full advantage of his contractual rights. In these circumstances, the court has powers to attach terms to the order that the contract be set aside. In effect, the original contractual rights and obligations are dissolved and replaced by fresh rights and obligations based on what the court thinks fair and just. But the court will not grant rescission if to do so would cause injustice to third parties. It seems that rescission on terms is available only where there has been a mistake common to both parties, and that it is not available in cases of mutual or unilateral mistake.

Cooper v. *Phibbs* (1867): an appeal from the Chancery Court to the House of Lords. The appellant had taken a three year lease of a salmon fishery from the respondent. At the time of the agreement, both parties believed that the fishery belonged to the respondent: indeed, he had spent a considerable amount of money on improvements to the property. It was subsequently discovered that the fishery was the property of the

VII. MISTAKE

appellant, who now sought to be relieved of the obligations he had incurred under the lease. HELD by the House of Lords: the appellant was entitled to have the lease rescinded on terms that the respondent would have a lien on the property to the extent of the money spent on improvements.

Solle v. *Butcher* (1949) : this was a dispute between landlord and tenant. The landlord had acquired a long lease of a war-damaged house, which had been let off in flats, subject to the *Rent Restriction Acts*. The landlord carried out repairs and considerable improvements to the house, and, in particular, to the flat which was the subject of this action. This flat was let to the tenant for £250 a year. Both parties were under the impression that the flat was no longer subject to the *Rent Restriction Acts*. Both parties knew that the controlled rent under the Acts would have been £140 a year. The landlord could have taken steps to have the controlled rent raised to £250 before entering into an agreement with any tenant, but he could not do this while an agreement was afoot. The tenant paid the agreed rent (£250) for more than a year, but then took proceedings in the County Court for a declaration that the flat was still subject to a controlled rent of £140 a year. The landlord contended that the dwelling had undergone a change of identity due to the bomb damage and the subsequent restoration and improvements, and that, accordingly, the Acts did not apply. He contended further that the lease should be rescinded on the grounds of mistake. The County Court judge held that the rent was controlled by the Acts at £140, and that the tenant was entitled to recover the sum overpaid. The landlord appealed. HELD by the Court of Appeal: (i) the structural improvements had not altered the identity of the flat so as to render it free from the provisions of the *Rent Restriction Acts*. (ii) The parties were under a common mistake of fact in believing that the flat was no longer subject to the Acts. (iii) The landlord was entitled to rescission on terms directed by the court, the terms being that he allow the tenant to enter a new lease at £250 a year.

Grist v. *Bailey* (1966): B entered into a written agreement with G for the sale of a house for £850. The agreement expressed the sale of the house to be "subject to the existing tenancy thereof." Both parties believed the house to be in the occupation of a statutory tenant but, unknown to them, the statutory tenant had died and the house was occupied by the tenant's son who did not wish to claim statutory tenancy. On discovering that there was no statutory tenancy and that the house was consequently worth about £2250, B refused to complete. G brought this action for specific performance of the contract and B counterclaimed for rescission on the grounds of common mistake. HELD: B was not at fault in not knowing that the statutory tenant had died. There was common mistake such as to entitle B to equitable relief. Specific performance refused and the contract rescinded on terms that B should enter a fresh contract with G, is required, at a proper vacant possession price.

15. Refusal of specific performance. Specific performance is a discretionary remedy and is not awarded as of right. The court will not usually award specific performance where the defendant entered the contract under some material misapprehension and

(a) it would be unduly harsh to force the defendant to comply specifically with the terms of the contract, or

(b) the mistake was caused by the misrepresentation of the plaintiff, or

(c) the plaintiff knew of the defendant's mistake.

If none of these conditions is satisfied, mistake is no defence to an action for specific performance.

Tamplin v. *James* (1880): an inn and an adjoining shop were put up for auction. Accurate plans showing the extent of the property were displayed in the auction room. The property was knocked down to J, who had not looked at the plans, and who wrongly thought that the lot included some gardens at the back of the inn. (J knew that the tenants of the inn had enjoyed the use of the gardens and, for this reason, thought they were included in the sale.) The vendor sought to have the contract specifically enforced against J. HELD: there was no excuse for the mistake and the contract should be specifically performed.

Webster v. *Cecil* (1861): W offered to buy certain land from C for £2000, but C rejected the offer. Then C wrote to W offering to sell the land for £1250, and W accepted by return of post. C immediately gave notice to W that he had written £1250 in error for £2250. Nevertheless, W claimed specific performance. HELD: W must have known of the mistake in the expression of C's offer. Specific performance refused.

Where specific performance is refused, the defendant may remain liable in damages for breach of contract. But where rescission is granted together with refusal of specific performance (*Grist* v. *Bailey*), there is no liability for breach.

16. Rectification. Where a written contract does not accurately express the agreement actually reached between the

VII. MISTAKE

parties, the court will rectify the written document so as to bring it into conformity with the actual agreement reached. A party claiming rectification must prove:

(a) that a complete and certain agreement was reached between the parties, and

(b) that the agreement was unchanged at the time it was put into writing, and the writing did not correspond with the agreement reached, *i.e.* there was a mistake in expressing the terms of the agreement.

Craddock Bros. v. *Hunt* (1923): C agreed orally to sell a house, exclusive of an adjoining yard, to H. The agreement was subsequently expressed in writing but, by mistake, the yard was included. Moreover, when the deed of conveyance was drawn up, it included the same mistake, and the deed was executed. When C discovered the mistake, he asked for rectification of (i) the written contract and (ii) the deed of conveyance. HELD by the Court of Appeal: there had been a complete oral agreement between the parties, and this agreement was not correctly expressed in the written contract, nor in the deed of conveyance. C was entitled to have the contract and the deed rectified to correspond with the oral agreement.

NOTE: rectification is never available where the written contract is identical to the antecedent oral agreement, even though one of the parties was under a misapprehension at the time of making the oral agreement.

Frederick E. Rose, Ltd. v. *Wm. H. Pim & Co., Ltd.* (1953): in this sale of goods case the buyers had received an enquiry from X for *"horsebeans described here as feveroles."* The buyers then asked the sellers what feveroles were. The sellers duly informed the buyers that feveroles and horsebeans were one and the same (in fact, feveroles are a special kind of horsebean). Suffering from this misapprehension, the parties entered into an oral agreement for the sale of 500 tons of horsebeans. The oral agreement was subsequently expressed accurately in writing. When the buyers discovered the mistake as to the nature of feveroles, they sought to have the written agreement rectified to read "horsebeans, feveroles." HELD by the Court of Appeal: the written contract correctly expressed the oral agreement. Therefore, the contract could not be rectified.

NOTE: the ultimate aim of the buyers in *Rose* v. *Pim*: if they had succeeded in getting rectification, the sellers would then have been in breach of contract (as rectified) and would thus have been liable to pay damages.

W. Higgins, Ltd. v. *Northampton Corporation* (1927): H submitted a tender to the Corporation for the building of certain houses. Due to faulty calculating, H stated the wrong price for the work in his tender. The tender was accepted without knowledge of the mistake. HELD: the contract could not be rectified because there had merely been a mistake by one party only in expressing his intention. (For the rules governing tenders *see* II, 11–13.)

Joscelyne v. *Nissen* (1970) C.A: this case concerned an agreement between a father and his daughter. The father lived in a house from where he carried on a car hire business. In 1960 he received notice to quit and the daughter then, in order to help her father, bought the house with the help of a mortgage. The daughter moved into the first floor with her husband and her parents occupied the ground floor. In 1963 the father ran into difficulties with his business with the result that the parties devised a scheme by which the daughter would take over the business on certain conditions. In 1964, there was a written contract by which the father transferred his business to his daughter and the daughter promised, *inter alia*, to permit the father to reside in the ground floor of the house "free of all rent and outgoings of every kind in any event." At first the daughter paid for the father's gas, electricity and coal and for his home help. When, later, the daughter refused to pay for these items, contending that she was not bound to do so under the contract, the father brought this action for rectification. HELD: the written contract did not express the accord between the parties that the daughter should pay all the outgoings of the house; since this was the agreement between the parties up to the time they executed the written contract, the court had jurisdiction to rectify the contract. It made no difference that there was no concluded and binding contract between the parties until the written contract was executed.

PROGRESS TEST 7

1. Distinguish between common mistake, mutual mistake, and unilateral mistake.

2. What is operative mistake? Give examples.

3. What kind of mistake does not affect the contract at common law?

4. Explain fully how mistaken identity may affect a contract.

5. In what circumstances may the defence of *non est factum* be pleaded?

6. Distinguish between mistake at law, and mistake in equity.

7. What do you understand by "rescission on terms"? Do you

VII. MISTAKE

consider that an order of rescission on terms is likely to achieve a more just result than a declaration that a contract is void *ab initio*?

8. "Rectification is concerned with contracts and documents, not with intentions. In order to get rectification, it is necessary to show that the parties were in complete agreement on the terms of their contract, but by an error wrote them down wrongly." Denning, L.J. (as he then was), in *Rose* v. *Pim* (1953). Comment on this statement.

9. There was a contract of sale between A, the seller, and B, the buyer, for 1000 Japanese cameras, described to be lying in A's warehouse in London. Immediately before the agreement, the cameras were destroyed in a fire in A's warehouse. A did not know about the fire until after the agreement. B, who had planned to make a large profit on a re-sale of the cameras, wishes now to claim damages from A for breach of contract. Advise B.

10. C and D thought they were married, but, unknown to them, their "marriage" was void. While they were under this misapprehension, they entered into a separation agreement under which C promised to make an allowance of £500 a year to D. C has now discovered that he was never married to D, and wishes to know whether he is bound by his agreement to pay the allowance. Advise him.

11. E agrees to buy F's horse Dobbin. At the time of the agreement, F intends to sell his grey horse called Dobbin. He does not know that E thinks he is buying F's white horse, which is also called Dobbin. Is there a binding contract between the parties?

12. G advertises in a newspaper for the sale of his motor car. H calls at G's house in response to the advertisement, introducing himself falsely as "Henry Jones." G agrees to sell his car to H and to take a cheque as payment. H drives off in the car, and the cheque is subsequently dishonoured. H sells the car to J, and then disappears. What must G prove in order to be able to recover the car from J?

13. K agrees orally with L that he will guarantee L's bank overdraft up to the sum of £100. K goes to L's bank and signs a form of guarantee, but he does not notice that the amount guaranteed, according to the form, is £1000. L then becomes overdrawn to the extent of £960. Advise the bank as to K's liability.

14. M attended the auction sale of a farm. He did not bother to examine the accurate plans exhibited at the sale, for he thought he knew the extent of the farm. M made the highest bid and the farm was knocked down to him. He subsequently discovered that the property sold did not include a certain field which he had always thought of as belonging to the farm. The vendor has asked for an order of specific performance, and M wishes to

resist this as he no longer wants the property. Advise him as to whether his mistake was of such a nature as to cause the court to refuse specific performance to the vendor.

15. In November 1964, N agreed orally to build a house for O, the work to be completed by August 1965. When the contract is reduced to writing, the typist makes an error—she types "August 1966," instead of "August 1965." The parties sign this contract without noticing the error. In January 1965, O notices the error. He tells N, who refuses to alter the written agreement, claiming that the written agreement was binding. O particularly wants the new house by August 1965, and he approaches you in February 1965, for advice. Advise him.

CHAPTER VIII

MISREPRESENTATION

REPRESENTATIONS DISTINGUISHED FROM EXPRESS TERMS

1. Material statements during negotiations. Business men often refer to statements made during negotiations as "representations." When a lawyer uses the word "representation" he usually intends a stricter and narrower meaning. The material statements made during the negotiations leading to a contract can be divided into two classes:

(*a*) Representations by which the parties intended to be bound. Such statements form the express terms of the contract and are not usually called "representations" by lawyers. These statements are either warranties or conditions.

(*b*) Representations by which the parties did not intend to be bound but which, nevertheless, helped to induce the contract. These statements are known as *representations* (using the word in its legal sense) or *mere representations*. The *'mere'* leaves no doubt as to the meaning intended.

2. Misrepresentation. Where a mere representation is a false statement there is misrepresentation. The word "misrepresentation" has two meanings. First, it means the false statement itself: second, it means the act of making the false statement. In order to arrive at a more complete definition of misrepresentation it is convenient to start by defining a mere representation. The various elements of the definition are considered in the next five paragraphs.

A mere representation is a statement

(*a*) of material fact;
(*b*) made by one party to another;
(*c*) during the negotiations leading to the agreement;

(d) which was intended to operate, and did operate, as an inducement to enter the contract;
(e) but was not intended to be a binding contractual term.

Where a statement of this class proves to be false, there is misrepresentation.

3. Statement of material fact. A representation is an assertion of the truth that a fact exists or did exist. It can, therefore, have no reference to future events or promises. The assertion must be materially connected to the contract. "There is a clear difference between a representation of fact and a representation that something will be done in the future. A representation that something will be done in the future cannot either be true or false at the moment it is made; and although you may call it a representation, if anything it is a contract or promise": *Beatty* v. *Ebury* (1872), *per* Mellish, L.J.

Points to note are:

(a) A promise to do something relates to the future. If it is material to the agreement, it will be a term and not a mere representation.

(b) A statement as to the state of a man's mind may be a statement of fact. In *Edgington* v. *Fitzmaurice* (1885), Bowen L.J. said, "The state of a man's mind is as much a fact as the state of his digestion." It is true that it is very difficult to prove what is the state of a man's mind at a particular time but, if it can be substantiated, it is as much a fact as anything else. A mis-statement of the state of a man's mind is misrepresentation of fact. A statement as to state of mind may be made with reference to intention or to opinion.

(i) An expression of intention may be a statement of fact.
(ii) An expression of opinion may be a statement of fact. If it is proved that the expressed opinion was not actually held, there is a misrepresentation. But if the expressed opinion was actually held there is no misrepresentation—even where the opinion was mistakenly held.

Bisset v. *Wilkinson* (1927): the vendor of a piece of land in New Zealand told a prospective purchaser that, in his opinion, the land would carry 2000 sheep. In fact, the land would not carry that number of sheep. HELD by the Privy Council: there

VIII. MISREPRESENTATION

was no misrepresentation, for the statement was one of opinion which was honestly held.

(c) *Simplex commendatio non obligat* (a simple commendation does not bind). The law allows a trader a good deal of latitude in his choice of language when commending his wares. Mere advertisement puff is not misrepresentation. The "desirable residence" advertised by the estate agent may leave much to be desired, but there is, nevertheless, no misrepresentation. However, statements of a specific nature will usually be either terms or representations.

(d) A statement of law must be distinguished from a statement of fact. If a legal principle is wrongly stated there is no misrepresentation: but a false statement as to the existence of a legal right may be a misrepresentation.

NOTE: A false statement as to the existence of an Act of Parliament is a misrepresentation of fact: *West London Commercial Bank* v. *Kitson* (1884).

4. Statement by one party to another. A statement made by a person who is not a party to the agreement cannot be a representation unless there is a principal–agent relationship (express or implied) between that person and one of the parties.

5. Statement made in negotiations. Any statement which was not made during the course of negotiations leading to the formation of an agreement cannot be a representation, *e.g.* a statement made after the agreement has been concluded.

6. Inducement to enter the contract. A statement cannot be a representation unless it was intended to be an inducement to the other party to enter the contract, and, in fact, operated as an inducement. There is no misrepresentation, therefore, where:

(a) The statement was not actually communicated to the other party; or
(b) The statement did not affect the other party's decision to enter the contract; or
(c) The statement was known to be untrue by the other party; or
(d) The other party did not believe the statement to be true.

Where a statement is made during negotiations leading to a contract for the purpose of inducing the other party to act on it, and that other party acts on it by entering the contract, then, *prima facie*, the statement was intended as a warranty. But the party making the statement can rebut the inference if he can by showing that it would not be reasonable to hold him bound to it.

In *Dick Bentley Productions* v. *Harold Smith* (1965), Lord Denning, M.R., said: "(T)he question whether a warranty was intended depends on the conduct of the parties, on their words and behaviour, rather than on their thoughts. If an intelligent bystander would reasonably infer that a warranty was intended, that will suffice." (*See* V, 2.)

7. No intention to be bound. A mere representation is a statement by which the parties did not intend to be bound. Intention is discovered, in cases of dispute, by the application of an objective test. Where a court finds an intention to be bound, the statement is a warranty and not a mere representation: see *Routledge* v. *McKay* (1954), and *Couchman* v. *Hill* (1947). (*See* V, 2.)

MISREPRESENTATION MAY BE INNOCENT OR FRAUDULENT

8. Innocent and fraudulent misrepresentation. Misrepresentation may be innocent or fraudulent and it is necessary to be able to distinguish between the two. Fraudulent misrepresentation is a false statement falling within the definition in *Derry* v. *Peek* and is explained in the next paragraph. Fraudulent misrepresentation is a *tort* and is sometimes known as deceit. A tort is a civil (as opposed to criminal) wrong for which damages is the usual remedy. The parties to an action in tort may or may not be parties to a contract. Accordingly, a fraudulent misrepresentation may or may not be connected with a contract. Innocent misrepresentation, however, is of legal significance only when connected with a contract.

9. Fraudulent misrepresentation. Where a statement is made fraudulently there is the tort of deceit, and an action for damages will lie at the suit of the person who has been misled.

The classic definition of fraud was made by Lord Herschell

in *Derry* v. *Peek* (1889), in the House of Lords. After a review of the authorities, he said, "First, in order to sustain an action of deceit, there must be proof of fraud, and nothing short of that will suffice. Secondly, fraud is proved when it is shown that a false representation has been made (i) knowingly, or (ii) without belief in its truth, or (iii) recklessly, careless whether it be true or false. Although I have treated the second and third as distinct cases, I think the third is but an instance of the second, for one who makes a statement under such circumstances can have no real belief in the truth of what he states. To prevent a false statement being fraudulent, there must, I think, always be an honest belief in its truth. And this probably covers the whole ground, for one who knowingly alleges that which is false has obviously no such belief. Thirdly, if fraud be proved, the motive of the person guilty of it is immaterial. It matters not that there was no intention to cheat or injure the person to whom the statement was made."

Derry v. *Peek* (1889): a tramway company was empowered by a special Act of Parliament to operate certain tramways by using animal power. The Act further provided that, with the consent of the Board of Trade, mechanical power might be used. The directors of the company, wishing to raise more capital, included the following statement in a prospectus: "... the company has the right to use steam or mechanical motive power instead of horses, and it is fully expected that by means of this a considerable saving will result...." P, relying on this representation, bought shares. The company was later wound up because the Board of Trade refused to allow the use of mechanical power over the whole of the company's tramway. P contended that there was fraud. HELD by the House of Lords: the false statement in the prospectus was not fraudulent.

Akerhielm v. *De Mare* (1959): in a prospectus issued by a company formed in Kenya, the following statement appeared: "About a third of the capital has already been subscribed in Denmark." This statement was untrue, but the directors of the company believed it to be true at the time of the issue of the prospectus. HELD by the Privy Council: the statement was not fraudulent. It was made in an honest belief in its truth.

10. Remedies for fraudulent misrepresentation. A party who has been deceived by fraudulent misrepresentation may sue for damages in tort for deceit, and in addition, he may either

(a) affirm the contract, or
(b) disaffirm the contract and refuse further performance.

Where a party disaffirms the contract, he may either

(i) *take no legal action*, and plead fraud as a defence and counterclaim for damages in the event of his being sued for breach of contract by the other party; or
(ii) *bring an action* for rescission of the contract.

11. Innocent misrepresentation. Any misrepresentation which is not caught by the definition of fraud in *Derry* v. *Peek* is an innocent misrepresentation. That is to say, where a representation is made with an honest belief in its truth, it is innocent. The test of honesty is a subjective one: the usual objective test of intention is not used in this distinction.

12. Remedies for innocent misrepresentation. A party who has suffered a misrepresentation and who is unable or unwilling to prove fraud may seek his remedy (a) at common law, (b) in equity or (c) under the *Misrepresentation Act*, 1967. These various remedies should now be considered separately.

(a) *At common law:* The party misled may affirm the contract and treat it as binding. At common law damages are not awarded for innocent misrepresentation.

(b) *In equity:* The party misled may disaffirm the contract either by notifying the other party to that effect, or by bringing an action (or counterclaim) for rescission. In either case he must be prepared to restore any money or property which has been transferred to him under the contract. Similarly, he can claim the recovery of property transferred to the other party, for equity requires mutual restoration. Where, under the contract, the party misled has assumed burdens which otherwise would have been the responsibility of the other party, these must also be taken back. In other words, the party who made the innocent misrepresentation must indemnify the other party for obligations assumed as a *direct result* of the contract. The obligations must have been created by the contract.

Whittington v. *Seale-Hayne* (1900): In an action for rescission of a lease, the lessees claimed an indemnity from the lessors under the following heads: (i) value of stock lost,

VIII. MISREPRESENTATION

(ii) loss of profits, (iii) loss of breeding season, (iv) rent and removal of stores, (v) medical expenses, (vi) rates and (vii) cost of repairs ordered by the local authority. HELD: Indemnity was payable for heads (vi) and (vii) only. No indemnity was payable under heads (i) to (v) because these losses were not related to obligations created directly by the contract.

Where a contract is disaffirmed by giving notice that further performance is refused, the innocent misrepresentation may be raised as a defence to any action for specific performance which the other party may bring.

Rescission is available to a party misled by an innocent misrepresentation notwithstanding that the misrepresentation has become a term of the contract: *Misrepresentation Act*, 1967, *s.* 1. Thus the Act has preserved the right of rescission in cases where the false statement was first made as a mere representation but subsequently became a term of the contract.

A party misled by an innocent misrepresentation is entitled to rescind even where the contract has been performed: *Misrepresentation Act*, 1967, *s.* 1. This provision abolishes the rule in *Seddon* v. *N.E. Salt Co. Ltd.* (1905).

Rescission is not open to a party who has affirmed the contract after becoming aware of the innocent misrepresentation. Nor is it open to a party who has delayed unreasonably either in giving notice or in bringing an action for rescission.

(c) *The Misrepresentation Act, 1967*: The common law rule that damages are not awarded for innocent misrepresentation has been amended by the *Misrepresentation Act*, 1967.

Section 2(1) of the Act provides that where a person has entered a contract after a misrepresentation has been made to him by another party and has thereby suffered loss, then, if the person making the misrepresentation would be liable in damages if the misrepresentation had been fraudulent, he is nevertheless liable in damages unless he proves that he had reasonable ground to believe and did believe up to the time the contract was made that the facts represented were true.

Section 2(2) provides that where a person has entered a contract after an innocent misrepresentation has been made to him giving him the right to rescind, then, if it is claimed that the contract has been rescinded, the court may declare the contract subsisting and award damages in lieu of rescission if it would be equitable to do so. The court must have regard to the nature of the misrepresentation, the loss that would be caused if the contract were upheld, and the loss that rescission would cause to the other party.

Section 2(3) relates *s.* 2(1) and *s.* 2(2) by providing that damages may be awarded under *s.* 2(2) whether or not there is liability under *s.* 2(1). But any award under *s.* 2(2) must be taken into account in assessing liability under *s.* 2(1).

13. The equitable remedy of rescission. A party who has been misled by a misrepresentation, fraudulent or innocent, may initiate proceedings for rescission of the contract. The object of this action is to obtain from the court an order that the contract is cancelled.

The remedy is equitable and is given (or withheld) entirely in the discretion of the court: it is not awarded as of right as in the case of damages at common law. Generally, rescission will be awarded only where *restitutio in integrum* (restoration to the original position) is still possible: *Lagunas* case. Thus the order will not be made if third parties have obtained rights in the subject-matter of the contract: *White* v. *Garden* (1851). Restitution involves the mutual restoration of all property transferred between the parties and also, where appropriate, an indemnity against obligations necessarily created by the rescinded contract: *Whittington* v. *Seale-Hayne* (1900). An action for rescission must be brought promptly, for delay defeats the equities.

Leaf v. *International Galleries* (1950): L bought a painting of Salisbury Cathedral, described by the sellers as a genuine Constable. Five years later, L discovered that the painting was not a genuine Constable and he brought this action for rescission on the grounds of innocent misrepresentation. HELD by the Court of Appeal: L's claim must fail. There can be no rescission of a contract of sale of goods after the buyer has taken possession, or at least within a reasonable time thereafter: five years is more than a reasonable time. (When this case was before the County Court, L's counsel asked for leave to amend by claiming damages for breach of warranty, but this request was refused.

If L had originally asked for damages instead of rescission, he would probably have succeeded.)

Lagunas Nitrate Co., Ltd. v. *Lagunas Syndicate, Ltd.* (1899): the Syndicate induced the Nitrate Company by means of an innocent misrepresentation to purchase nitrate grounds from it. The Nitrate Company worked the property vigorously as soon as it could and called upon the Syndicate to make large outlays on it. For a time the Nitrate Company made large profits from working the nitrate grounds until the market price of nitrate fell permanently. The Nitrate Company then brought this action to rescind the contract of sale of the nitrate grounds. HELD by the Court of Appeal: rescission could not be granted because it was impossible to restore the parties to their original position.

14. Exemption clauses. If a contract contains an exemption clause purporting to protect a party from liability for misrepresentation or purporting to exclude or restrict any remedy available to the other party, the clause will be void unless the court allows reliance on it as being fair and reasonable in the circumstances: *Misrepresentation Act*, 1967, *s.* 3.

15. Exceptions to the common law "no damages" rule. The common law rule that no damages will be awarded for an innocent misrepresentation has now been almost eaten away by exceptions. The most important of these is the provision contained in *s.* 2 of the *Misrepresentation Act*, 1967, which has already been considered. There are, in addition, the following exceptions.

(*a*) *Company prospectus:* where the innocent misrepresentation is included in a prospectus inviting the public to buy shares in a company, *compensation* is payable: *Companies Act*, 1948, *s.* 43.

(*b*) *Estoppel:* where the innocent misrepresentation is made in such a way as to give rise to an estoppel. (Estoppel is a rule of evidence which precludes, *i.e.* estops, a person from denying the truth of a representation made by him where another person has changed his position on the faith of the representation.)

Silver v. *Ocean Steamship Co., Ltd.* (1929): goods were loaded on to a ship and the master signed the bill of lading to the effect that the goods were "in apparent good order and condition." The goods were, in fact, seriously damaged. The master was estopped from denying the truth of the representation that the goods were in good order and condition when loaded on to the ship.

Holland v. *Manchester & Liverpool District Banking Co.* (1909): a bank represented to one of its customers that he had a credit balance of £70 when, in fact, he was only entitled to a credit balance of £10. On the faith of this representation, he drew a cheque for £65 which was dishonoured. The customer sued for wrongful dishonour of the cheque. HELD: the bank was estopped from denying that there were sufficient funds to meet the cheque.

(c) *Negligent mis-statement:* where, in the ordinary course of business, a person seeks information or advice from another person who is not under a contractual or fiduciary obligation to give that information or advice, in circumstances where a reasonable man would know that he was being trusted or that his skill or judgment was being relied upon, the giving of the information or advice involves a duty of care. Failure to exercise care in giving the information or advice amounts to negligence and the person misled by the advice or information may claim damages in tort for any loss he has suffered by relying on it. It is a good defence, however, for the person giving the advice or information to show that he qualified his statement by saying that he does not accept legal responsibility for it: *Hedley Byrne & Co., Ltd.* v. *Heller & Partners, Ltd.* (1963). Where a negligent mis-statement of this kind has been made by a party during negotiations leading to a contract, he may be sued under the provisions of *s.* 2 of the *Misrepresentation Act,* 1967.

WHERE NON-DISCLOSURE CONSTITUTES MISREPRESENTATION

16. No general duty to disclose. There is no general duty to disclose material facts during negotiations leading to a contract. Thus, in the case of contracts of sale of goods, the common law rule is *caveat emptor*. In *Bell* v. *Lever Bros.* (*see* VII, 8.) the House of Lords held that Bell was under no duty to disclose to Lever Bros. his misconduct in making the secret profit through private trading. In that case, Lord Atkin said, "Ordinarily the failure to disclose a material fact which might influence the mind of a prudent contractor does not give the right to avoid the contract. The principle of *caveat emptor* applies outside contracts of sale." Lord Atkin then went on to mention the main exceptions to this general rule. He said, "There are certain contracts, expressed by the law to be contracts of the utmost good faith, where material facts must be disclosed; if not the contract is voidable. Apart from special fiduciary relationships contracts for partnership and contracts of insurance are the leading instances. In such cases the duty does not arise out of contract; the duty of a person proposing an insurance arises before a contract is made, so of an intending partner."

Hands v. *Simpson, Fawcett & Co. Ltd.* (1928): a commercial traveller applied for, and obtained, a post without informing his new employer that he was disqualified from driving a car. The employer regarded driving as an essential part of the traveller's duties, and he brought this action, contending that his silence about the driving disqualification amounted to misrepresentation. HELD: the traveller was under no duty to volunteer information about his driving disqualification. Mere silence cannot be a misrepresentation where there is no duty to speak.

17. Where there is a duty to disclose. In the following circumstances the withholding of a material fact may constitute misrepresentation:

(*a*) Contracts *uberrimae fidei*.

(*b*) Contracts affected by the *uberrima fides* principle.

(*c*) Where a part-truth amounts to a falsehood.

(*d*) Where there is a fiduciary element in the relationship between the contracting parties.

There is also a duty of disclosure in the following circumstances:

(*e*) Where a statement, true at the time it was made, becomes untrue during the course of negotiations: *Davies* v. *London Provincial* (1878).

(*f*) Where a party who made a statement in the belief that it was true subsequently discovers that it was false: *With* v. *O'Flanagan* (1936).

18. Uberrima fides (utmost good faith). In contracts of insurance of all kinds, disclosure of all material facts must be made to the insurer. A fact is material if it would affect the judgment of a prudent insurer in deciding whether to accept the risk or in deciding what shall be the premium. It has been held that there was a duty to disclose in the following cases:

(a) Where the insured goods were carried on the deck of a ship instead of in the hold: *Hood* v. *West End Motor Car Packing Co.* (1917).

(b) Where it is not disclosed that a proposal has been refused by another insurance company: *Locker and Woolf, Ltd.* v. *Western Australian Insurance Co., Ltd.* (1936).

(c) Where a ship was insured and it was not disclosed that her cargo was insured at a value exceeding the real value: *Ionides* v. *Pender* (1874).

Where there has been a material non-disclosure, the insurer may avoid the contract.

19. Contracts affected by the uberrima fides principle. There are also the following classes of contract in which the principle of *uberrima fides* operates.

(a) *Company prospectuses*. The *Companies Act*, 1948, provides that certain matters shall be included in prospectuses inviting the public to subscribe for shares or debentures. Any person responsible for the non-disclosure of the stipulated matters shall be liable to a fine: *s.* 38. Also, a contract to buy shares is voidable where there is a material non-disclosure in the prospectus.

(b) *Contracts for sale of land*. The vendor of an estate or interest in land is under a duty to the purchaser to show good title to the estate or interest he has contracted to sell. All defects in *title* must, therefore, be disclosed. This duty does not extend to physical defects in the property itself.

(c) *Family arrangements* are agreements or arrangements between members of a family for the protection or distribution of family property. If any member of the family has withheld material information, the agreement or arrangement may be set aside: *Gordon* v. *Gordon* (1821); *Greenwood* v. *Greenwood* (1863).

(d) *A confidential relationship* between the contracting parties gives rise to a duty to disclose material facts. This

VIII. MISREPRESENTATION

rule is sometimes known as the equitable doctrine of constructive fraud, and is closely connected with undue influence.

Tate v. *Williamson* (1866): A, who was a young man heavily in debt, sought the advice of B. B advised A to sell certain land in order to raise money to repay the debts. B then offered to buy the land for half its real value. Certain facts which were material to the value of the land were known to B and he did not disclose them to A. HELD: the contract could be set aside for constructive fraud.

(*e*) *Suretyship and partnership contracts.* Contracts of suretyship (guarantee) and contracts of partnership do not require *uberrima fides*: but they do create a relationship between the parties which requires a measure of good faith (*i.e.* disclosure of material facts) in their dealings after the contract has been made.

PROGRESS TEST 8

1. Define carefully a "mere representation," distinguishing it from a contractual term.
2. "The state of a man's mind is as much a fact as the state of his digestion." Comment on this statement.
3. How do the courts distinguish between innocent misrepresentation and fraudulent misrepresentation?
4. What are the remedies available for

   (*a*) innocent misrepresentation, and
   (*b*) fraudulent misrepresentation?

5. In what circumstances will damages be awarded for an innocent misrepresentation?
6. Is there a general duty to disclose material facts during negotiations preceding a contract?
7. What kinds of contracts are affected by the *uberrima fides* principle?
8. A, the vendor of a small general store, told B, the purchaser, that he thought trade would double within twelve months because four large blocks of council flats were nearing completion and would soon be occupied. A year after the contract, the trade in B's store had not increased at all. The flat-dwellers, when they arrived, hardly used the store at all. B wishes to know whether he has any claim against A with respect to his statement that trade would double within twelve months. Advise him.

9. Eight years ago, C bought a painting from D, a dealer. D had described the painting as a genuine Picasso, and C paid a high price accordingly. C has just discovered that the painting is not a Picasso, and is almost worthless. There is no evidence that D's false statement was fraudulent. What steps would you advise D to take?

10. E went to his bank and asked what was the state of his current account. The cashier made enquires and then gave E a slip of paper on which was written, "Current account credit balance—£210·55." In fact, there was a clerical error, and the correct balance should have been £120·55. However, on the strength of the information, E drew a cheque for £160, which was dishonoured in due course. E has decided to sue the bank for wrongful dishonour of the cheque. Will he succeed? If so, on what grounds? If not, why not?

11. Compare the tactical position of the plaintiff seeking damages for fraudulent misrepresentation with that of a plaintiff bringing an action under the *Misrepresentation Act*.

CHAPTER IX

DURESS AND UNDUE INFLUENCE

1. Coercion. Where a person has been coerced into a contract so that he did not enter it of his own free will he may apply to the court to have the contract avoided or set aside. He will seek his remedy either at common law or in equity, according to whether the coercion amounts to duress or undue influence. If he can prove duress, the contract will be avoided as a matter of right: but if he proves undue influence, the contract will be set aside in the discretion of the court. The remedies for duress, on the one hand, and undue influence, on the other, are distinct. The one is at common law and the other is in equity. Where there is doubt as to whether any particular act of coercion is duress or undue influence, the plaintiff should bring his action to have the contract avoided for duress and, in the alternative, to have the contract set aside for undue influence. If the plaintiff follows this procedure and proves duress, the contract will be avoided and the court does not have to consider whether to exercise its equitable jurisdiction to set the contract aside. If, however, the plaintiff fails to prove duress, the court will consider whether there has been undue influence and whether the circumstances warrant the exercise of the equitable jurisdiction to set the contract aside.

DURESS

2. What constitutes duress. Duress at common law occurs where a party enters a contract under violence or threatened violence to himself or to his immediate family; or where he is threatened with false imprisonment; or where he is threatened with the dishonour of a member of his family. Coercion of this kind is legal duress when it is exercised by another party to the contract, or by the agent of another party, or by any person to the knowledge of another party. Cases of duress are rare in modern times.

NOTE: duress is exercised against persons only, and not goods.

3. Legal effect of duress.

Where there is duress, the assent is not freely given, and the contract is voidable at the option of the party who has been coerced.

> *Cumming* v. *Ince* (1847): an inmate of a private lunatic asylum agreed to make certain arrangements as to her property in return for the suspension of the commission of lunacy which was being held on her. HELD: the agreement was not binding as the consent was not freely given.
>
> *Kaufman* v. *Gerson* (1904): G had taken money which K had entrusted with him. K threatened to prosecute G, unless G's wife made good the loss out of her own property. G's wife agreed to do so, in order to save her husband's honour. HELD: G's wife was not bound by her promise. She was entitled to avoid the contract which she had entered under duress.

UNDUE INFLUENCE

4. What constitutes undue influence.

Undue influence in equity occurs where a party enters a contract under any kind of influence which prevents him from exercising a free and independent judgment. The courts have always taken care not to define undue influence, for a definition would cramp their equitable jurisdiction in this connection. "As no court has ever attempted to define fraud, so no court has ever attempted to define undue influence, which includes one of the many varieties": *per* Lindley, L.J., in *Allcard* v. *Skinner* (1887). Where undue influence is alleged, the court regards itself as a court of conscience with full discretion to make its findings accordingly. There is a rebuttable presumption of undue influence where a fiduciary or confidential relationship exists between contracting parties: in all other cases, the onus is on the party alleging undue influence to prove it.

5. Legal effect of undue influence.

A contract (or gift under seal) may be set aside at the suit of a party who contracted under influence. This relief is equitable and, therefore, discretionary. It may be disallowed where the plaintiff has delayed making his claim, for *delay defeats the equities*: *Allcard* v. *Skinner*. Also, it may be disallowed where the plaintiff's conduct has been tricky, for *he who comes to equity must come with clean hands*.

IX. DURESS AND UNDUE INFLUENCE

6. Presumed influence. Where the relationship between contracting parties is such that one is entitled to rely upon the confidential advice of the other, undue influence is presumed to have been exercised, until it is proved to the contrary.

The presumption arises, for example, where the contracting parties are in any of the following relationships: solicitor and client, trustee and *cestui que trust*, doctor and patient, parent and child, guardian and ward, religious adviser and person over whom religious influence is exercised. It is not clear whether the presumption arises in the case of engaged couples, but it certainly does not arise in the case of husband and wife. Evidence required to rebut the presumption will vary according to the circumstances, but it is usually necessary to show

(a) that the consideration moving from the dominant party was at least adequate;

(b) that the plaintiff had the benefit of competent, independent advice, in the light of a full disclosure of all material facts;

(c) that, in the case of a gift by deed, the gift was made spontaneously.

Allcard v. *Skinner* (1887): in 1868 the plaintiff, an unmarried woman, was introduced to a Church of England sisterhood. In 1870 she became a novice and in 1871 she was admitted a full member of the sisterhood, embracing the vows of poverty, obedience and chastity. The plaintiff, without independent advice, made gifts of money and stock to the defendant, who was the lady superior of the sisterhood. In 1879 the plaintiff left the sisterhood and became a member of the Church of Rome. Soon afterwards, she spoke to her brother about getting back her money and he told her that it would be better to leave it alone. She was similarly advised by a Roman Catholic priest. Then, in 1880, her solicitor advised her that the sum was too large to leave with the sisterhood without asking for its return, but she replied that she preferred not to bother about it. In 1884 the plaintiff heard that one of the sisters had left the sisterhood and that her money had been returned to her at her request. As a result of this news, the plaintiff decided to make an attempt to get her money back from the sisterhood. In the same year, 1884, the plaintiff asked for her money. The lady superior refused to return it and the plaintiff brought this action against her for its recovery in 1885. The plaintiff claimed to recover the entire capital sum which she had given to the lady superior, but the trial judge gave judgment for the defendant. The plaintiff appealed, limiting her appeal to certain railway stock which was transferred to the lady superior and was still standing in the lady superior's name. HELD, by the Court of Appeal: (i) the lady superior's equitable title was imperfect because, at the time of the gift, the plaintiff was bound by her vows, and the rules of the sisterhood, to make absolute submission to the defendant as lady superior; but (ii) the plaintiff was not entitled to recover the funds because of the delay in making her claim.

In *Allcard* v. *Skinner* Lindley, L.J., said: "It would obviously be to encourage folly, recklessness, extravagance, and vice if persons could get back property made away with, whether by giving it to charitable institutions, or by bestowing it on less worthy objects. On the other hand, to protect people from being forced, tricked, or misled, in any way by others into parting with their property, is one of the most legitimate objects of all laws; and the equitable doctrine of undue influence has grown out of and been developed by the necessity of grappling with insidious forms of spiritual tyranny and with the infinite varieties of fraud. As no court has ever attempted to define fraud, so no court has ever attempted to define undue influence, which includes one of the many varieties. The undue influence which courts of equity endeavour to defeat is the undue influence of one person over another; not the influence of enthusiasm or the enthusiast who is carried away by it, unless indeed such enthusiasm is itself the result of external undue influence. But the influence of one mind over another is very subtle, and of all influences religious influence is the most dangerous and the most powerful. To counteract it courts of equity have gone very far. They have not shrunk from setting aside gifts made to persons in a position to exercise undue influence over the donors, although there has been no proof of the actual exercise of such influence; and the courts have done this on the avowed ground of the necessity of going this length in order to protect persons from the exercise of such influence under circumstances which render proof of it impossible. The courts have required proof of its non-exercise, and, failing that proof, have set aside gifts otherwise unimpeachable."

Inche Noriah v. *Shaik Alli Bin Omar* (1928): a nephew was managing the affairs of his aged aunt and he persuaded her to give him property by deed of gift. The lawyer who drew up the deed of gift explained to the aunt that it was irrevocable and asked whether she was signing it voluntarily. He did not know that the gift constituted practically the whole of her property, nor did he advise her that she could have left the property to her nephew by will instead of making the gift. HELD by the Privy Council: the nephew was unable to rebut the presumption of undue influence and the gift should be set aside.

Lancashire Loans Ltd. v. *Black* (1933): A daughter who was of full age, married and living in her own home, was persuaded by her mother to enter into an agreement with a money lender. The agreement was in the mother's interest but against the daughter's interest. The mother was also a party to the agreement. The daughter did not have independent legal advice nor did she understand her obligations under the transaction. The money lender sued for money due under the agreement, but the daughter contended that the agreement should be set aside for undue influence. HELD by the Court of Appeal: the marriage of the daughter and her departure from the parental home did not necessarily put an end to the parental influence. It is impossible to lay down any hard and fast rule in the matter. In the present case, the daughter had the benefit of a presumption that the influence continued after her marriage, and since the presumption was not rebutted, she was entitled to have the contract set aside.

7. Where undue influence must be proved. Where there is no relationship between the parties giving rise to the presumption of undue influence, a party alleging undue influence must prove that the other party had a dominant influence over his mind so that there was no exercise of independent will in entering the contract. Where the existence of the influence is proved, the court will assume that it was exercised, unless the contrary is proved.

Williams v. *Bayley* (1866): B was induced to settle property on a bank which had been defrauded by B's son. At the time of making the settlement, B thought that if he did not do this, his son would be prosecuted; although the bank had not actually threatened this. HELD by the House of Lords: at the time of making the settlement, B was not a free voluntary agent, and the settlement must be set aside.

PROGRESS TEST 9

1. Explain carefully what you understand by duress at common law. Mention whether or not duress may be exercised against goods.

2. What constitutes undue influence? In what circumstances is undue influence presumed?

3. What is the legal effect where a contract has been entered into (a) under duress, and (b) under undue influence?

4. A suspects that B's son has taken some money from him. He threatens B that he will prosecute unless B promises to pay the sum taken. If B promises to pay this, will he be bound by the promise?

5. Upon recovering from a serious illness, C, by deed of gift, transferred certain valuable property to D, his medical adviser. The motive for the gift was gratitude. C now regrets his generosity, and wishes to know whether the deed of gift is binding on him. Advise him

   (a) on the footing that the deed of gift was made twelve years ago, and
   (b) on the footing that the deed of gift was made eight months ago.

6. E is a solicitor and he wishes to buy a Georgian house from F, one of his clients. Would you advise E to arrange for F to be independently advised before the sale?

CHAPTER X
CAPACITY

CONTRACTUAL CAPACITY

1. Capacity and persons. In law, persons may be natural or artificial. Natural persons are human beings: artificial persons are corporations. Contractual capacity (or the lack of it) is an incident of personality. It is not possible for contractual capacity to attach to animals or inanimate objects.

(*a*) *Natural persons:* The general rule is that all natural persons have full contractual capacity. But there are exceptions in the case of infants, drunken persons, insane persons, and enemy aliens.

(*b*) *Corporations:* The contractual capacity of a corporation depends on the manner in which it was created.

2. Capacity and rights and obligations. In order to benefit from a contractual right, or to incur a contractual obligation, a contracting party must have the appropriate capacity. Rights and obligations can exist only where there is capacity to support them. Incapacity may, therefore, affect the apparent rights and obligations created by a contract.

INFANTS AS CONTRACTING PARTIES

3. Infants' contracts. By *s.* 1 of the *Family Law Reform Act*, 1969, the age of capacity for the purpose of any rule of law is eighteen years. Section 9 provides further that a person will be deemed to attain the age of eighteen at the commencement of the eighteenth anniversary of his birth. A person below the age of capacity may be referred to as an infant or as a minor. A contract entered into by an infant will fall into one of the four following classes:

(*a*) Contracts rendered void by statute.
(*b*) Contracts voidable by the infant.
(*c*) Contracts binding on the infant.

(d) Contracts enforceable by the infant but not against him.

4. Void contracts. The *Infants' Relief Act*, 1874, section 1, provides that: "All contracts, whether by specialty or by simple contract, henceforth entered into by infants for the repayment of money lent or to be lent, or for goods supplied or to be supplied (other than contracts for necessaries), and all accounts stated with infants, shall be absolutely void."

NOTE: *an account stated* is an agreed balance payable between parties resulting from a series of transactions: *e.g.* where the following three transactions occur—X sells to Y £300 worth of goods; Y sells to X £100 worth of goods; Y supplies £50 worth of services to X, if the parties agree in writing that, on balance, Y owes X £150, that is an account stated. In this example, Y would be able to base his action on the account stated, and it would not be necessary for him to prove the previous contracts. But if Y were an infant, the account stated would be void under the Act, and no action would lie.

Where a person of full age agrees to repay a loan contracted during infancy, the agreement is void: *Betting and Loans (Infants) Act*, 1892.

5. Effect of infants' contracts rendered void. Contracts governed by the *Infants' Relief Act*, 1874, and the *Betting and Loans (Infants) Act*, 1892, are void and cannot be enforced in any circumstances. Points to note are:

(a) Where an infant has borrowed money, no action is available to the lender to recover it. Where the infant fraudulently states that he is of full age so as to induce the other party to lend the money, no action in tort will lie against the infant for his fraud, for to allow this would open the door to a serious inroad upon the statutory provisions of the *Infants' Relief Act* and the *Betting and Loans (Infants) Act*.

Leslie v. *Sheill* (1914): an infant borrowed £400 from a firm of moneylenders by fraudulently stating that he was of full age. He did not repay the money and the moneylenders brought this action to recover it. HELD by the Court of Appeal: the plaintiffs could not recover the money by an action for fraud, for this would be an indirect way of enforcing a contract which was void by statute. Nor was there any rule of equity by which the infant could be compelled to restore the money he had obtained by fraud.

(b) A person who guarantees an infant's debt cannot be made liable on the guarantee: *Coutts & Co.* v. *Browne-Lecky* (1946), a decision of the King's Bench Division. But the Court of Appeal has held that a person giving an indemnity to an infant's creditor is liable on the indemnity: *Yeoman Credit* v. *Latter* (1961). (The fundamental distinction between a guarantor and a person giving an indemnity is that the guarantor is only secondarily liable on the default of the principal debtor, whereas a person who gives an indemnity makes himself primarily liable.)

(c) The contracts characterised as "absolutely void" by the *Infants' Relief Act*, 1874, includes contracts "for goods supplied or to be supplied." The Act, therefore, applies to goods supplied to the infant by way of sale, loan, exchange or hire-purchase.

Stocks v. *Wilson* (1913): an infant, by fraudulently stating that he was of full age, induced the plaintiff to sell him certain goods for £300. The infant then sold some of the goods and mortgaged the rest, obtaining a total of £130. HELD: the plaintiff could recover the £130. (But this decision appears to be at odds with *Leslie* v. *Sheill*.)

Pearce v. *Brain* (1929): P, an infant, exchanged his motor cycle for B's motor car. A few days later, the car broke down and P brought this action for the recovery of the motor cycle on the ground that the contract of exchange was void under the *Infants' Relief Act*. HELD: the contract of exchange was governed by the *Infants' Relief Act* but the infant could not recover the motor cycle because there had not been a total failure of consideration, the infant having had the use of the car for a few days. (In this case the court followed *Valentini* v. *Canali* (1889), in which it was held that an infant could not recover money paid under a void contract unless there had been a total failure of consideration.)

Yeoman Credit, Ltd. v. *Latter* (1961): an infant entered into a hire-purchase agreement with a finance company for a motor car. X entered into a collateral agreement by which he undertook to indemnify the finance company against any loss arising out of the hire-purchase agreement. The infant defaulted in his payments to the finance company. The company brought this action against the infant and X. HELD by the Court of Appeal: the hire-purchase agreement was void under

112   THE LAW OF CONTRACT

s. 1 of the *Infants' Relief Act*, 1874, but the indemnity given by X was binding.

(*d*) Where an infant obtains possession of goods under a contract void under the 1874 Act, he may be liable in tort if he deals with the goods in a manner outside the terms of the contract, *e.g.* by parting with possession of them.

Ballet v. *Mingay* (1943): The owner of certain radio equipment lent this equipment to an infant. The infant then lent the equipment to a third party. The owner brought this action against the infant in detinue. HELD by the Court of Appeal: notwithstanding that the loan agreement was void under the Act of 1874, the infant was liable in tort (detinue). When the infant parted with possession of the equipment he was acting right outside the loan agreement and his liability in tort was quite independent of the void contract.

(*e*) Section 1 of the *Infants' Relief Act* will not be construed so as to allow an infant to recover money paid by him for something he has used.

Valentini v. *Canali* (1889): the plaintiff, who was an infant at that time, agreed to take a lease of the defendant's restaurant, at a yearly rent of £32, payable quarterly. The plaintiff also agreed to buy from the defendant the fixtures and furniture of the shop for £102 6s. 9d. The plaintiff entered into possession and paid £68 15s. towards the cost of the fixtures and furniture, giving the defendant a promissory note for the balance. The plaintiff remained in occupation for several months using the furniture. The plaintiff then left the premises and brought this action in which he claimed (i) that the agreement should be set aside; (ii) that the promissory note should be delivered up to him for cancellation; and (iii) repayment of the moneys which had been paid to the defendant by him. The county court found in the plaintiff's favour on the first two counts, but refused to order repayment by the defendant. The plaintiff appealed. HELD on appeal to the Queen's Bench Division: section 1 of the *Infants' Relief Act*, 1874, is not to be construed so as to allow an infant to recover money paid by him for something he has consumed or used. *Per* Lord Coleridge, C.J.: "The learned counsel for the plaintiff has relied upon *s*. 1 of the *Infants' Relief Act*, 1874. Let us examine this Act of Parliament. The words of the section no doubt are very strong: 'All contracts whether by specialty or simple contract henceforth entered into by infants for the repayment of money lent, or to be lent, or for goods supplied ... shall be absolutely void.' But these words must be construed so as to give a sensible and reasonable construction to the Act which was passed for the purpose of protecting young people. It is obvious that if the plaintiff's construction of the section be the correct one there are many cases in which it would give rise to the grossest violations of natural justice. I think that the old rule of law on this point was just, and that it has not been altered by the Act. That rule was that where an infant had received something for which he had given consideration, if he was unable to return that for which the consideration had passed he could not recover the consideration. In other words, he was not allowed to recover money paid for what he had consumed or used."

6. Restitution by the infant. The cases show that, in equity, an infant may be compelled to give up the benefit he has received under a void contract. This is a special aspect of the equitable doctrine of restitution and its limits are not at all clearly defined. But restitution is not the same as repayment of money lent. In *Leslie* v. *Sheill*, Lord Sumner said, "I think that the whole current of decisions down to 1913, apart from dicta which are inconclusive, went to show that when an infant obtained an advantage by falsely stating himself to be of full age, equity required him to restore his ill-gotten gains or to release the party deceived from obligations or acts in law induced by the fraud, but scrupulously stopped short of enforcing against him a contractual obligation entered into while he was an infant even by means of fraud." However, if *Stocks* v. *Wilson* is rightly decided, an infant may be forced to disgorge the proceeds of sale or mortgage of goods obtained under a void contract. There is early authority to support the contention that restitution will be ordered where an infant obtains goods by fraud and remains in possession of them: see *Lemprière* v. *Lange* (1879). But where the infant parts with possession contrary to the terms of his agreement, he will be liable in tort: *Ballett* v. *Mingay*.

7. Infants' voidable contracts. Where an infant enters a contract of continuing obligation, the contract is voidable at the option of the infant before, or within a reasonable time after, reaching his majority.

Contracts in this class include tenancy agreements, marriage settlements, partnership agreements, and agreements to take shares which are not fully paid up. Where an infant repudiates a contract during infancy, he may cancel his repudiation and treat it as binding on reaching the age of 18.

Edwards v. *Carter* (1893): an infant covenanted by a marriage settlement, dated 16 October 1883, to settle after-acquired property. The infant came of age on 19 November 1883. In 1887 the infant became entitled under his father's will to a large sum of money to which the covenant in the marriage settlement should have applied. But in July 1888 the infant repudiated the settlement. The trustees of the settlement brought this action to enforce the covenant to settle after-acquired property. It was held by the Court of Appeal (reversing a decision of Romer, J.) that an infant must repudiate, if at all, within a reasonable time after he attains his majority, and what is a reasonable time is a question of fact to be determined in the light of all the circumstances, and in the circumstances of the present case, four and a half years was not a reasonable time. The respondent then appealed to the House of Lords. HELD by the House of Lords: the law gives an infant the privilege of repudiating obligations undertaken during minority within a reasonable time after coming of age. The law lays no obligation upon the infant, it merely confers upon him a privilege which he might or might not avail himself of as he chooses. If he chooses to be inactive his opportunity is lost, if he chooses to be active the law comes to his assistance. In the present case the period of four years and eight months which the infant permitted to elapse before he took any steps in the matter could not possibly be regarded as a reasonable time and, therefore, the covenant was binding.

In *Edwards* v. *Carter* Lord Herschell said: "It is said that in considering whether a reasonable time has elapsed you must take into account the fact that he did not know what were the terms of the settlement and that it contained this particular covenant. He knew that he had executed a deed—he must be taken to have known that the deed though binding upon him could be repudiated when he came of age, and it seems to me that in measuring a reasonable time whether in point of fact he had or had not acquainted himself with the nature of the obligations which he had undertaken is wholly immaterial —the time must be measured in precisely the same way whether he had so made himself acquainted or not. I do not say that he was under any obligation to make himself acquainted with the nature of the deed, which, having executed it as an infant, he might or might not at his pleasure repudiate when he came of age—all I say is this, that he cannot maintain that the reasonable time when measured must be a longer time because he has chosen not to make himself acquainted with the nature of the deed which he has executed."

8. Effect of repudiation. The general rule is that where an infant repudiates a contract of continuing obligation, he can recover money paid or property transferred only where there has been a complete failure of consideration. Where the infant has received any benefit at all, he cannot recover. In the case of partnership agreements, however, an infant partner can claim to recover his share of the partnership assets after the payment of partnership debts: *i.e.* he will have to share in the payment of partnership debts.

Steinberg v. *Scala (Leeds), Ltd.* (1923): an infant who had bought partly paid up shares in a company sought to repudiate the contract and recover her money. HELD: (i) she was entitled to repudiate and have her name removed from the register of members; and (ii) since the shares had some value, there was no failure of consideration, and she could not recover money paid.

NOTE: in *Steinberg* v. *Scala*, the infant was entitled to repudiate her obligation to pay further calls.

9. Contracts binding the infant. An infant is bound when he enters contracts of the following kinds:

(*a*) Contracts for *necessaries*.
(*b*) Contracts of *education*, training, or beneficial service.

10. Contracts for necessaries. An infant is liable to pay for necessaries that have been supplied to him. At common law, the concept of "necessaries" includes goods and services necessary to the infant and his dependants according to his position in life: *Peters* v. *Fleming* (1840); *Chapple* v. *Cooper* (1844). Articles of mere luxury are always excluded though luxurious articles of utility may be allowed according to the infant's station in life: *Chapple* v. *Cooper* (1844). "Necessaries" would accordingly include such things as medical attendance, lodgings, and food for the infant and also for any wife and children of the infant.

Section 2 of the *Sale of Goods Act*, 1893, defines "necessaries" as goods suitable to the condition in life of the infant and suitable to his actual requirements at the time of sale and delivery. The section provides further that where necessaries are sold and delivered to an infant he must pay a reasonable price. The infant's liability under the Act to pay a reasonable price for necessaries is quasi-contractual. He is not liable on an executory contract for necessaries, such liability being excluded by the use of the words "sale or delivery" and "sold and delivered" in *s*. 2 of the *Sale of Goods Act*, 1893.

Where a person sues an infant under *s*. 2 of the *Sale of Goods Act*, 1893, for the recovery of a reasonable price for goods sold and delivered, he must prove (i) that the goods were suitable to the condition in life of the infant, and (ii) that the goods were suitable to the infant's actual requirements at the time of sale and delivery.

Nash v. *Inman* (1908): the plaintiff had supplied to the defendant clothing to the value of £145 10*s*. 3*d*. at a time when the defendant was a Cambridge undergraduate. The clothes supplied by the plaintiff included eleven fancy waistcoats. The defendant raised the defence of infancy at the time of goods were supplied and that the goods were not "necessaries." The defendant's father had amply supplied the defendant with proper clothes according to his condition in life. It was held by Ridley, J. that there was no evidence that the goods were "necessaries" and entered judgment for the defendant. The plaintiff appealed. HELD by the Court of Appeal: there was no evidence that the goods supplied were necessary to the defendant's requirements. That, on the contrary, the defendant was amply supplied with suitable and necessary clothes. The trial judge was correct in the view that he took. *Per* Sir Herbert Cozens-Hardy, M.R.: "In substance the position is this. The plaintiff sues the defendant for goods sold and delivered. The defendant pleads infancy at the date of the sale, and his plea is proved. What is the consequence of that? The consequence of that is that the contract may turn out to be void, for since the *Infants' Relief Act*, 1874, all contracts for goods supplied to infants are absolutely void, subject, *inter alia*, to these provisions of *s*. 2 of the *Sale of Goods Act*, 1893: 'Capacity to buy and sell is regulated by the general law concerning capacity to contract, and to transfer and acquire property: Provided that where necessaries are sold and delivered to an infant, or minor, or to a person who by reason of mental incapacity or drunkenness is incompetent to contract, he must pay a reasonable price therefor.' The section then defines 'necessaries' as follows: 'Necessaries in this section means goods suitable to the condition in life of such infant, or minor, or other person, and to his actual requirements at the time of the sale and delivery.' What is the effect of that? The plaintiff, as I have already stated, sues for goods sold and delivered and the defendant pleads infancy. The plaintiff must then reply, 'the goods sold were "necessaries" within the meaning of the definition in *s.* 2 of the *Sale of Goods Act*, 1893.' It is not sufficient, in my view, for him to say, 'I have discharged the onus which rests upon me if I simply show that the goods supplied were suitable to the condition in life of the infant at the time.' There is another branch of the definition which cannot be disregarded. Having shown that the goods were suitable to the condition in life of the infant he must then go on to show that they were suitable to his actual requirements at the time of the sale and delivery. Unless he establishes that fact either by evidence adduced by himself or by cross-examination of the defendant's witnesses, as the case may be, in my opinion he has not discharged the burden which the law imposes upon him."

It has been held that where a person provides an infant with money to buy necessaries, that person may recover the amount from the infant notwithstanding the provision of the *Infants' Relief Act*, 1874, *s.* 1: *Martin* v. *Gale* (1876).

11. Contracts of education, training, or beneficial service.
An infant is bound by a contract under which he obtains education, or training for a trade or profession, or beneficial experience in a trade or profession. He is bound to pay a reasonable price for training where a price is agreed. The following contracts have been held to be beneficial:

(*a*) A contract by which an infant boxer undertook to abide by the rules of the British Boxing Board of Control; *Doyle* v. *White City Stadium Ltd.* (1935).

(*b*) A contract by which an infant billiards professional undertook to go on tour with a well-known player. *Roberts* v. *Gray* (1913).

NOTE: where an infant is engaged in trade, an ordinary trading contract is not binding on him, even though it may be for his benefit: *Mercantile Union Corporation Ltd.* v. *Ball* (1937).

12. Contracts enforceable by the infant but not against him.
Infants' contracts which are not void, voidable, or binding

form a residual class of contracts which are enforceable by the infant but are not enforceable against him.

13. Infants' Relief Act, 1874, s. 2. Section 2 of the *I.R.A.*, 1874, provides that, "No action shall be brought whereby to charge any person upon any promise made after full age to pay any debt contracted during infancy, or upon any ratification made after full age of any promise or contract made during infancy, whether there shall or shall not be any new consideration for such promise or ratification after full age."

This provision amended the common law rule that where a person enters a contract during infancy and subsequently ratifies the contract after reaching full age, he is bound by the terms of the original contract. Section 2 provides that no action shall be brought against a person upon any ratification of any contract made during infancy. Any such purported ratification is unenforceable. The statutory rule applies to *all* categories of contract which are not binding on an infant. But the rule does not apply where the former infant enters a fresh contract, for this is different from ratification of the old contract. The distinction is illustrated by the two cases below.

Coxhead v. *Mullis* (1878): M, an infant, became engaged to marry C. After reaching full age, M continued to treat himself as C's fiancé for several months. M refused to marry C, who then brought this action for breach of promise of marriage. M pleaded infancy. HELD: M's conduct in behaving towards C as her fiancé after he had reached full age constituted a mere ratification of his promise to marry her. Section 2 of the 1874 Act applied, therefore C's action could not succeed.

Northcote v. *Doughty* (1878): D, an infant, agreed to marry N, subject to obtaining his parents' approval. On coming of age, D went to N and told her that his parents approved of the marriage and that he would marry her as soon as he could. Subsequently D changed his mind and refused to marry N, who then brought this action for breach of promise. HELD: D's promise made after reaching full age was not mere ratification of his earlier promise made in infancy. It was a new promise and he was liable on it, s. 2 of the *Infants' Relief Act*, 1874 not being applicable.

CONTRACTS MADE BY INSANE OR DRUNKEN PERSONS

14. Incapacity through insanity or drunkenness. Where a person who is drunk or insane, and thus does not understand what he is doing, enters into a contract, the contract is voidable at his option, provided that the other party knew of his condition. Lopes, L.J., summed up the position in *Imperial Loan* v. *Stone* (1892) as follows: "A contract made by a person of unsound mind is not voidable at that person's option if the other party to the contract believed at the time he made the contract that the person with whom he was dealing was of sound mind. In order to avoid a fair contract on the ground of insanity the mental incapacity of the one must be known to the other party. A defendant must plead and prove both his insanity and the knowledge of the plaintiff; the burden of proof of both those facts lies on the defendant."

NOTE:

(i) Mentally unbalanced persons are bound by contracts made during periods of lucidity.

(ii) Voidable contracts may be ratified and made binding after the period of incapacity has ended.

(iii) Insane and drunken persons are bound to pay a reasonable price for necessaries according to the same rules as apply to infants: *Sale of Goods Act*, 1893, *s.* 2.

CONTRACTUAL CAPACITY OF CORPORATIONS

15. How capacity may be determined. The contractual capacity of a corporation may be determined as follows:

(*a*) *Chartered corporations:* there are no legal limits to the contractual capacity of a chartered corporation. There are, however, limits imposed by the artificial nature of the corporation, *e.g.* it cannot contract to have its hair cut, or to have its appendix removed. Where a chartered corporation enters into a contract beyond the powers granted in the charter, the act is valid and binding. But a member of a chartered corporation may apply for an injunction to restrain an act beyond the powers granted in the charter.

(b) *Statutory corporations:* the contractual capacity of a statutory corporation is defined expressly or by implication by the statute under which the corporation was created. Any contract which is beyond the powers conferred by the statute is void.

(c) *Registered corporations:* the contractual capacity of a company registered under the *Companies Act*, 1948, is defined by the objects clause in the company's memorandum of association.

Any act going beyond the capacity thus defined was formerly *ultra vires* (beyond its powers).

Section 9 (1) of the *European Communities Act*, 1972, now provides that a third party who is *bona fide* may assume that any transaction decided on by the directors is both *intra vires* and within the directors' authority and enables him to enforce the contract accordingly. Although the memorandum of association is a public document which every company formed under the *Companies Act* must lodge with the Registrar of Companies, a third party no longer has constructive notice of its contents, as was formerly the case.

PROGRESS TEST 10

1. What do you understand by the expression "contractual capacity"?
2. Into what classes may infants' contracts be divided?
3. State and explain the provisions of *s.* 1 of the *Infants' Relief Act*, 1874.
4. Is a person of full age bound by a promise to repay a loan which he contracted as an infant? Give an authority for your answer.
5. Where an infant fraudulently states that he is of full age so as to induce a person to lend money to him, does an action in tort lie against the infant for his fraud?
6. What kinds of contracts entered into by infants are voidable at the option of the infant? Where an infant exercises his option to repudiate, may he recover money paid to the other party under the contract?
7. In what circumstances is an infant contractually bound?
8. Define "necessaries," giving an authority.
9. Where an infant is engaged in trade, is an ordinary trading contract ever binding on him?
10. State and explain the provisions of *s.* 2 of the *Infants' Relief Act*, 1874.

X. CAPACITY

11. Compare fully the contractual capacity of an infant with that of a person who is insane.

12. To what extent is a drunken person bound contractually?

13. Define carefully an enemy alien. Make sure to mention whether nationality is relevant.

14. Why do you think a corporation is sometimes called an artificial person?

15. Explain the difference between

   (a) A chartered corporation; and
   (b) A statutory corporation; and
   (c) A company registered under the *Companies Act*, 1948.

16. X, an infant, enters into the following contracts. Explain whether he is bound by them:

   (a) A contract of hire-purchase of a television set.
   (b) A contract of apprenticeship with C, a gardener.
   (c) An account stated with D to the effect that X owes D the sum of £21.
   (d) A contract for a new pair of spectacles delivered to the infant, price £10.

17. XYZ Ltd. is a company registered under the *Companies Act*, 1948. The company is empowered by the objects clause in the Memorandum of Association to engage in business as retailers of fresh fish. The company owns a chain of fish shops for this purpose. The board of directors have now decided to expand the scope of their trade by retailing frozen vegetables. Following this decision, negotiations are taking place with Freezo Ltd., for the purchase of 150 refrigerators, designed for frozen packaged vegetables. Advise Freezo Ltd. as to their position if the contract is entered into.

18. E, aged 17, entered an agreement with F, under which E hired a sports car for one week. E then lent the car to a friend G, who took it to a disused airfield and raced the car around the perimeter track. Owing to the high speed of the car and the poor surface of the disused perimeter track, the car overturned and was completely wrecked. G died as a result. F wishes to know whether he may recover the value of the car from E. Advise him.

19. H, aged 17, is married and has one child. He is a commercial traveller earning approximately £20 a week. He receives bills for the following goods which have been delivered to him:

   (a) A mink coat for his wife, price £1100.
   (b) A small saloon car, price £600.
   (c) A push-chair for his child, price £6.50.

(d) A new suit made for H by a Savile Row tailor, price £90.
(e) Groceries used by his family, price £13.

Advise him as to his liability on each of these transactions.

20. J, aged 16, is a millionaire. His pocket is picked and his binoculars are stolen while he is at a race meeting, so he borrows £50 from an adult friend, K. Next day he quarrels with K and, out of spite, refuses to repay the £50. K needs this money badly. Advise him as to whether he can recover it from J. Give your answer on the footing that J spent £30 on betting and the remaining £20 on a pair of binoculars.

CHAPTER XI

ILLEGAL CONTRACTS

CONTRACTS ILLEGAL IN INCEPTION

1. Ex turpi causa non oritur actio. It is against public policy, *i.e.* against the policy of the common law, to allow an action on a contract containing an illegal or wrongful element. The maxims upon which this policy is founded are:

(a) *Ex turpi causa non oritur actio:* no action arises from a base cause. (Sometimes expressed as *ex dolo malo non oritur actio.*)

(b) *In pari delicto potior est conditio defendentis:* where there is equal fault, the defendant is in the stronger position.

A clear explanation of the two maxims was given by Lord Mansfield, C.J. in *Holman* v. *Johnson* (1775). He said, "The objection, that a contract is immoral or illegal as between plaintiff and defendant, sounds at all times very ill in the mouth of the defendant. It is not for his sake, however, that the objection is ever allowed; but it is founded in general principles of policy, which the defendant has the advantage of, contrary to the real justice, as between him and the plaintiff, by accident, if I may say so. The principle of public policy is this: *ex dolo malo non oritur actio.* No court will lend its aid to a man who founds his cause of action upon an immoral or illegal act. If, from the plaintiff's own stating or otherwise, the cause of action appears to arise *ex turpi causa*, or the transgression of a positive law of this country, there the court says he has no right to be assisted. It is upon that ground the court goes; not for the sake of the defendant, but because they will not lend their aid to such a plaintiff."

Where the plaintiff's cause of action arises from the breach of an illegal contract, the general rule is that the court will refuse its aid and will drive the parties from its presence making no order as to damages or costs. In *Archbolds, Ltd.* v. *S. Spanglett, Ltd.* (1961), Pearce, L.J., said, "If a contract is expressly or by necessary implication forbidden by statute, or if it is *ex facie* illegal, or if both parties know that though *ex facie* legal it can only be performed by illegality or is intended to be performed illegally, the law will not help the plaintiffs in any way that is a direct or indirect enforcement of rights under the contract; and for this purpose both parties are presumed to know the law." In the same case Devlin, L.J., said, "The effect of illegality on a contract may be three fold. If at the time of making the contract there is an intention to perform it in an unlawful way, the contract, although it remains alive, is unenforceable at the suit of the party having that intent; if the intent is held in common, it is not enforceable at all. Another effect of illegality is to prevent a plaintiff from recovering under a contract if in order to prove his rights under it he has to rely on his own illegal act; he may not do that even though he can show that at the time of making the contract he had no intent to break the law and that at the time of performance he did not know that what he was doing was illegal. The third effect of illegality is to avoid the contract *ab initio*, and that arises if the making of the contract is expressly or impliedly prohibited by statute or is otherwise contrary to public policy."

2. Examples of illegal contracts. A contract is illegal if it involves the transgression of a rule of law (statutory or otherwise) or where it is base or immoral. Examples are:

(a) Contracts prohibited by statute.
(b) Contracts to defraud the Revenue.
(c) Contracts involving the commission of a crime or tort.
(d) Contracts with a sexually immoral element.
(e) Contracts against the interests of the United Kingdom or a friendly state.
(f) Contracts leading to corruption in public life.
(g) Contracts which interfere with the course of justice.

3. Contracts prohibited by statute. A contract which contravenes the terms or policy of a statute is illegal. Where a statutory provision expressly or by implication prohibits a particular kind of contract, the rules discussed in this chapter apply to contracts of that kind. But where a statute declares a particular class of contractual term to be void or of no effect, the rules of illegality are not thereby invoked: the effect is merely that if any such void terms are found in a contract, they will be struck out.

Where a contract is *ex facie* legal and one of the parties performs his side of it in a manner forbidden by statute, the illegal performance does not debar the other party from relief provided he did not know of the other's intention to perform in an illegal manner.

Archbolds, Ltd. v. *Spanglett, Ltd.* (1961): there was a contract between the plaintiffs and the defendants by which the defendants agreed to carry by road certain goods owned by a third party. The vehicle in which the goods were carried had a "C" licence. The *Road and Rail Traffic Act*, 1933, prohibits the use of goods vehicles on a road except with an "A" licence. The defendants knew at the time of the contract that a vehicle with the "C" licence was to be used, but the plaintiffs did not know this. As a result of negligence on the part of the defendants, the goods were stolen in transit. The plaintiffs claimed damages for breach of contract and negligence. HELD by the Court of Appeal: the contract was *ex facie* legal. The plaintiffs could succeed in their claim for damages for negligence because they did not know that the vehicle to be used had only a "C" licence.

4. Contracts to defraud the Revenue.
A contract which is designed to defraud the Revenue or a rating authority is illegal.

Napier v. *National Business Agency, Ltd.* (1951): N was employed by the company at a salary plus £6 a week for expenses. As both parties knew, N's expenses were never more than £1 a week. The company dismissed N summarily and he claimed his salary for a period in lieu of notice. HELD by the Court of Appeal: the part of the agreement relating to expenses was tax evasion and illegal: the rest of the agreement was tainted with the illegality and, accordingly, unenforceable.

Alexander v. *Rayson* (1936): in July 1929 the defendant, Mrs Rayson, approached the plaintiff with a view to taking an under lease of a flat at a rent of £1200 a year, the rent to cover the provision of services. The plaintiff, accordingly, sent to the defendant two documents. The first being a draft sub-lease of the flat at a rent of £450 a year. The second being a draft agreement for various services in connection with the flat for the payment of an additional sum of £750 a year. The sub-lease itself provided for services which were substantially the same as those in the service agreement with the exception of the provision and maintenance of a frigidaire. (The plaintiff had stated to the rating assessment committee that £450 was the only amount he received for rent, services and rates. His assessment was then reduced from £720 to £270. But the committee subsequently discovered the existence of the agreement and the assessment of £720 was restored.) The annual sum of £1200 was paid by the defendant quarterly up to and including the instalment due at midsummer 1934. But the defendant refused to pay the quarterly instalment of the £750 which fell due in September 1934, contending that the plaintiff had failed to comply with his obligations in respect of the services to be rendered under the sub-lease and under the agreement. The defendant tendered the sum of £112 10s. as the quarterly rent due under the sub-lease. The plaintiff refused this tender and brought this action claiming the sum of £300, being the quarterly instalment payable under the two documents. The defendant contended, *inter alia*, that the agreement was void for illegality and that its enforcement would be contrary to public policy in that its execution was obtained by the plaintiff for the purposes of defrauding the Westminster City Council by deceiving them as to the true rateable value of the premises and by inducing them to believe that the true rent received by the plaintiff was £450 and by concealing from them the terms of the agreement. The trial judge held that the agreement was not unenforceable for illegality. The defendant appealed. HELD by the Court of Appeal: the landlord had intended to use the sub-lease and the agreement for an illegal purpose and had, accordingly, put himself in the same position in law as though he had intended that the flat, when let, should be used for an illegal purpose. He was, therefore, not entitled to enforce the sub-lease or the agreement. It made no difference that he had failed to defraud the rating authority and could no longer use the documents for an illegal purpose.

In *Alexander* v. *Rayson*, Romer, L.J., in reading the judgment of the Court, said: "It is settled law that an agreement to do an act that is illegal or immoral or contrary to public policy, or to do any act for a consideration that is illegal, immoral, or contrary to public policy, is unlawful and therefore void. But it often happens that an agreement which, in itself, is not unlawful, is made with the intention of one or both parties to make use of the subject-matter for an unlawful purpose, that is to say, a purpose that is illegal, immoral, or contrary to public policy. The most common instance of this is an agreement for the sale or letting of an object, where the agreement is unobjectionable on the face of it, but where the intention of one or both of the parties is that the object shall

XI. ILLEGAL CONTRACTS

be used by the purchaser or hirer for an unlawful purpose. In such a case any party to the agreement who had the unlawful intention is precluded from suing upon it *ex turpi causa non oritur actio*. The action does not lie because the court will not lend its help to such a plaintiff."

5. Contracts to commit a crime or a tort.
Where the consideration in, or the purpose of, a contract is criminal or tortious, the contract is illegal.

> *Beresford* v. *Royal Insurance Co., Ltd.* (1938): R shot himself a few minutes before his life insurance policy expired. His personal representatives claimed on the policy. HELD: it would be against public policy to allow a man to benefit his estate by committing a crime. The sum assured was not recoverable.

Contracts involving maintenance or champerty fall into this class, *i.e.* contracts whereby a person promises to support another improperly in bringing an action at law.

6. Contracts with a sexually immoral element.
A contract is illegal for immorality as follows:

(*a*) Where the consideration is an act of sexual immorality, *e.g.* an agreement for future illicit co-habitation. (N.B. An agreement with respect to *past* illicit co-habitation is not illegal, and is binding if made under seal.)

(*b*) Where the purpose of the contract is the furtherance of sexual immorality, and both parties know this.

> *Pearce* v. *Brooks* (1866): there was a contract under which a firm of coachbuilders hired out a carriage to a prostitute. It was known that she intended to use the vehicle as part of her display to attract men. The prostitute fell into arrears with the hire payments, and the coachbuilders claimed the sum due. HELD: the contract was illegal and the sum claimed could not be recovered.

7. Contracts against the interest of the State.
Any contract which is detrimental to the interests of the United Kingdom is illegal, *e.g.* a trading contract which would benefit a country at war with the United Kingdom.

The rule also covers agreements which might disturb the friendly relations between the U.K. and other states. Thus the court once refused to recognise an agreement to export whisky to the U.S.A. contrary to the prohibition laws of that country in the 1920s: *Foster* v. *Driscoll* (1929).

8. Contracts leading to corruption in public life.

Contracts involving the bribery of officials, or attempts to buy honours, are illegal. Such contracts are void even though no crime has been committed.

Parkinson v. *College of Ambulance, Ltd.* (1925): one Harrison, the second defendant in this case, was the secretary of the defendant company. He fraudulently represented to the plaintiff that he had power to nominate persons to receive titles of honour and that he or the company could arrange for the grant to the plaintiff of a knighthood if the plaintiff would make a donation to the company funds. In response to this false and fraudulent representation, the plaintiff made a donation of £3000 to the company. The plaintiff brought this action to recover £3000 as damages for deceit, or, in the alternative, as money had and received by the defendants to the use of the plaintiff, or, in the further alternative, as damages for breach of warranty of authority. HELD: the contract between the plaintiff and the defendants by which the plaintiff gave the money on the strength of representations that he would receive a knighthood, was against public policy and, therefore, illegal; as the parties were *in pari delicto* an action for damages could not be maintained by the plaintiff, nor could he recover the money on the ground that it was had and received by the defendant to his use.

9. Contracts which interfere with the course of justice.

Any contract which tends to pervert the course of justice is illegal. A contract not to prosecute, or to compromise, in criminal proceedings is illegal, unless the proceedings could have been initiated in the civil courts for tort. Also, a contract under which an accused person indemnifies a person who has gone bail for him is illegal: *Herman* v. *Jeuchner* (1885).

Kearley v. *Thomson* (1890): A petition in bankruptcy was presented by B aganst C, a friend of the plaintiff. The plaintiff paid £40 to the defendants, a firm of solicitors, in consideration of an undertaking by them not to appear at C's public examination and not to oppose his discharge. The defendants, in accordance with the agreement, did not appear at the public examination. Before C applied for his order of discharge, the plaintiff brought this action to recover the £40.

HELD by the Court of Appeal: the agreement was illegal and the sum could not be recovered. *Per* Fry, L.J.: "The tendency of such an undertaking as that which was given by the defendants is obvious; it tends to pervert the course of justice. The defendants were not bound to appear, but they were bound not to enter an agreement which would fetter their liberty of action as to appearing or not."

THE CONSEQUENCES OF ILLEGALITY

10. The general rule. The general rule is that no action can be brought by a party to an illegal contract: *ex turpi causa non oritur actio*. The following points should be noted:

(*a*) No action will lie for the recovery of money paid or property transferred under an illegal contract: *Parkinson's Case; Kearley* v. *Thomson*.

(*b*) No action will lie for the breach of an illegal contract: *Pearce* v. *Brooks; Beresford's Case*.

(*c*) Where part of an illegal contract would have been lawful by itself, the court will not sever the good from the bad. The whole contract becomes tainted with illegality: *Napier's Case*.

(*d*) Any contract which is collateral to an illegal contract is also tainted with illegality, and is treated as being illegal, even though it would have been lawful by itself.

Fisher v. *Bridges* (1854): there was an illegal contract under which F agreed to sell certain land to B. B paid the purchase price except for £630, and the land was conveyed to him. By a separate deed B promised to pay £630 to F. HELD: the collateral agreement under seal was tainted with the illegality.

(*e*) Title of goods may pass under an illegal contract if it is executed. There is no rule that the court will not look at an illegal contract: *Belvoir Finance Co* v. *Stapleton* (1971).

NOTE: although illegal contracts are sometimes said to be void, it should be noticed that the consequences of illegality are different from those where a contract is merely void.

11. Exceptions to the general rule of no recovery. A party to an illegal contract may sue to recover money paid or property transferred as follows:

(a) Where the parties are not *in pari delicto*, *i.e.* not equally at fault, the "innocent" party may recover. This circumstance may arise in two ways:

(i) Where the contract is prohibited by statute in order to protect the class of person to which the plaintiff belongs.

(ii) Where a party has been induced to enter an illegal contract by fraudulent misrepresentation, or where an ignorant man enters an illegal contract under the influence of a cleverer man.

Hughes v. *Liverpool, etc. Friendly Society* (1916): H was induced by the fraudulent mispresentation of an insurance agent to enter an illegal contract of life insurance. H sought to recover the premiums paid. HELD by the Court of Appeal: the parties were not *in pari delicto* and the premiums were recoverable.

(b) Where no substantial part of the illegal act has been performed, a party who is truly repentant may recover. In this way, the law encourages repentance. But a party seeking to take advantage of this rule must show that his repentance is genuine, and that he is not repudiating the contract for mere reasons of convenience: *Bigos* v. *Bousted* (1951).

(c) Where a contract is apparently lawful in its actual formation, but there is an illegal purpose known to one party and not to the other, the innocent party may recover: *Cowan* v. *Milbourn* (1867). But a contract which is *ex facie* lawful will be treated as illegal if both parties knew of the illegal purpose: *Pearce* v. *Brooks* (1866).

(d) Where a party to an illegal contract is able to frame his action so as not to depend on contract, he may succeed in recovering property: *Bowmakers, Ltd.* v. *Barnet Instruments, Ltd.* (1944); *Sajan Singh* v. *Sardara Ali* (1960).

ILLEGAL PERFORMANCE OF A LAWFUL CONTRACT

12. Participation in illegal performance. Where a contract is lawful in its inception but is performed in an illegal manner, any party who participated in the illegal performance will be

XI. ILLEGAL CONTRACTS

debarred from claiming damages for breach of contract. This principle was expounded by Atkin, L.J., in *Anderson Ltd.* v. *Daniel* (1924) in a passage which was quoted by Devlin, J., in *St. John Shipping Corpn.* v. *Joseph Rank Ltd.* (1956), and approved by Lord Denning in *Ashmore, Ltd.* v. *Dawson, Ltd.* (1973): "The question of illegality in a contract generally arises in connection with its formation, but it may also arise, as it does here, in connection with its performance. In the former case, where the parties have agreed to do something which is prohibited by Act of Parliament, it is indisputable that the contract is unenforceable by either party. And I think that it is equally unenforceable by the offending party where the illegality arises from the fact that the mode of performance adopted by the party performing it is in violation of some statute, even though the contract as agreed upon between the parties was capable of being performed in a perfectly legal manner."

Ashmore, Ltd. v. *Dawson, Ltd.* (1973): the plaintiffs had manufactured a piece of engineering equipment weighing 25 tons which the defendants, a road haulage company, agreed to carry to a port of shipment. The plaintiffs' transport manager was present when the equipment was loaded on to the defendants' vehicle. He knew that the vehicle provided by the defendants was overloaded contrary to the statutory regulations governing the carrying of loads on motor vehicles. He made no objection to the use of this vehicle, nor did he explain (what he well knew) that the appropriate vehicle for the load in question was a "low loader." On its way to the port, the vehicle toppled over and the loaded equipment was damaged. The plaintiffs brought this action for damages contending that there was negligence and/or breach of contract on the defendants' part. HELD by the Court of Appeal: even if the contract was lawful in its inception, it was performed in an unlawful manner and the plaintiffs, through their transport manager, had participated in the illegality. Accordingly, the plaintiffs were debarred from claiming damages.

PROGRESS TEST 11

1. Explain the maxims *ex turpi causa non oritur actio* and *in pari delicto potior est conditio defendentis*.
2. Give some examples of the kinds of contract which are illegal.
3. Where a party to a lawful contract performs his side of the

LAW OF CONTRACT

agreement in a manner forbidden by statute, is the contract rendered illegal?

4. "Any contract which is collateral to an illegal contract is tainted with illegality." Explain this statement and illustrate your answer with a case.

5. The general rule is that there is no recovery of money paid or property transferred under an illegal contract. Give a careful account of the exceptions to this rule.

6. A entered a contract of service with an employer, B. According to the terms of the contract, B agreed to pay A £18 a week salary and £10 a week by way of expenses. The agreement was designed to defraud the Revenue, for it was never envisaged that A should require more than £2 a week as expenses. B has just dismissed A summarily, giving no reason for doing so. A seeks your advice as to whether he can claim three weeks' arrears of salary and expenses. Advise him.

7. C agrees to let D have the use of C's motor yacht for a week. C knew at the time of the agreement that D intended to use the yacht for smuggling dope into England. D paid C £2000 deposit before going aboard the yacht, and when he got aboard, he found that C had removed some vital parts of the engine, so that it was impossible to put to sea. Advise D as to whether he can recover the £2000.

8. E has co-habited with his mistress, F, for the past five years. E tells F that he wishes to leave her, and then takes her to his solicitor's office, where he makes a promise under seal to pay her £500 per annum for the rest of her life, in consideration for what she has done for him. Advise F as to whether she can enforce E's promise in the event of non-payment.

9. G is anxious that his dull son, H, shall be admitted into Dotheboys College. G knows that competition is keen and that H has not the intelligence to pass the entrance examination; so he arranges to meet J, the college bursar, privately and agrees to pay him (J) the sum of £2000 on the understanding that H shall be admitted in the following Michaelmas term. When J received the £2000 from G, he immediately sent it to his favourite charity. He then wrote to G, telling him that on no account would H be admitted into the college. G now wishes to recover the £2000. Advise him.

10. K enters a contract with L for the purchase of 100 packets of cigarettes which he knows that L has recently stolen. K pays £5 to L under the agreement, but when, later, L tries to deliver the cigarettes, K refuses to accept them. K's refusal was due to a sudden fear that the stolen cigarettes would be traced to him. L now refuses to return the £5. Will K be able to recover the money? Would your answer be different if K's refusal had been out of true repentance?

CHAPTER XII

VOID CONTRACTS

VOID CONTRACTS GENERALLY

1. Distinction between void and illegal contracts. A contract which is void does not give rise to rights and obligations, but the full consequences of illegality are not present.

2. Grounds on which a contract may be void. A contract may be void in any of the following circumstances:

(a) Where a statute renders contracts of that class void.

(b) Where the contract is void at common law as being against public policy.

(c) Where the Restrictive Trade Practices Court declares that the contract is against the public interest.

(d) Where the contract is void at common law generally, *e.g.* for operative mistake, or for lack of capacity of one of the parties. (This class is outside the scope of this chapter, but *see* VII and X.)

CONTRACTS MADE VOID BY STATUTE

3. Examples of contracts in this class.

(a) Assignments of retired pay by officers of the army, navy, or air force. Also, assignments of pensions by teachers, policemen, and old age pensioners.

(b) Infants' contracts rendered absolutely void by *s.* 1 of the *Infants' Relief Act*, 1874. (These contracts are considered in Chapter X.)

(c) Wagering contracts. Under the *Gaming Act*, 1845, all contracts by way of gaming or wagering are null and void.

(d) Contracts made void by the *Resale Prices Act*, 1964: *see* **33** *below*.

4. Consequences where a contract is void by statute. No enforceable rights arise from a void contract. However, the

134 THE LAW OF CONTRACT

transaction may not be entirely without legal effect. For example, a contract by an infant to repay money lent to him is "absolutely void," but the legal effect is that the lender is unable to recover his loan. Similarly, money paid under a wagering contract cannot be recovered.

WAGERING CONTRACTS

5. Definition. "A wagering contract is one by which two persons, professing to hold opposite views touching the issue of a future uncertain event, mutually agree that, dependent upon the determination of that event, one shall win from the other, and that other shall pay or hand over to him, a sum of money or other stake; neither of the contracting parties having any interest in that contract other than the sum or stake he will so win or lose, there being no other real consideration for the making of such contract by either of the parties": *per* Hawkins, J., in *Carlill* v. *Carbolic Smoke Ball Co.* (1892), approved by the Court of Appeal in *Ellesmere* v. *Wallace* (1929).

NOTE: *a gaming contract* is a wager upon the result of a game or sporting event. It matters not whether the game or sporting event involves skill or chance.

6. Analysis of the definition. A contract is a wager if the following elements are present:

(*a*) Two persons must profess to hold opposite views touching the issue of a *future uncertain event*. The uncertainty must lie in the minds of the contracting parties. It is possible, for example, for two parties to wager as to the height of Nelson's Column. Now, although the height of the column is not a future uncertain event, the actual height as subsequently determined by the parties, *is* a future uncertain event.

(*b*) On the determination of the event, one party shall win from the other party the agreed sum of money or other stake. Notice that the consideration for a wager may be any form of property.

(*c*) There must be two parties, each of whom will win or lose according to the determination of the event. There cannot be more than two parties unless there be two groups of persons.

(*d*) Neither party must have an interest in the contract other than the sum or stake he will win or lose.

Thus if X bets Y £5 that he (Y) will not pass the Bar Finals at first attempt, there is no wager. In this example, Y has an interest in the contract other than the £5.

NOTE:

(i) *In insurance contracts* the interest, other than the money consideration, is known as the insurable interest.

(ii) *In contracts between stockbroker and client* for the purchase of shares, there is a wager if the parties did not intend the delivery of the shares, but rather that the client should be credited or debited according whether the shares rose or fell by the next settling day. (The normal purchase and delivery of shares is not a wagering contract.)

7. The Gaming Acts, 1845 and 1892. The 1845 Act provides that, "All contracts or agreements, whether by parole or in writing, by way of gaming or wagering, shall be null and void; and no suit shall be brought or maintained in any court of law and equity for recovering any sum of money or valuable thing alleged to have been won upon any wager, or which shall have been deposited in the hands of any person to abide the event on which any wager shall have been made."

The 1892 Act further provides that, "Any promise, express or implied, to pay any person any sum of money paid by him under or in respect of any contract or agreement rendered null and void by the *Gaming Act*, 1845, or to pay any sum of money by way of commission, fee, reward, or otherwise in respect of such contract, or of any services in relation thereto or in connection therewith, shall be null and void, and no action shall be brought or maintained to recover any such sum of money."

NOTE: the 1892 Act makes void any contract collateral to a wagering contract, *e.g.* a contract by which a betting agent is to receive commission.

8. Cheques given in a wager. Where a party to a wagering contract gives a cheque or other negotiable instrument by way of payment, the legal consequence will depend upon whether the contract was (*a*) a gaming contract, or (*b*) any *other* kind of wagering contract.

(*a*) *Cheques given in gaming contracts:* any cheque given by way of payment in a gaming contract shall be *deemed* to have been given for an illegal consideration: *Gaming Act,* 1835. The effect of this provision is that the winner to whom the cheque is given cannot maintain an action on it in the event of dishonour.

But if the winner negotiates the cheques to a holder in due course, that holder has full rights on the instrument, and can maintain an action against any prior party to the cheque (*i.e.* the holder must have taken the cheque in good faith, and without notice of the fact that it was given in a wager, and he (or some prior party) must have given consideration for it). See *Bills of Exchange Act,* 1882, *s.* 29, for a definition of "holder in due course"; also XV, **17**.

(*b*) *Cheques given in other wagering contracts:* any cheque given by way of payment in a wagering contract other than a gaming contract is given for no consideration because the wager is void. The difference is that it is not deemed to have been given for an illegal consideration as in the case of gaming contracts.

In the event of dishonour in the hands of the winner, he could claim against the loser, and the burden of proving the absence of consideration would lie on the loser: for consideration is presumed in bills of exchange. But if the winner negotiated the cheque for value, the new holder would have full rights on the cheque: in the event of dishonour, he could sue all prior parties.

9. Loans for wagering. Where money is lent for wagering purposes the right of the lender to recover depends, primarily, on whether the money was used for a lawful or an illegal wager.

In *M'Kinnell* v. *Robinson* (1838) it was held that money lent for betting on an illegal game is not recoverable. The position is not free from doubt where money is lent for the purpose of a lawful wager. In *Carlton Hall Club* v. *Laurence* (1929) it was held that the lender could not recover. This decision, which was founded on a very free construction of the *Gaming Acts* of 1710 and 1835, has been doubted by the Court of Appeal in *C.H.T., Ltd.* v. *Ward* (1965) where it was asserted *obiter* that a loan for lawful wagering is recoverable.

CONTRACTS VOID AT COMMON LAW AS BEING AGAINST PUBLIC POLICY

10. Contracts offending public policy. Certain contracts which offend against public policy are illegal, and have been dealt with in Chapter XI. There are, however, certain remaining contracts against public policy which have escaped the full stigma of illegality. These contracts are void, but only so far as they are against public policy. They are:

(a) Contracts to oust the courts from their jurisdiction.
(b) Contracts striking at the sanctity of marriage.
(c) Contracts impeding parental duties.
(d) Contracts in restraint of trade.

11. Contracts to oust the jurisdiction. The court is the final arbiter on questions of law, and this jurisdiction cannot be ousted by any agreement between the parties. Thus, although a party may bind himself to submit to the findings of fact by a competent arbitrator or domestic tribunal, he cannot bind himself to refrain from submitting questions of law to the courts: *Lee* v. *Showmen's Guild* (1952). Similarly, an agreement not to refer disputes as to interpretation to the courts is void: *Baker* v. *Jones* (1954).

12. Contracts striking at the sanctity of marriage. The institution of marriage is protected by the policy of the courts. Contracts in undue restraint of marriage, contracts which impede a party in his marital duties, and marriage brokage contracts are void.

EXAMPLES:

(i) A contract by which a party undertakes not to marry at all is void. A partial restraint is not necessarily void, *e.g.* where X contracts not to marry Y, the restraint does not necessarily make the contract void; but where X promises not to marry at all, the contract is void. A contract not to marry for six years has been held to be void.

(ii) A contract between husband and wife for a definite or possible future separation is void. But a contract between husband and wife for an immediate separation is valid.

(iii) Where a party, whose present spouse is still alive, contracts to marry another, the contract is void, *e.g.* X, who is married to Y, contracts with Z that he will marry her after the death of Y—the contract is void. But a contract to marry, entered into after a decree nisi and before the decree absolute of divorce, is not void.

13. Contracts impeding parental duties. A contract by which a party deprives himself of the custody of his child is void. But note that a court order to the same effect is binding.

14. Contracts in restraint of trade. A contract in restraint of trade is one whereby a party undertakes to suffer some restriction as to carrying on his trade or profession. There is an agreement in restraint of trade:

(a) Where an employee, apprentice, or articled clerk undertakes not to set up in business, or enter the service of another, within a specified area.

(b) Where the vendor of the goodwill of a business undertakes not to compete with the purchaser.

(c) Where merchants or manufacturers give mutual undertakings for the regulation of their business relations: e.g. by agreeing (i) to regulate the output of any commodity, (ii) to control prices or (iii) to regulate the trading use of a particular piece of land.

15. Contracts in restraint of trade are prima facie void. Although a contract in restraint of trade is *prima facie* void, it will be upheld by the court if it can be shown that the restraint is:

(a) reasonable as between the parties, in particular, the restraint must be no wider than is necessary to protect the proper interests of the person whom it is designed to benefit; and also

(b) reasonable as regards the interests of the public, *i.e.* not injurious to the public.

The essential law on this point was stated by Lord MacNaghten in the *Nordenfelt* case as follows: "Restraints of trade and interference with individual liberty of action, may be justified by the special circumstances of a particular case. It is sufficient justification, and indeed, it is the only justification, if the restriction is reasonable—reasonable, that is, in reference to the interests of the parties concerned and reasonable in reference to the interests of the public, so framed and so guarded as to afford adequate protection to the party in whose favour it is imposed, while at the same time it is in no way injurious to the public."

16. Reasonableness in contracts in restraint of trade. The question of whether a restraint is reasonable is decided by the judge. The duty of the jury is to find any facts which are necessary to the judge's decision. The concept of *reasonableness* should be considered separately with reference to restraints in contracts of (a) employment, (b) sale of goodwill and (c) trading agreements.

17. Reasonableness in contracts of employment. An employer is entitled to the benefit of a restraint clause protecting confidential information or a proprietary interest, *e.g.* goodwill or trade secrets. Where an employer can show that the restraint is no wider than this, the presumption that the contract is void is rebutted. The test is whether the stipulated restraint exceeds what is necessary for the protection of both parties, taking into account the interest of the public.

A restraint clause which purports to restrict an employee from using his *skill* in competition with his master (after leaving his master's employment) is always void, even where the skill was acquired in that master's service: *Morris* v. *Saxelby* (1916). In deciding whether a restraint is reasonable, the courts will consider all the relevant circumstances, in particular the following:

(a) The nature of the employer's business.
(b) The status of the employee.
(c) The geographical area covered by the restraint clause.
(d) The duration of the restraint clause in time.

Mason v. *Provident Clothing Co. Ltd.* (1913): a canvasser contracted not to be employed in any business similar to his employer's within 25 miles of London within three years of the termination of his employment. HELD by the House of Lords: the restriction was wider than reasonably necessary and, therefore, void.

NOTE: an employee can be restrained from using a list of customers made while in the employment of his former master: *Robb* v. *Green* (1895).

Herbert Morris, Ltd. v. *Saxelby* (1916): In his contract of employment with Herbert Morris, Ltd., S undertook not to be concerned with the sale or manufacture of pulley blocks, overhead runways, or overhead travelling cranes during a period of seven years from the date of ceasing to be employed by the company. S left the company's service and the company subsequently brought this action to restrain him from breach of the restrictive undertaking in the contract of employment. HELD by the House of Lords: having regard to all the circumstances, the undertaking was not reasonable in reference to the interests of the parties and was prejudicial to the interests of the public. The undertaking by S was therefore void and unenforceable by the company. All restraints on trade of themselves, if there is nothing more, are contrary to public policy, and, therefore, void. It is not that such restraints must of themselves necessarily operate to the public injury, but that it is against the policy of the common law to enforce them except in cases where there are special circumstances to justify them. To be valid a restraint must be reasonable in the interests of the contracting parties, and secondly, it must be reasonable in the interests of the public. To be reasonable in the interests of the parties the restraint must afford adequate protection to the party in whose favour it is imposed and be to the advantage of the covenantee who otherwise might lose such advantages as obtaining the best terms on the sale of a business or the possibility of obtaining employment or training under competent employers. . . . The only reason for upholding a restraint on an employee is that the employer has some proprietary right, whether in the nature of trade connection or trade secrets, for the protection of which such a restraint is, having regard to the duties of the employee, reasonably necessary.

Fitch v. *Dewes* (1921): the respondent was a solicitor practising in Tamworth in Warwickshire. In 1899 the appellant entered the employment of the respondent as a junior clerk and continued in that employment until 1914. In 1903 the appellant was articled to the respondent. In 1908 there was an agreement between the respondent and the appellant which provided that if the appellant was successful in his final law examination he should serve the respondent as managing clerk. There was a further agreement made in 1912 by which the appellant agreed to serve the respondent as managing clerk for a period of three years from 31 December 1911. This agreement contained the following restraint clause: "The said Thomas Birch Fitch hereby expressly agrees with the said John Hunt Dewes that he will not on the expiration or sooner determination of the said term of three years or any extended term as herein provided either alone or jointly with any other person or persons directly or indirectly be engaged or manage or concerned in the office, profession or business of a solicitor within a radius of seven miles of the town hall of Tamworth, but nothing herein contained shall at any time prevent the said Thomas Birch Fitch from carrying on the legal business of the North Warwickshire Miners' Association at Tamworth or within the aforesaid radius thereof." When the respondent sought to enforce the restraint clause the appellant contended that it was against public policy and void. HELD, by the House of Lords: the question whether or not the unlimited restriction as to time was void as being in restraint of trade and so against public policy, depended on (i) whether it was against the public interest and (ii) whether it exceeded what was required for the respondent's protection. And that, on the facts of this case, the unlimited restriction as to time was not against the public interest and it was reasonable to give the respondent the specified protection.

Home Counties Dairies Ltd. v. *Skilton* (1970) C.A.: in June 1963 the respondent became employed as a roundsman in a dairyman's business. The agreement made between employer and employee in July 1964, when the employee had already been employed for one year contained the following two clauses among others. Clause 12 provided that: "During his employment hereunder the Employee shall not, without the previous consent of the Employer, enter the service of or be employed in any capacity or for any purpose whatsoever by any person, firm or company carrying on any dairy business." Clause 15 provided that: "The Employee expressly agrees not at any time during the period of one year after the determination of his employment under this agreement (whether the same shall have been determined by notice or otherwise) either on his own account or representative or agent of any person or company, to serve or sell milk or dairy produce to, or solicit orders for milk or dairy produce from any person or company, who at any time during the last six months of his employment shall have been a customer of the Employer and served by the Employee in the course of his employment." In March 1969, the employer sold the goodwill of his business to the appellant company which agreed to take over all employees. At the end of March the employee gave a week's notice to end his employment with the employer. In April, he entered the employment of another dairyman whose business was in the same area and immediately began to serve the same milk round that he had worked during the course of his previous employment. The respondent company then brought this action to enforce clause 15 of the agreement. HELD by the Court of Appeal: the agreement, on its true construction, was an agreement not to serve another employer as a milk roundsman calling on the customers of the old milk round whom he had served in the previous six months, and that the restraint contained in clause 15 was not unreasonable and was binding on the respondent.

18. Reasonableness in sale of goodwill.

Where the vendor of the goodwill of a business undertakes not to compete with the purchaser, the courts are more likely to uphold the restraint than in the case of the restraint imposed on an employee. Nevertheless, restraints of this class are void unless they protect a definite proprietary interest. When the goodwill of a business is sold, one of the main items will always be the trade connections and the buyer is entitled to the protection of a restraint clause by which the vendor has agreed not to set up in competition with the very business he has sold.

Nordenfelt v. *Maxim Nordenfelt Co., Ltd.* (1894): N had established a business for the manufacture and sale of guns and ammunition. His dealings were world-wide. He entered a contract by which he sold the business to a company formed for the purpose of buying it. The contract included a restraint clause intended to protect the business in the hands of the company. Two years later, the company transferred the business to the Maxim Nordenfelt Company with the concurrence of N. On the occasion of the transfer, N entered another restraint agreement in substitution for that entered into with the original purchasers. The restraint stipulated was that N should not, during the term of twenty-five years from the formation of the company engage in the trade or business of a manufacturer of guns, explosives or ammunition. N subsequently engaged in business contrary to his undertaking to the company, which then brought this action claiming an injunction to restrain him from further breach. N contended in his defence that the undertaking was void as being in restraint of trade and going beyond what was reasonably necessary for the protection of the company's interests. HELD by the House of Lords: N's undertaking was valid because the area supplied by the company was practically unlimited, the customers being states all over the world, and so the restraint was not wider than the protection of the company required.

British Reinforced Concrete Co., Ltd. v. *Schelff* (1921): in 1918, a partnership firm engaged in a small business of supplying steel reinforcements for concrete roads contracted to sell to the plaintiff company a patent, the goodwill of the firm and certain stock. The contract contained a restraint clause to the effect that none of the partners would engage in a similar business until three years after the end of the war. One of the partners took employment with a company as manager of its reinforced materials department. The plaintiff company sought an injunction to restrain this breach of the agreement for the sale of the firm's goodwill. HELD: in an agreement for the sale of the goodwill of a business, the reasonableness of the vendor's restrictive undertaking was to be judged by the extent and circumstances of the *business sold* and its need of protection in the hands of the purchaser and not by the extent or range of any business of the purchaser. The restraint clause in the present case was wider than necessary for the reasonable protection of the transferred business in the hands of the plaintiff company. Injunction refused.

19. Reasonableness in contracts regulating trade. Agreements between merchants and manufacturers to regulate trade will not be considered reasonable unless each party derives some advantage from it. Thus, it has been held, on the highest authority, that the quantum of consideration may enter into the question of reasonableness. Where experienced men of business are bargaining on an equal footing, it is unlikely that the court will presume to know the parties' interests better than they do themselves. The court is more likely to interfere in cases where the bargaining has not taken place on an equal footing, for example, where conditions have been incorporated into a contract but which have not been carefully negotiated.

Esso Petroleum Co., Ltd. v. *Harper's Garage (Stourport), Ltd.* (1968): the respondent garage company had entered into what is known as a solus agreement with the appellants in respect of each of the respondents' two garages. By these agreements, the respondents undertook, *inter alia*, to sell Esso petrol and no other in each of their garages. The first agreement (the Corner Garage agreement) was expressed to remain in force for a period of twenty-one years from 1 July 1962. In October 1962 the respondents charged the Corner Garage by way of legal mortgage, covenanting to repay the appellants £7000 with interest by quarterly instalments over a period of twenty-one years, and undertaking that they would not be entitled to redeem the mortgage otherwise than by payments over the full period of twenty-one years. The respondents covenanted by the same deed to sell Esso petrol and no other during the continuance of the mortgage. The second agreement (the Mustow Green agreement) was expressed to remain in force for a period of four years and five months from 1 July 1963. By this agreement, the respondents undertook, *inter alia*, to keep open at all reasonable hours to sell Esso petrol and not to dispose of the garage except to a person willing to enter into a similar solus agreement with the appellant. The appellants appealed to the House of Lords against the Court of Appeal decision that the doctrine of restraint of trade could apply to covenants in mortgage deeds and that the restrictions in the solus agreements and the mortgage deed were unreasonable and, consequently, void. (At the time of the action, the respondents had tendered repayment of the mortgage.) HELD by the House of Lords: contracts or covenants regulating the trading use made of a particular piece of land are not necessarily outside the doctrine of restraint of trade and the doctrine may apply to mortgages; the solus agreements and the provisions in the mortgage deed relating to trading were within the scope of the doctrine of restraint of trade and must therefore be justified if they are to be enforceable; a restriction is justified only if it is reasonable; the Mustow Green restrictions were reasonable because the period of four years and five months was reasonable, taking into account the advantages derived by the respondents; the Corner Garage agreement and the restrictive provisions in the mortgage deed were unreasonable because the period of duration, twenty-one years was unreasonable, and these provisions were, accordingly, unenforceable.

CONSEQUENCES WHERE A CONTRACT IS VOID AS BEING AGAINST PUBLIC POLICY

20. General consequences. Contracts to oust the jurisdiction, or which are prejudicial to marriage, or which impede parental duties, or which are in restraint of trade, are not illegal in the full sense: they are merely void in so far as public policy is contravened. Contracts of this kind are binding except as to clauses which do not satisfy public policy. Points to note are:

(*a*) Such contracts are severable.

(*b*) Collateral transactions are not necessarily void.

(*c*) Money paid or property transferred is recoverable.

21. Severance. Contracts in this class are said to be severable, *i.e.* the void part (if any) is rejected and the rest of the contract is valid and enforceable. But note *Attwood* v. *Lamont* (1920).

Attwood v. *Lamont* (1920): L, who was a tailor's cutter, entered a contract of employment as head of the tailoring department of A's general outfitting shop. Under the contract, L covenanted not to engage in "the trade of a tailor, dressmaker, general draper, milliner, hatter, haberdasher, gentlemen's, ladies' or children's outfitter at any place within a radius of 10 miles of [A's] place of business." HELD by the Court of Appeal: (i) no part of this clause could be severed because it constituted a single covenant for the protection of A's entire business. It must stand or fall in its unaltered form. (ii) The clause as a whole was wider than necessary in the circumstances and was void.

Contracts which are void by statute are also severable, but contracts illegal at common law are not severable.

22. Collateral transactions. Where a contract is void, in part or in whole, as being against public policy, collateral transactions remain unaffected.

23. Recovery of money. In *Hermann* v. *Charlesworth* (1905) it was held that money paid under a marriage brokage contract was recoverable upon total failure of consideration. It would seem to follow that money paid, or property transferred, under a contract merely void as contravening public policy, is always recoverable.

THE RESTRICTIVE TRADE PRACTICES ACTS

24. The Registrar. The *Restrictive Trade Practices Act*, 1956, s. 1, provides for the appointment of an officer to be known as the Registrar of Restrictive Trading Agreements. It is the duty of the Registrar to prepare, compile and maintain a register of agreements subject to registration under the Act, and to take proceedings before the Restrictive Practices Court in respect of the registered agreements. The general part of the register is open to public inspection. By *s*. 11, the Registrar must maintain a special section of the register containing particulars the publication of which in the opinion of the Secretary of State for Trade and Industry would be contrary to the public interest and information the publication of which would in the opinion of the Secretary of State substantially damage the legitimate business interests of any person. The special section is not open to public inspection.

The Registrar must be furnished with the names of the parties to every registrable agreement and the whole of the terms of the agreement: *s.* 10. Any person who furnishes false information or who suppresses or destroys a document that he is required to furnish is guilty of an offence.

25. The Restrictive Practices Court. The Act provides for the establishment of the Restrictive Practices Court and that the Court is a superior court of record: *s.* 2. The Court has jurisdiction, on application made in accordance with the Act, to declare whether restrictions contained in registered agreements are contrary to the public interest: *s.* 20. Where the Court finds a restriction to be contrary to the public interest, the agreement is void in respect of that restriction.

26. Registrable agreements. The provisions as to registration apply to any agreement between two or more persons carrying on business within the United Kingdom in the production or supply of goods, or in the application to goods of any process of manufacture, whether with or without other parties, if it is an agreement under which restrictions are accepted by two or more parties in respect of the following matters:

(*a*) the prices to be charged, quoted or paid for goods supplied, offered or acquired, or for the application of any process of manufacture to goods;

(*b*) the terms or conditions on or subject to which goods are to be supplied or acquired or any such process is to be applied to goods;

(*c*) the quantities or descriptions of goods to be produced, supplied or acquired;

(*d*) the process of manufacture to be applied to any goods, or the quantities or descriptions of goods to which any such process is to be applied; or

(*e*) the persons or classes of persons to, for or from whom, or the areas or places in or from which goods are to be supplied or acquired, or any such process applied: *s.* 6(1).

In this context, "agreement" includes any agreement or arrangement, whether or not it is or is intended to be enforceable by legal proceedings: *s.* 6(3). It follows that the Act is not merely concerned with written agreements for there may always be a relevant "arrangement" to be taken into account: see *Re Schweppes, Ltd.'s Agreement* (1965). It was held in *Re British Basic Slag, Ltd.'s Agreements* (1963) that the expression "arrangement" is to be broadly construed so that it includes the situation which arises when each of the parties intentionally arouses in the other an expectation that he will act in a particular way.

27. Excepted agreements. By *s.* 8, the following agreements are not subject to the provisions as to registration:

(*a*) Any agreement which is expressly authorised by Parliament.

(*b*) Any agreement forming part of a scheme certified by the appropriate Minister under the *Income Tax Act*, 1952.

(*c*) Any agreement for the supply of goods between two persons, neither of whom is a trade association, being an agreement to which no other person is party and under which no such restrictions as are described in *s.* 6(1) are accepted (i) by the party supplying the goods, in respect of the supply of goods of the same description to other persons; or (ii) by the party acquiring the goods, in respect of the sale, or acquisition for sale, of other goods of the same description.

(*d*) Any grant of a licence of a patent or registered design, or any assignment of a patent or registered design, where the licence or assignment contains no restrictions as are described in *s.* 6(1) except in respect of (i) the invention to which the patent or application for a patent relates, or articles made by use of that invention; or (ii) articles in respect of which the design is or is proposed to be registered and to which it is applied, as the case may be.

(*e*) Any agreement between two persons, neither of whom is a trade association, for the exchange of information relating to the operation of process of manufacture (whether patented or not), if it is an agreement to which no other person is party and under which no such restrictions as are described in *s.* 6(1) are accepted except in respect of the descriptions of goods to be produced by those processes or to which those processes are to be applied.

(*f*) Any agreement made in accordance with regulations approved by the Secretary of State for Trade under the *Trade Marks Act*, 1938, authorising the use of a trade mark if it is an agreement under which no restrictions as are described in *s.* 6(1) are accepted, other than restrictions permitted by the regulations.

(g) Any agreement between the registered proprietor of a trade mark (other than a certification trade mark) and a person authorised by the agreement to use the mark subject to registration as a registered user, if it is an agreement under which no restrictions as are described in s. 6(1) are accepted except in respect of the descriptions of goods bearing the mark which are to be produced or supplied or the processes of manufacture to be applied to the goods or to goods to which the mark is to be applied.

(h) Any agreement under which any restrictions as are described in s. 6(1) relate exclusively (i) to the supply of goods by export from the United Kingdom; (ii) to the production of goods, or the application of any process of manufacture to goods, outside the United Kingdom; (iii) to the acquisition of goods to be delivered outside the United Kingdom and not imported into the United Kingdom for entry for home use; or (iv) to the supply of goods to be delivered outside the United Kingdom otherwise than by export from the United Kingdom.

28. Further exemptions. The *Restrictive Trade Practices Act*, 1968, (which amends the Act of 1956), provides for the exemption from registration of certain agreements of importance to the national economy and agreements for holding down prices.

29. Agreements of importance to the national economy. By s. 1 of the 1968 Act, if it appears to the Secretary of State for Trade, on consideration of an agreement proposed to be made by any parties, that certain conditions are complied with in respect of the proposed agreement, he may, by order made on or before the conclusion of the agreement, approve the agreement. Any agreement so approved will be exempt from registration under the Act of 1956 during the continuance in force of the order.

The conditions referred to above (the conditions of exemption) are:

(a) that the agreement is calculated to promote the carrying out of an industrial or commercial project or scheme of substantial importance to the national economy;

(b) that its object or main object is to promote efficiency

in a trade or industry or to create or improve productive capacity in an industry;

(c) that the object cannot be achieved or achieved within a reasonable time except by means of the agreement or of an agreement for similar purposes;

(d) that no relevant restrictions are accepted under the agreement other than such as are reasonably necessary to achieve that object; and

(e) that the agreement is on balance expedient in the national interest;

and in considering the national interest for the purpose of (e) above, the Secretary of State must take into account any effects which an agreement is likely to have on persons not parties to it as purchasers, consumers or users of any relevant goods.

30. Agreements holding down prices. Certain specified government departments are authorised by s. 2 of the 1968 Act to approve by order any agreement which relates exclusively to the prices to be charged in connection with transactions of any description and is designed either to prevent or restrict increases or to secure reductions in those prices. Where an agreement is approved by order under s. 2 of the 1968 Act, the agreement will be exempt from registration under the Act of 1956 during the continuance in force of the order. An order under s. 2 will continue in force for the period specified by the order itself: but the period specified may not exceed two years, and the period may not be extended for more than two years at a time.

31. Presumptions as to the public interest. For the purposes of proceedings before the Restrictive Practices Court to decide whether restrictions contained in a registered agreement are contrary to the public interest, a restriction accepted in pursuance of any agreement will be deemed to be contrary to the public interest unless the Court is satisfied of any one or more of the following circumstances:

(a) that the restriction is reasonably necessary, having regard to the character of the goods to which it applies, to protect the public against injury (whether to persons or to premises) in connection with the consumption, installation, or use of those goods;

(b) that the removal of the restriction would deny to the public as purchasers, consumers, or users of any goods other specific and substantial benefits or advantages enjoyed or likely to be enjoyed by them as such, whether by virtue of the restriction itself or of any arrangements or operations resulting therefrom;

(c) that the restriction is reasonably necessary to counteract measures taken by any one person not party to the agreement with a view to preventing or restricting competition in or in relation to the trade or business in which the persons party thereto are engaged;

(d) that the restriction is reasonably necessary to enable the persons party to the agreement to negotiate fair terms for the supply of goods to, or the acquisition of goods from, any person not party thereto who controls a preponderant part of the trade or business of acquiring or supplying such goods, or for the supply of goods to any person not party to the agreement and not carrying on such trade or business who, either alone or in combination with any other such person, controls a preponderant part of the market for such goods;

(e) that, having regard to the conditions actually obtaining or reasonably foreseen at the time of the application, the removal of the restriction would be likely to have a serious and persistent adverse effect on the general level of unemployment in an area, or in areas taken together, in which a substantial proportion of the trade or industry to which the agreement relates is situated;

(f) that, having regard to the conditions actually obtaining or reasonably foreseen at the time of the application, the removal of the restriction would be likely to cause a reduction in the volume or earnings of the export business which is substantial either in relation to the whole export business of the United Kingdom or in relation to the whole business (including export business) of the said trade or industry;

(g) that the restriction is reasonably required for purposes connected with the maintenance of any other restriction accepted by the parties, whether under the same agreement or under any other agreement between them, being a restriction which is found by the Court not to be contrary to the public interest upon grounds other than those specified in this paragraph, or has been so found in previous proceedings before the Court; or

(*h*) that the restriction does not directly or indirectly restrict or discourage competition to any material degree in any relevant trade or industry and is not likely to do so. (Sub-paragraph (*h*) was added by the 1968 Act.)

Section 21 of the 1956 Act provides that the Court must be further satisfied in any such case that the restriction is not unreasonable having regard to the balance between those circumstances and any detriment to the public or to persons not parties to the agreement resulting or likely to result from the operation of the restriction.

32. Consequences of failure to register. By *s*. 8 of the 1968 Act, if particulars of any registrable agreement are not duly furnished to the Registrar,

(*a*) the agreement will be void in respect of all relevant restrictions;

(*b*) it will be unlawful for any person party to the agreement who carries on business within the United Kingdom to give effect to, or enforce or purport to enforce, the agreement in respect of any such restrictions;

(*c*) the obligation to comply with (*b*) above is a duty owed to any person who may be affected by a contravention of it and any breach of that duty is actionable accordingly subject to the defences and other incidents applying to actions for breach of statutory duty;

(*d*) upon the application of the Registrar, the Court may make an order in the nature of an injunction restraining any party from giving effect to or enforcing a restriction.

33. Price maintenance of goods. Resale price maintenance agreements are those by which manufacturers seek to control the retail price of their goods. Such agreements are usually made between manufacturer and wholesaler, the wholesaler giving an undertaking not to sell to any retailer except on an undertaking by the retailer that he will not sell to the public below the manufacturer's list price. At common law, this kind of agreement was not enforceable by the manufacturer against the retailer because there was no privity of contract between them. *See* XIV.

The common law doctrine of privity of contract as applied to resale price maintenance must now be seen against the *Restrictive Trade Practices Act*, 1956, ss. 24 and 25, and the *Resale Prices Act*, 1964.

34. Collective enforcement of resale prices. Section 24 of the *Restrictive Trade Practices Act*, 1956, provides that it is unlawful for two or more persons carrying on business as suppliers of goods to make an agreement by which they undertake:

(a) to withhold supplies of goods for delivery from dealers who resell in breach of any condition as to the price at which those goods may be resold:

(b) to refuse to supply goods for delivery to such dealers except on terms less favourable than those applicable to other dealers; or

(c) to supply goods only to persons who undertake to withhold supplies of goods from dealers who resell in breach of any condition as to the price at which the goods may be resold.

35. Individual enforcement of resale prices. While *s.* 24 prohibits the collective enforcement of resale price maintenance, the *individual* enforcement is permitted by *s.* 25, as an exception to the doctrine of privity of contract. Section 25 provides that where goods are sold by a supplier subject to a condition as to the price at which those goods may be resold, that condition may be enforced by the supplier against any person not party to the sale who subsequently acquires the goods with notice of the condition. In other words, the Act provides that the privity rule does not apply to the *Dunlop* v. *Selfridge* situation. But *s.* 25 has now been much modified by *s.* 1 of the *Resale Prices Act*, 1964, which provides that any stipulation purporting to establish a minimum resale price of goods shall be void. Section 25 of the 1956 Act still applies to agreements for the maximum retail price of goods.

The Restrictive Practices Court may, however, direct that goods of any class shall be exempt from the provisions of the 1964 Act.

PROGRESS TEST 12

1. Outline the different grounds on which contracts may be rendered void.
2. Give some examples of contracts made void by statute.
3. Define carefully a wagering contract. Does your definition include gaming contracts?
4. Can a bet by which one party stands to win but not to lose be a wagering contract?
5. What is an insurable interest in a contract of insurance?
6. In what circumstances is a contract between a stockbroker and client a wagering contract?
7. The *Gaming Act*, 1845, provided that wagering contracts shall be null and void. In what way was this provision extended by the *Gaming Act*, 1892?
8. "Where a party to a wagering contract gives a cheque by way of payment, the legal consequences will depend upon whether the contract was (*a*) a gaming contract, or (*b*) any other kind of wagering contract." Explain this statement.
9. Which kinds of contract are void at common law as being against public policy?
10. Is it possible for contracting parties to make a binding agreement to refrain from submitting to the courts (*a*) any dispute on a matter of law, or (*b*) any dispute on a matter of the construction of a document?
11. Give some examples of contracts which are considered to strike at the sanctity of marriage.
12. Into which classes can contracts in restraint of trade be divided?
13. In what circumstances will a contract in restraint of trade be upheld by the court?
14. What is the rule as to consideration in contracts in restraint of trade?
15. Consider the concept of "reasonableness" in connection with a restraint clause in a contract between employer and employee.
16. Distinguish between the legal consequences of (*a*) a contract which is void as being against public policy, and (*b*) an illegal contract.
17. What do you understand by "severance" in contracts which contain a void clause?
18. Outline the main provisions of the *Restrictive Trade Practices Acts*, 1956 and 1968, and the *Resale Prices Act*, 1964.
19. What kinds of contract must be registered with the Registrar of Restrictive Trading Agreements?
20. What powers has the Restrictive Practices Court?
21. A is about to drive from London to Brighton in a vintage

motor car. B bets A that he (A) will not reach Brighton without a breakdown. According to the agreement, if A reaches Brighton without a breakdown, B will pay £100 to A: but if there is a breakdown, A will pay £100 to B. Is this a wager? Give reasons for your answer.

22. C loses a wager with D on a horse race, and he pays D his winnings with a cheque. D negotiates the cheque to E, by way of payment for a debt, which D has owed to E for a month. When E presents the cheque for payment, it is dishonoured. Advise E as to his rights, if any, against C and D.

23. F enters into a written agreement with G. The agreement includes the following clauses:

(a) "This agreement is binding in honour only and is not intended to give rise to legal rights and obligations."

(b) "The contracting parties hereby agree that, in the event of a dispute as to the interpretation of this agreement, no recourse shall be had to any court of law."

Comment on the validity of these clauses.

24. H, who is married to J, agrees to marry K, if and when he, H, can get a divorce from J. Is the agreement between H and K in any way binding on the parties?

25. L entered into a contract under seal whereby he (L) became articled to M, a chartered accountant. There was a clause in the agreement by which L covenanted not to be concerned in any chartered accountant's business within six miles of M's office during his (L's) lifetime. L wishes to know whether the restraint is binding on him. Advise him.

26. N sold his tobacconist retail shop to Universal Tobaccos Ltd., a company owning a chain of tobacco shops throughout the country. In the agreement of sale, N covenanted not to engage in the trade of tobacconist within ten miles of any of the branch shops of Universal Tobaccos Ltd. N has opened a new tobacco shop a hundred miles from the one he sold to the company, but within ten miles of one of their numerous branches. The company now wish to take action against N to enforce the restraint. Advise the company.

27. O entered a contract under seal by which P, a goldsmith, undertook to teach him the trade of goldsmith during a period of five years. One of the terms of the agreement was that O should not, after the five year period, engage in the trade of goldsmith or jeweller within 50 miles of P's workshop. One year after the agreement, P dismissed O, claiming that he was not bound to continue to teach O, because the contract was void as being in restraint of trade. Advise O as to whether he has an action against P for breach of contract.

CHAPTER XIII

CONTRACTS UNENFORCEABLE UNLESS EVIDENCED BY WRITING

UNENFORCEABLE CONTRACTS

1. Note or memorandum. Certain contracts are not enforceable unless the plaintiff can produce a sufficient note or memorandum of the agreement. The note must be signed by the defendant or his agent.

2. Unenforceable contracts. The most important contracts in this class are:

(a) Contracts of guarantee.
(b) Contracts for the sale or other disposition of land or any interest in land.

3. Contracts of guarantee. A contract of guarantee is made where one party, the guarantor, promises to answer for the "debt, default, or miscarriage" of another person. The expression "debt, default, or miscarriage" is taken from *s.* 4 of the *Statute of Frauds*, 1677, and covers the guarantee of a contractual liability or a tortious liability. In most cases, however, the liability guaranteed is a contractual debt.

NOTE: contracts of guarantee are sometimes called contracts of suretyship: a guarantor is sometimes called a surety.

4. Three parties. In any contract of guarantee, there is a principal creditor, a principal debtor and a guarantor. Thus, where G guarantees D's debt to C, there is a triangular relationship in which three collateral contracts may be distinguished:

(a) As between C and D there is a contract out of which the guaranteed debt arises.
(b) As between G and C there is the contract by which G makes himself secondarily liable to pay D's debt. G promises that he will pay D's debt in the event of D's default.

(c) As between G and D there is always a contract by which D indemnifies G. Thus, if G pays C according to the guarantee, then D will be liable to G. This contract is always implied if it is not expressed between the parties.

NOTE: it is the contract between the guarantor and the principal creditor which includes the promise to answer for the debt, default or miscarriage of another. But there must always be the other two contracts collateral.

5. Indemnity distinguished from guarantee. A contract of indemnity must be distinguished from a contract of guarantee. There are the following points of difference:

(a) A guarantor makes himself secondarily liable.
(b) A person giving an indemnity makes himself primarily liable.

The distinction depends entirely upon the intention of the parties.

THE STATUTORY PROVISIONS

6. Statute of Frauds, 1677. Section 4 of the *Statute of Frauds*, 1677, provides that, "No action shall be brought whereby to charge the defendant upon any special promise to answer for the debt, default, or miscarriage of another person unless the agreement upon which such action be brought, or some memorandum or note thereof, shall be in writing and signed by the party to be charged therewith or some other person thereunto by him lawfully authorised."

NOTE: this section applies to contracts of guarantee and *not* to contracts of indemnity.

7. Law of Property Act, 1925. Section 40 of the *Law of Property Act*, 1925, provides that, "No action may be brought upon any contract for the sale or other disposition of land or any interest in land, unless the agreement upon which such action is brought, or some memorandum or note thereof, is in writing and signed by the party to be charged or by some other person thereunto by him lawfully authorised."

NOTE: contracts to which *s.* 40 applies will include those for sale, lease, and mortgage of land.

8. The note or memorandum.

Any contract of guarantee, or any contract for the sale or other disposition of land or any interest in land, which is not itself in writing, must be evidenced by a sufficient note or memorandum, or the agreement will be unenforceable. Points to note are:

(a) The memorandum need not be in any special form. It may consist of several documents provided there is evidence to connect them. The memorandum may have been made at any time after the contract was made.

(b) The memorandum must be signed by the defendant or his agent.

(c) The memorandum must contain the material terms of the agreement. Thus included are:

(i) *The Parties:* the parties must be named or described sufficiently in the note.

(ii) *The subject-matter of the agreement:* e.g. in the case of a lease—the address of the premises, the duration of the lease, the rent to be paid.

NOTE: in the case of contracts of guarantee, the consideration need not appear in the memorandum: *Mercantile Law Amendment Act*, 1856. But there must be consideration.

9. Absence of sufficient memorandum.

Where a party cannot produce in evidence a sufficient note or memorandum, the agreement is unenforceable at his suit. The legal consequences of unenforceability should be viewed from the standpoint of a party who cannot produce the memorandum:

(a) No action can be brought for damages at common law for breach of contract.

(b) No action can be brought for specific performance of the contract in equity, unless there is a sufficient act of part performance.

(c) All rights which do not require action in the courts are retained, *e.g.* where the purchaser is in breach of an unenforceable contract for the sale of land, the vendor may keep the deposit: *Thomas* v. *Brown* (1876).

10. Part performance.

The *Statute of Frauds*, 1677, and *s.* 40 of the *Law of Property Act*, 1925, were designed to prevent fraud. Therefore, where a party to an unenforceable contract has partly, or wholly, performed his side of the agreement, trusting the other party to do the same, the court has a discretion to order specific performance of the contract, notwithstanding the absence of a memorandum.

The court will make the order on the grounds that, in these circumstances, the defendant's breach of the unenforceable contract is fraudulent, and equity will not allow a statute to be used as an engine of fraud. The court will not make the order unless the following conditions are satisfied:

(a) The contract must be one for which specific performance would be a proper remedy apart from the matter of the absence of the memorandum; *see* Chapter XVIII.

(b) The act of part performance must have been performed by the plaintiff.

(c) The act of part performance must be exclusively referable to the unenforceable contract. This means that the act must be such as could not have been done with any other purpose in view.

Dickinson v. *Barrow* (1904): there was an oral contract for the sale of a house to be built by the vendor. The purchaser made frequent visits to the building site and made suggestions for alteration and improvement as the work progressed. The vendor complied with these suggestions, but when the house was finished, the purchaser refused to buy. HELD: the acts of the vendor constituted sufficient part performance. The purchaser must specifically perform her side of the agreement. This decision was followed in *Rawlinson* v. *Ames* (1925).

(d) The defendant's refusal to perform his side of the agreement must amount to fraud, bearing in view the plaintiff's act of part performance in reliance on the agreement: *Dickinson* v. *Barrow* (1904); *Rawlinson* v. *Ames* (1925).

(e) There must be sufficient oral or other evidence of the material terms of the agreement.

NOTE: the mere payment of money is never a sufficient act of part performance because it is an act which is not unequivocally referable to any particular agreement.

FORMAL REQUIREMENTS UNDER THE HIRE-PURCHASE ACT, 1965

11. The Hire-Purchase Act, 1965. The main purpose of the Act is to protect the interests of the hirer under a hire-purchase agreement and the buyer under a conditional sale or a credit sale agreement, by providing *inter alia* that, unless certain formalities are present, the contract is unenforceable against the hirer or buyer. The Act applies to agreements under which the price does not exceed £2000.

A contract of hire-purchase is a bailment of goods coupled with an option to purchase. The option may or may not be exercised, and there is no sale unless and until it is exercised. A "conditional sale agreement" is an agreement for the sale of goods under which the price is payable by instalments and the property in the goods is to remain in the seller until such conditions as to the payment of instalments or otherwise as may be specified in the agreement are fulfilled. A "credit-sale agreement" is an agreement for the sale of goods, not being a conditional sale agreement, under which the purchase price is payable by five or more instalments. But the Act does not apply to contracts in which the hirer or buyer, as the case may be, is a corporation.

12. H.-P. and conditional sale agreements. Before any hire-purchase or conditional sale agreement is entered into the owner or seller must state in writing otherwise than in the agreement a price at which the goods may be purchased for cash. It is sufficient if the hirer or buyer sees a price tag on the goods clearly stating the cash price, or if he selects the goods by reference to a catalogue or advertisement which clearly states the cash price.

The agreement is unenforceable by the owners or seller unless it is signed by the hirer or buyer as the case may be. Thus, although the Act does not expressly require the agreement to be in writing, there is an inescapable implication that writing is required.

13. Credit-sale agreements. A credit-sale agreement where the purchase price exceeds thirty pounds is not enforceable by the seller unless the agreement is signed by the buyer and by or on behalf of the seller.

PROGRESS TEST 13

1. Which contracts are unenforceable unless the plaintiff can produce a sufficient note or memorandum of the contract?

2. Describe fully a contract of guarantee.

3. How does a contract of indemnity differ from a contract of guarantee?

4. What are the provisions of the *Statue of Frauds*, 1677 *s.* 4?

5. What are the provisions of the *Law of Property Act*, 1925 *s.* 40?

6. What are the requirements of a sufficient note or memorandum? Is consideration necessary?

7. Explain and illustrate the equitable doctrine of part performance.

8. Is the payment of money ever an act of part performance?

9. Consider the consequences of the absence of a note or memorandum as evidence of contracts governed by the *Statute of Frauds, s.* 4, and the *Law of Property Act*, s. 40.

10. Compare the requirements as to form under the *Hire-Purchase Act*, 1965, with those under the Statute of Frauds, 1677.

11. A agreed orally to buy Blackacre from B, and following the agreement he paid to B £700, being 10% of the purchase price agreed on. A has now informed B that he does not want Blackacre after all. Advise the parties:

 (*a*) Whether B can bring an action to claim specific performance of the contract.
 (*b*) Whether A can recover the £700.

12. C entered an oral agreement to take a ten year lease of D's villa, Whiteoaks. Following the agreement, D has spent £350 on internal redecorations in Whiteoaks, entirely to the requirements of C. During the course of the redecoration, C made several visits to Whiteoaks, to make sure that his taste was satisfied. D complied with all his suggests as to wallpapers, paint, etc. C has now written to D to say that he does not intend to take the lease after all. Advise D.

13. By an oral agreement, E undertook to supply a car to F on terms that the price of £400 should be paid in ten equal instalments. Is the agreement binding on F?

CHAPTER XIV

PRIVITY OF CONTRACT

1. The doctrine of privity. A contract creates rights and obligations only between the parties to it. A contract does not confer rights on a stranger, nor does it impose obligations on a stranger. It is a fundamental principle of the common law, therefore, that no person can sue or be sued on a contract unless he is a party to it.

Per Lord Haldane in *Dunlop* v. *Selfridge* (1915): "Our law knows nothing of a *jus quaesitum tertio* arising by way of contract." (Third party rights.)

> *Scruttons, Ltd.* v. *Midland Silicones, Ltd.* (1962): there was a contract between X and Y for the carriage of a cargo of goods belonging to Y. There was another contract between X and Z for the unloading of the goods from X's ship. The goods were damaged through Z's negligence during unloading. Y claimed damages from Z. Z relied on an exemption clause in the contract between X and Y. HELD by the House of Lords: Z was a stranger to the contract between X and Y, and could not rely on the exemption clause. Z's defence therefore failed.

2. Rights and benefits compared. Although a contract cannot confer a substantive right upon a stranger, it is possible for a contract to confer a benefit upon him. In these circumstances it has been held that the stranger cannot sue in the event of his not receiving the benefit: *Tweddle* v. *Atkinson* (1861). But the matter is now open to doubt. The Law Revision Committee recommended in 1937 (Cmnd. 5449) that "where a contract by its express terms purports to confer a benefit directly on a third party it shall be enforceable by the third party in his own name." In *Beswick* v. *Beswick* (1966), Lord Denning, M.R., said that, "Where a contract is made for the benefit of a third person who has a legitimate interest to enforce it, it can be enforced by the third person in the name of the contracting party or jointly with him or, if he refuses to join, by adding him as a defendant." Accordingly, a person specified to benefit from a contract to which he is a stranger may have a procedural right of action, notwithstanding that he has no substantive rights under the contract. However, when *Beswick* v. *Beswick* was heard on appeal to the House of Lords in 1967, their Lordships declined to deal with the point because it was not essential in that case. But Lord Reid said that if one had to contemplate a further long period of parliamentary procrastination, the House of Lords might have to deal with the matter. See also *Snelling* v. *John G. Snelling* (1972).

Dunlop Pneumatic Tyre Co., Ltd. v. *Selfridge & Co. Ltd.* (1915): there was a contract dated 12 October 1911 by which Dew & Co., agreed to purchase a quantity of tyres and other goods from Dunlop. By this contract, Dew & Co., undertook not to sell at prices below the current list prices except to genuine trade customers, to whom they could sell at a discount. The contract provided that such discount would be substantially less than the discount that Dews themselves were to receive from Dunlop's. Where such sales took place, Dews undertook, as the agents of Dunlop, to obtain from the customer a written undertaking that he similarly would observe the terms so undertaken to be observed by themselves. On 2 January 1912 Selfridges agreed to purchase goods made by Dunlop from Dew & Co., and gave the required undertaking to resell at the current list prices. Selfridge's broke this agreement and Dunlop sued for breach of contract. HELD by the House of Lords: the agreement of 2 January 1912 was between Selfridge and Dew only, and that Dunlop was not a party to that contract because no consideration moved from them to Selfridges.

NOTE: this case illustrates the general common law rule as to privity of contract but cases of this kind are now governed by statute, *see* **6** below.

Beswick v. *Beswick* (1968): in March 1962 a coal merchant, Peter Beswick, agreed to sell his business to his nephew John in return for the following undertakings: (i) that John should pay to Peter the weekly sum of £6 10*s*. during the rest of Peter's life: (ii) that, in the event of Peter's wife surviving him, John should pay her an annuity of £5 weekly. Peter died intestate in November 1963 and in 1964 his widow took out letters of administration. After Peter's death, John made one payment of £5 only to the widow, refusing to make any further payments. The widow, who brought this action as administratrix of her husband's estate and also in her personal capacity, claimed arrears of the annuity and specific performance of the contract between Peter and John. It was held by the Court of Appeal that she was entitled, as administratrix, to specific performance of the contract. Lord Denning and Danckwerts, L.J., held further that she could succeed under *s*. 56 (1) of the *Law of Property Act*, 1925. (Section 56 (1) provides that: "A person may take an immediate or other interest in land or other property, or the benefit of any condition, right of entry, covenant or agreement over or respecting land or other property, although he may not be named as a party to the conveyance or other instrument." The Act further provides, by *s*. 205, that: "unless the context otherwise requires, the following expressions have the meaning hereby assigned to them respectively, that is to say . . . 'Property includes any thing in action, and any interest in real or personal property.' ") John appealed to the House of Lords. HELD by the House of Lords: the widow, as administratrix, was entitled to specific performance of the agreement to which her deceased husband was a contracting party; but the statute gave her no right of action in her personal capacity against John.

In *Beswick* v. *Beswick*, Lord Hodson said: "Section 56 had as long ago as 1937 received consideration by the Law Revision Committee presided over by Lord Wright, then Master of the Rolls, and containing a number of illustrious lawyers. The committee was called on to report specially on consideration including the attitude of the common law towards the *jus quaesitum tertio*. . . . By its report (Cmd. 5449) it impliedly rejected the revolutionary view, for it recommended that— 'Where a contract by its express terms purports to confer a benefit directly on a third party, it shall be enforceable by the third party in his own name.' Like my noble and learned friend, Lord Reid, whose opinion I have had the opportunity of reading, I am of opinion that *s*. 56, one of the twenty-five sections of the Act of 1925 appearing under the cross-heading 'Conveyances and other instruments,' does not have the revolutionary effect claimed for it, appearing as it does in a consolidation Act. I think, as he does, that the context does otherwise require a limited meaning to be given to the word 'property' in the section."

3. Privity and consideration. The rule that consideration must move from the promisee is closely related to the wider doctrine of privity of contract. The two common law principles combine to produce a rule that no person can sue on a simple contract unless (i) he is a party, and (ii) he gave consideration to the defendant in return for his promise.

4. Exceptions to the privity doctrine. Although the doctrine of privity of contract has been regarded as fundamental to the English law of contract, there are, nevertheless, circumstances where there is conflict with other principles. This gives rise to certain exceptions, the most important of which are as follows:

(a) *The Law of Property Act*, 1925, *s.* 56.
(b) *Restrictive Trade Practices Act*, 1956, *s.* 25.
(c) *Road Traffic Act*, 1960, *s.* 207.
(d) The law of agency.
(e) Negotiable instruments.
(f) Trusts.
(g) Restrictive covenants.
(h) Assignment of contractual rights.
(i) Guarantor's right of subrogation.

5. The Law of Property Act, 1925. Section 56 (1) of the Act provides that, "A person may take an immediate or other interest in land or other property or the benefit of any condition, right of entry, covenant or agreement over or respecting land or other property although he may not be named as a party to the conveyance or other instrument," and by *s.* 205, "property" includes "any thing in action, and any interest in real or personal property." Although the plain meaning of the words used in these two sections appears to restore the common law rule prevailing before *Tweddle* v. *Atkinson* (1861), dicta and decisions show that this is not the effect of the provision: *Re Sinclair's Life Policy* (1938); *Re Millers Agreement, Uniacke* v. *A.-G.* (1947) and *Beswick* v. *Beswick* (1967).

6. The Restrictive Trade Practices Act, 1956. Section 25 (1) of the Act provides that, "Where goods are sold by a supplier subject to a condition as to the price at which those goods may be resold, either generally or by or to a specified class or person, that condition may, subject to the provisions of this section, be enforced by the supplier against any person not party to the sale who subsequently acquires the goods with notice of the condition as if he had been party thereto."

In *Goodyear Tyre and Rubber Co., Ltd.* v. *Lancashire*

Batteries, Ltd. (1958), it was held by the Court of Appeal that a circular issued by a manufacturer to retailers constituted a sufficient notice under *s.* 25 of the Act.

NOTE: Section 25 (1) is modified by the *Resale Prices Act*, 1964, see XII, **34**.

7. The Road Traffic Act, 1960. Section 207 of this Act provides that in a compulsory third-party motor insurance contract effected between the insurer and the car user, certain persons who are not privy to the contract may sue the insurer.

8. The law of agency. Where the relationship of principal and agent exists, the principal is bound by contracts entered into by the agent with third parties. Moreover, where an agent contracts without authority on behalf of a named principal, the person named as principal may ratify the contract so that it becomes binding as between himself and the third party. Also, where an agent contracts with a third party, without disclosing the existence of his principal, a contract is created between the principal and the third party. *See* XVI.

9. Trusts. Where, as a result of a binding contract, a person agrees to act as a trustee, the beneficiaries under the trust (not being parties to the contract) will have an action against the trustee in the event of a breach of trust. This is merely an apparent exception to the *common law* doctrine of privity, because the rights of the beneficiaries are equitable.

Where a contract confers a mere benefit upon a stranger, the courts are reluctant to imply a trust unless there is a clear intention to create a trust: thus, the doctrine of constructive trusts does not generally operate as a method of evading the privity rule.

10. Negotiable instruments. In the event of the dishonour of a bill of exchange, the holder in due course may sue any prior party to the bill who has signed as drawer, indorser, or acceptor. This right is in addition to the contractual right against the person who transferred the bill to him for value: *e.g.* where X sells goods to Y, and takes a bill of exchange as conditional payment, if the bill is dishonoured, X may either sue Y or any prior party to the bill, or he may sue Y for the price of the goods, *i.e.* he may either sue on the bill or sue in contract. *See* XV.

11. Restrictive covenants. A restrictive covenant is a promise under seal made between neighbouring landowners by which the promiser binds himself not to use his land in some stipulated manner. A restrictive covenant is enforceable as follows:

(*a*) At common law a restrictive covenant is enforceable as between the covenantee and covenantor in the same way as any specialty contract.

(*b*) In equity the benefit of a restrictive covenant may generally be enforced by an assignee of the covenantee.

(*c*) In equity the burden of a restrictive covenant may devolve upon an assignee of the covenantor.

Although restrictive covenants may "run with the land," they do not run with goods. It is unlikely that the Privy Council decision in the *Strathcona Case* (1926), will be followed. (In that case it was held that a purchaser of a ship was bound by the terms of a charterparty between the vendor and a third party.)

12. Assignment. Where A is under a contractual obligation to B, and B assigns his contractual right to C, it may be possible for C to sue A on his promise to B. *See* XV.

13. Guarantor's right of subrogation. Where a guarantor has paid the principal creditor, he is subrogated to the rights of the principal creditor against the debtor, *i.e.* the guarantor "stands in the principal creditor's shoes."

PROGRESS TEST 14

1. "Our law knows nothing of a *jus quaesitum tertio* arising by way of contract." Comment on this statement.
2. State in simple terms the doctrine of privity of contract.
3. Distinguish between a right and a benefit conferred by a contract on a stranger.
4. Mention some exceptions to the doctrine of privity of contract.
5. State the provisions of the *Restrictive Trade Practices Act*, 1956, *s.* 25 (1).
6. In what circumstances is a restrictive covenant enforceable?

XIV. PRIVITY OF CONTRACT

7. How has the court interpreted s. 56 (1) of the *Law of Property Act*, 1925?

8. A contract was made between A and B. One of the terms of the contract was that B should pay £100 to C. B now refuses to pay C, and A declines to sue B. Advise C as to whether he can claim against B.

9. E enters a contract with F. E contracted, with full authority, as G's agent, but he did not inform F that he was an agent. F has now broken his agreement. Can G sue F for breach of contract?

CHAPTER XV

ASSIGNMENT

THE ASSIGNMENT OF CONTRACTUAL RIGHTS

1. Contractual rights as a form of property. A right under a contract has a certain economic value and may, therefore, be regarded as a personal right of property. In property law, contractual rights belong to a class known as choses in action or things in action.

2. Choses in action. "Chose in action" has been defined as "an expression used to describe all personal rights of property which can only be claimed or enforced by action, and not by taking physical possession": *per* Channell, J., in *Torkington* v. *Magee* (1903). Choses in action may be legal or equitable, according to whether they are founded on legal or equitable rules.

(*a*) Legal choses in action include debts and other contractual rights, company shares, insurance policies, bills of lading, patents, and copyrights.

(*b*) Equitable choses in action include rights under a trust and legacies.

3. Assignment of choses in action. A valid assignment of a chose in action may take place in one of three ways:

(*a*) Statutory (or legal) assignment.
(*b*) Equitable assignment.
(*c*) Assignment by operation of the law.

NOTE: the doctrine of privity of contract prevents any assignment at common law of a contractual right.

STATUTORY ASSIGNMENT

4. Law of Property Act, 1925, s. 136. A statutory assignment is one which complies with the provisions of s. 136 of the *L.P.A.*

XV. ASSIGNMENT

1925. Statutory assignments are sometimes called legal assignments. Section 136 provides that:

"Any absolute assignment by writing under the hand of the assignor (not purporting to be by way of charge only) of any debt or other legal thing in action, of which express notice in writing has been given to the debtor, trustee or other person from whom the assignor would have been entitled to claim such debt or thing in action, is effectual in law (subject to equities having priority over the right of the assignee) to pass and transfer from the date of such notice:

(*a*) the legal right to such debt or thing in action;
(*b*) the legal and other remedies for the same; and
(*c*) the power to give a good discharge for the same without the concurrence of the assignor."

5. Analysis of s. 136. In order to comply with *s*. 136, the assignment must

(*a*) be in writing;
(*b*) be signed by the assignor;
(*c*) be absolute, *i.e.* the entire chose must be assigned and not merely a part of it;
(*d*) not purport to be by way of charge only; and
(*e*) be accompanied or followed by express notice in writing to the debtor or other person from whom the assignor would have been entitled to claim the chose in action.

Further points to note are:

(*a*) The expression legal thing in action in its context in *s*. 136, means lawful thing in action. Thus, the section applies to equitable as well as to legal choses in action.

(*b*) It is not necessary that the assignee should have given consideration to the assignor.

(*c*) The assignment takes effect from the date when written notice was given to the debtor.

(*d*) Statutory assignments are subject to the equities (as indeed are equitable assignments). This means that:

(i) Any defence or counter-claim which would have been available to the debtor against the assignor at the time of notice of the assignment is available against the assignee.

(ii) If there have been two or more assignments of the same chose in action, the rights of the second and subsequent assignees are postponed to the first.

EQUITABLE ASSIGNMENT

6. Equity looks to the intent rather than to the form. If, in any transaction, there was an intent to assign a chose in action, but *s.* 136 was not complied with, there may be a valid assignment in equity.

> NOTE: there is no statutory assignment, *e.g.* where the assignment is not in writing, or where the assignment is not signed by the assignor, or where the assignment is of part only of a chose in action, or where no written notice was given to the debtor. In all these circumstances there may be a valid equitable assignment.

7. Equitable assignments of equitable choses in action. Equity has always allowed the assignment of equitable choses in action so that the assignee can bring an action in his own name without joining the assignor. Note that:

(*a*) The assignment is subject to the equities. Thus, although notice to the person liable is not essential, it is highly desirable, for where there are two or more assignees, they take priority each according to the date on which notice was given.

(*b*) Consideration is necessary unless the assignment is complete and perfect, *i.e.* unless all necessary formalities are completed according to the nature of the equitable right assigned.

8. Equitable assignments of legal choses in action. Provided the assignee can show that there was an intention to assign a legal chose in action, there may be a good equitable assignment. Points to note are:

(*a*) The assignment is subject to the equities.

(*b*) The assignee must join the assignor in any action he takes against the debtor. (If the assignor refuses to be co-plaintiff, he will be made a co-defendant.)

(*c*) The assignee must show that he gave consideration to the assignor.

> NOTE: these rules do not apply where title has passed to the assignee.

ASSIGNMENT BY OPERATION OF LAW

9. Automatic assignment. An involuntary assignment of choses in action will take place automatically on the death or bankruptcy of the owner.

10. Assignment on death. The general rule is that all contractual rights and obligations pass to the personal representatives of a party who dies. Thus, the personal representatives may sue or be sued on a contract to which the deceased was privy. The rule does not, however, apply to contracts of personal services.

11. Assignment on bankruptcy. The principal aim of bankruptcy law is to provide for a fair distribution of the debtor's property between the creditors. When a debtor has been adjudicated bankrupt, his property vests in the trustee in bankruptcy and becomes divisible between the creditors.

ASSIGNMENT OF CONTRACTUAL OBLIGATIONS

12. Obligations cannot be assigned. There can be no effective assignment at common law or in equity of contractual obligations without the creditor's consent. The need for the creditor's consent means, in effect, that the assignment may be achieved only through a new contract. This process is known as *novation*.

For example, a partner in a firm will usually wish to assign his liabilities to the firm as newly constituted on his retirement. Any such assignment of a liability is ineffective unless the creditor is a party. Novation is a tri-partite agreement.

13. Vicarious performance. Where A is under a contractual obligation to perform services of a personal nature for B, A cannot be discharged if the services are vicariously performed by C. B is entitled to the personal performance by A.

> *Robson and Sharpe* v. *Drummond* (1831): a coachbuilder contracted to hire out, maintain, and repaint a carriage. He purported to assign this contractual obligation. HELD: there could be no vicarious performance of this obligation. The other

party was entitled to the taste and judgment of the coach-builder.

Where, however, the obligation does not involve a personal element, the law permits vicarious performance on the principle that *qui facit per alium facit per se* (he who does anything by another does it himself): *British Waggon Co.* v. *Lea* (1880).

NOTE: where a party arranges for his obligations to be vicariously performed, he is not thereby discharged. He remains liable until the vicarious performance is complete. For example, where X is under an obligation to Y, and X arranges with Z for Z to perform the obligation, X is not discharged merely because Z has promised performance. He remains liable until Z's performance is complete.

NEGOTIABLE INSTRUMENTS

14. Negotiability. Negotiability is a characteristic which should be distinguished from assignability. It is a characteristic which has been conferred on certain instruments, mainly bills of exchange and promissory notes.

A cheque is a particular kind of bill of exchange.

15. Definitions. The following definitions are taken from the *Bills of Exchange Act,* 1882:

(*a*) "A bill of exchange is an unconditional order in writing, addressed by one person to another, signed by the person giving it, requiring the person to whom it is addressed to pay on demand or at a fixed or determinable future time a sum certain in money to or to the order of a specified person, or to bearer": *s.* 3 (1).

(*b*) "A cheque is a bill of exchange drawn on a banker payable on demand": *s.* 73.

(*c*) "A promissory note is an unconditional promise in writing made by one person to another signed by the maker, engaging to pay, on demand or at a fixed or determinable future time, a sum certain in money, to, or to the order of, a specified person or to bearer": *s.* 83 (1).

16. Meaning of negotiability. The special legal qualities of a negotiable instrument are as follows:

(*a*) *Transfer of ownership:* the rights of ownership of the instrument are transferred thus:

XV. ASSIGNMENT 173

(i) Where the instrument is drawn payable to order, or is specially indorsed, ownership is transferred by indorsement and delivery to the transferee.

(ii) Where the instrument is payable to bearer or indorsed in blank, ownership is transferred by mere delivery.

(b) *Free from the equities:* where an instrument is negotiated, the transferee takes the rights of ownership free from the equities, provided he is a holder in due course.

(c) *Holder may sue in own name:* the holder of a negotiable instrument may, in the event of dishonour, sue all prior parties to the instrument, *i.e.* the drawer, the acceptor, and all persons who transferred the instrument by indorsement and delivery.

17. Holder in due course. "A holder in due course is a holder who has taken the bill, complete and regular on the face of it, under the following conditions, namely:

(a) that he became the holder of it before it was overdue, and without notice that it had been previously dishonoured, if such was the fact;

(b) that he took the bill in good faith and for value, and that at the time the bill was negotiated to him he had no notice of any defect in the title of the person who negotiated it." *Bills of Exchange Act*, 1882, *s.* 29 (1).

PROGRESS TEST 15

1. What is a chose in action?
2. On what grounds does the common law forbid an assignment of a chose in action?
3. What are the requirements of a statutory assignment of a contractual right? Is consideration necessary?
4. How may an equitable assignment of a chose in action take place?
5. Is it possible to assign a contractual obligation?
6. Define a bill of exchange.
7. What are the main characteristics of a negotiable instrument?
8. What is a holder in due course?
9. A owes B the sum of £50. B owes A the sum of £20. B assigns his right to the £50 to C, and the assignment satisfies the requirements of *s.* 136 of the *Law of Property Act*, 1925. Comment on C's rights against A.

10. D owes E the sum of £100. E assigns his rights against D to F by way of gift. The assignment is in writing, but E has not signed it. Written notice has been given to D. F wishes to know whether he can claim against D for the £100. Advise him.

CHAPTER XVI

AGENCY

THE PRINCIPAL–AGENT RELATIONSHIP

1. The essential characteristic. The essential characteristic of an agent is that he is invested with a legal power to establish contractual relations between his principal and third parties.

2. The creation of the relationship. The relationship of principal and agent may be created in the following ways:

(a) By express appointment.
(b) By implication of the law, which may arise

  (i) from the conduct of the parties, *i.e.* agency by estoppel, or
  (ii) from the necessity of the case, *i.e.* agency of necessity.

(c) By subsequent ratification of an unauthorised act.
(d) By a partnership agreement.
(e) By the *Hire-Purchase Act*, 1965 (*see* V, **26**.)

3. Express appointment. Where the principal expressly appoints his agent, and the agent accepts the appointment, the relationship is based on contract and is sometimes known as contractual agency. No particular form of appointment is needed unless the agent is required to enter into contracts under seal, in which case the authority must be given under seal. An authority given under seal is known as a *power of attorney*.

4. Contractual capacity of an agent. Usually, though not always, the agent incurs no contractual obligations towards the third party. Thus the general rule is that an agent need not have contractual capacity, although, of course, the principal must have capacity.

5. Kinds of appointed agents. Appointed agents may be divided into three classes:

176   THE LAW OF CONTRACT

(a) *Special agents*, who are appointed to perform a particular act, after which their authority comes to an end.

(b) *General agents*, who have a continuous authority to act in some particular trade or business.

(c) *Universal agents*, who have unlimited authority to act for their principals.

6. Implication of law.
The law may infer an agency from the conduct of the parties or from the necessity of the case. The former gives rise to agency by estoppel and the latter to agency of necessity.

7. Agency by estoppel.
Consider the following generalised example: as a result of X's conduct, Y appears to be X's agent, and on the faith of this appearance, Z contracts with Y and suffers consequent loss. If Z has a cause of action arising from the contract, he may sue X, who will be estopped from denying that Y is his agent, and may thus be liable.

Spiro v. *Lintern* (1973): the defendant owned a house which he wished to sell. He arranged with his wife that she should find a purchaser, but he did not give her authority to enter into a contract of sale. His wife found a purchaser, the plaintiff, and entered into a contract of sale with him. The defendant, with knowledge of this, allowed the plaintiff to have repairs carried out to the house. The defendant refused to convey the house to the plaintiff, contending that his wife had no authority to enter the contract. The plaintiff brought this action for specific performance. HELD by the Court of Appeal: as the defendant knew that the plaintiff had acted under a misapprehension as to the extent of the authority of his (the defendant's) wife and had not disabused him, he was estopped from denying her authority to enter the contract of sale.

Agency by estoppel sometimes arises after the actual authority of an agent has been determined—for if a former agent continues to deal with third parties who believe the agency to be afoot, the former principal will be estopped from denying that he is principal. Thus a principal should be careful to give notice of the determination of his agent's authority to all possible third parties.

Trueman v. *Loder* (1840): A dealt with T on behalf of his principal, P. The agency was determined but notice of this was not given to T. A subsequently dealt with T in his own name.

T suffered loss as a result of A's breach of contract and he sued P. HELD: P was estopped from denying that A was still his agent. Damages awarded against P.

An apparent agency brought about by the procedural rule of estoppel has all the effects of an agency deliberately created by an express appointment.

8. Agency of necessity.

An authority may be conferred by law in circumstances where property is in jeopardy, and, at the time of the emergency, the instructions of the owner cannot be obtained. In such cases, there is a legal implication that the owner has consented to the creation of an agency, or to the extension of an existing authority. It may be regarded as yet another example of the law giving effect to the presumed intentions of the parties.

An agency of necessity arises when all the following conditions are satisfied:

(a) The person claiming to be an agent of necessity must have been driven by a real emergency, and not by mere convenience.

Prager v. *Blatspiel* (1924): X bought skins as agent for Y, but was unable to send them to Y because of war conditions in Europe: nor was X able to communicate with Y. X sold the skins before the war was over. Y brought this action against X, who pleaded that he had acted as agent of necessity. HELD: the skins could have been stored until the end of hostilities. There was no real necessity for the sale because the goods were never in jeopardy. X was not an agent of necessity.

(b) It must be practically impossible to obtain fresh instructions from the owner.

Springer v. *Great Western Railway* (1921): a consignment of fruit was found by the carrier to be going bad. The carrier sold the consignment instead of delivering to the destination. HELD: the carrier was not an agent of necessity for he could have obtained instructions from the owner of the fruit.

(c) An agent of necessity must act *bona fide* in the interests of all concerned: if he does not, he will be personally liable for his action.

9. Ratification of an unauthorised act. Where A acts in the name of, or professedly on behalf of, B, without B's authority, B may ratify the act and make it as valid as if it had been done with his authority. The result is the same whether A had no authority at all to act for B, or whether A merely acted in excess of an authority conferred by B. Ratification is effective only subject to the following conditions:

(*a*) The only person having power to ratify is the person on whose behalf the act was done: and this person must then

(i) have existed,
(ii) have been named or described,
(iii) have been competent, and must have remained competent to be principal.

(*b*) There must have been an act capable of ratification.
(*c*) Ratification must take place within a reasonable time.
(*d*) The person ratifying must have full knowledge of all material facts, or be prepared to ratify in any event.

NOTE: ratification is an expression of intention, and may be express or implied from conduct.

10. Partnership agreements. The law of partnership was amended and declared by the *Partnership Act*, 1890. The Act defines partnership as "the relation which subsists between persons carrying on a business in common with a view to profit." The agreement creating a partnership may be made with or without formality. It may be oral or written, and may or may not be under seal. Section 5 of the Act provides that every partner is an agent of the firm and his other partners for the purpose of the business of the partnership. Partnership firms enter into contracts through the agency of one of the partners and the acts of every partner who does any act for the carrying on in the usual way business of the kind carried on by the firm are binding on the firm unless (*a*) the partner so acting has in fact no authority to act in the particular matter, *and* (b) the person with whom he is dealing either (i) knows that he has no authority to act in the particular matter, or (ii) does not know or believe him to be a partner: *Partnership Act*, 1890, *s*. 5.

THE POSITION OF PRINCIPAL AND AGENT WITH REGARD TO THIRD PARTIES

11. Three possible circumstances. Here it is necessary to consider whether a third party (with whom the agent has contracted) is capable of suing, or of being sued by, the agent or the principal. On the footing that the agent was authorised to enter the contract, there are three circumstances to examine:

(a) Where both the fact of agency and the name or description of the principal are disclosed to the third party.
(b) Where the agent discloses the existence of the principal, but not his name or description.
(c) Where the existence of the principal is not disclosed.

12. Where the name of the principal is disclosed. Where the agent discloses the fact of the agency and the name or description of the principal to the third party, the general rule is that the agent incurs no rights or obligations. The contract is made between the principal and the third party, and it is between these that the rights and obligations are created. The legal effect is the same as if the principal had contracted directly with the third party.

NOTE: this general rule will be modified by any term, express or implied, to the effect that the agent is to be liable to the third party or to the principal. In particular:

(i) The agent is always liable on a deed executed in his own name.
(ii) The agent is always liable on a bill of exchange signed in his own name, without any words showing that he signed as agent.
(iii) The agent is liable where he is made so by custom of a trade, *e.g.* in a contract of marine insurance, the broker is liable to the insurer for the amount of the premium.

13. Where the existence but not the name of the principal is disclosed. Where the agent clearly contracts as agent, but does not disclose the name or sufficient description of his principal, the third party and the principal are contractually bound. The legal position is the same as where the principal is named, *i.e.* the agent does not incur personal liability: *Universal Steam Navigation Co., Ltd.* v. *McKelvie* (1923).

14. Where the principal is undisclosed. Where a principal has conferred authority on an agent and the agent subsequently contracts with a third party, but does not disclose the fact of the agency, so that the third party does not know of the existence of the principal, the doctrine of the undisclosed principal will apply. According to this doctrine, the parties have rights as follows:

(a) If a cause of action accrues to the third party, he may elect to sue either the agent or the undisclosed principal, if he can find him. A judgment against one is a bar to action against the other.

(b) If a cause of action accrues to the undisclosed principal against the third party, his rights will be subject to the following limitations:

  (i) The agent's authority must have existed at the time of the contract with the third party.
  (ii) The agent must not have contracted in terms incompatible with agency, *e.g.* in a contract of sale or hire he must not have described himself as "owner": *Humble* v. *Hunter* (1848).

If conditions (i) and (ii) are not satisfied, the undisclosed principal cannot intervene.

(c) An undisclosed principal cannot ratify (*see* **9** above): only a principal whose existence has been disclosed can ratify: *Keighley Maxsted & Co.* v. *Durant* (1901).

THE POSITION AS BETWEEN PRINCIPAL AND AGENT

15. General. The relationship between a principal and his agent is partly contractual and party fiduciary. The fiduciary element is important. There are always certain rights and obligations existing between principal and agent, apart from those which clearly stem from their contractual relationship. It must be remembered that the relationship is essentially a confidential one.

16. Obligations of the agent. In addition to his express contractual obligations, an agent is always under the following duties to his principal. These may, of course, be regarded as giving corresponding rights to the principal, who may sue for damages in the event of a breach of duty by the agent:

(a) To exercise diligence and whatever skill is professed, *e.g.* a salesman must sell his principal's property at the best possible price: *Keppel* v. *Wheeler* (1927).

(b) To render accounts to the principal as required.

(c) Not to let his own interests conflict with his obligations to the principal, *e.g.* an agent must not take any secret profit or bribe from any party with whom he deals on behalf of the principal. Where this occurs to the knowledge of the third party, the contract is voidable at the option of the principal: *Armstrong* v. *Jackson* (1917).

(d) Not to make use of confidential information obtained during the course of his duties as agent: *Lamb* v. *Evans* (1893).

(e) Not to delegate his duties to a sub-agent without authority, express or implied: *delegatus non potest delegare* (a delegate has no authority to delegate): *De Bussche* v. *Alt* (1878).

(f) To comply with the principal's instructions and to notify him when compliance becomes impossible. But where an agent is given ambiguous instructions, he is not liable if he interprets them otherwise than as intended by his principal: *Ireland* v. *Livingstone* (1872).

Principals have three rights as against agents who fail in their duty: (i) they can recover damages for want of skill and care, and for disregard of the terms of the mandate; (ii) they can obtain an account and payment of secret and illicit profits; and (iii) they can resist an agent's claims for commission and for indemnity by showing that the agent has acted as a principal himself and not merely as an agent. Each of these three remedies is distinct and available for a specific irregularity: *Christoforides* v. *Terry* (1924).

17. Obligations of the principal. The principal has always the following duties towards his agent. From these duties the agent derives corresponding rights which he can enforce against his principal:

(a) To pay remuneration and expenses as agreed; or, failing agreement, as is customary; or, failing a custom, to pay what is reasonable.

(b) To indemnify the agent against losses arising from the execution of his authority.

(c) To indemnify the agent against losses and liabilities arising out of an unauthorised act subsequently ratified.

(d) An agent has a lien on goods of his principal lawfully in his possession where the principal has not paid remuneration or expenses properly due.

NOTE: an agent is not entitled to be indemnified against the consequences of his own negligence, default or breach of duty; nor is he entitled to be indemnified against the consequences of an unlawful act except where he is entitled to a contribution towards damages in cases of his liability in tort towards a third party.

BREACH OF WARRANTY OF AUTHORITY

18. The warranty of authority. A person who purports to act as an agent is deemed to warrant that he has his principal's authority. Where a person contracts as agent without any authority, or where an agent contracts in excess of his authority, there is a breach of warranty of authority.

19. Who may bring the action? Any person who has relied on the warranty of authority and has acted upon that reliance and has thereby suffered loss may bring an action for damages against the agent. The remedy is available even where the third person was not induced to enter the contract by the warranty of authority: *Starkey* v. *Bank of England* (1903). But no person who knew of the agent's lack of authority, or did not believe him to be an agent, may sue.

It is no defence for the agent to plead that he acted in good faith and that he did not know his authority to be at an end: *Yonge* v. *Toynbee* (1910). The agent's liability arises independent of fraud or negligence, but where this is present, the party who has suffered loss may bring his action for breach of warranty and also in tort in the alternative.

20. The action arises ex contractu. The action for breach of warranty of authority arises out of contract, and damages is the usual remedy.

A breach of warranty of authority should not be regarded

as a misrepresentation, for which damages are not awarded at common law.

TERMINATION OF THE AGENCY RELATIONSHIP

21. Ways in which authority may be ended. The relationship of principal and agent may be terminated by acts of the parties or by operation of law as follows:

(a) By notice of revocation given by the principal to the agent.

(b) By notice of renunciation given to the principal by the agent.

(c) By the completion of the transaction, where the authority was given for that transaction only, *i.e.* in the case of a special agency.

(d) By the expiration of the period stipulated in the contract of agency.

(e) By mutual agreement, by which the principal discharges the agent from further liability and duty in consideration for a reciprocal discharge from the agent.

(f) Generally, by death, lunacy, or bankruptcy of the principal or agent.

(g) By dissolution, where the principal is a corporation. (Probably also where the agent is a corporation.)

(h) By the destruction of the subject-matter of the agency.

(i) By the contract becoming unlawful.

22. Unilateral termination of agency. Where there is a contract of agency, summary unilateral termination, unless within the terms of the contract, will be in breach of contract, and damages may be awarded against the party revoking or renouncing. However, if there is no period of notice stipulated in the contract of agency, either party may give reasonable notice at any time.

NOTE: although the general rule is that an agency agreement is always revocable and will not be specifically enforced, where the agency is coupled with an interest, the authority is irrevocable: *e.g.* if A owes money to B and subsequently gives him a power of attorney to sell certain property and to discharge the debt from the purchase money, the power is coupled with an interest and is, therefore, irrevocable: *Gaussen* v. *Morton* (1830).

23. Ostensible authority. The termination of an agent's actual authority does not necessarily mean that the principal is not bound by future acts of the former agent. Where notice of revocation has not been given to third parties, they may still regard the former agent as having actual authority to enter contracts for the former principal. If such a third party enters a contract with a former agent, on the faith of his ostensible authority, the former principal will be liable if a cause of action accrues to the third party: *Trueman* v. *Loder* (1840). A prudent principal will therefore give notice of the termination of agency to all who have dealt with his former agent as agent.

PROGRESS TEST 16

1. What is the essential characteristic of an agent?
2. Explain the different ways in which the relationship of principal and agent may be created.
3. In what circumstances does an agent who has contracted within his authority remain liable on the contract?
4. Explain the doctrine of the undisclosed principal.
5. What rights and duties exist between principal and agent?
6. In what circumstances may an action be brought for breach of warranty of authority? Who may bring the action?
7. In what ways may the principal-agent relationship be terminated?
8. Distinguish between the actual authority and the ostensible authority of an agent.
9. A dealt with B in the course of his (A's) duties as C's agent. The agency relationship has now been brought to an end, but A continues to deal with B. A has always used his own name in his dealings with B, but B knew that he was acting as C's agent. B has not yet been informed of the termination of A's agency. Advise C as to his liabilities towards B.
10. D, a carrier, discovers that a consignment of tomatoes owned by E has deteriorated badly before the destination has been reached. He therefore sells the consignment for what he can get: this is about a third of the market price for good tomatoes. E has now brought an action against D for damages. D wishes to know whether he can claim that he was an agent of necessity. Advise him.
11. F and G are partners in a building business. G contracts to buy a quantity of bricks from H. If G dies before payment is made, is F liable to H? Give full reasons for your answer.

CHAPTER XVII

DISCHARGE

THE END OF A CONTRACT

1. Discharge of obligations. Every contractual obligation gives rise to a corresponding contractual right. Thus, where the obligation of one party is discharged, the corresponding right of the other party is extinguished. Where all obligations which arose under a contract are discharged—and all rights are thus extinguished—the contract is said to be discharged.

2. Ways in which a contract may be discharged. A contract may be discharged in any of the following ways:

  (*a*) Performance.
  (*b*) Agreement.
  (*c*) Acceptance of breach.
  (*d*) Frustration.

DISCHARGE BY PERFORMANCE

3. Performance must be complete. A contractual obligation is discharged by a complete performance of the undertaking. The promisee is entitled to the benefit of complete performance exactly according to the promisor's undertaking. Where the promisor is unable or unwilling to give more than a partial performance, the general rule is that there is no discharge.

The practical effect of this rule is that where a contract provides for payment by one party after performance by the other, no action to recover payment may be maintained until the performance is complete. Nor will an action for a proportional payment be available on the basis of *quantum meruit*.

Cutter v. *Powell* (1795): the plaintiff sued as administratrix of her deceased husband's estate. The defendant had, in Jamaica, subscribed and delivered to T. Cutter, the intestate, a note as follows: "Ten days after the ship Governor Parry, myself master, arrives at Liverpool, I promise to pay to Mr T. Cutter the sum of thirty guineas, provided he proceeds, continues and does his duty as second mate in the said ship from hence to the port of Liverpool. Kingston, July 31, 1793." The Governor Parry sailed from Kingston on 2 August 1793 and arrived in Liverpool on 9 October. But T. Cutter died on 20 September, until which date he did his duty as second mate. The plaintiff claimed payment on a *quantum meruit*. HELD: according to the express terms of the contract, the sum of thirty guineas was payable only on completion of the whole voyage. A term to the effect that proportional payments should be made in case of partial performance could not be implied. The plaintiff could not, therefore, succeed in her claim on a *quantum meruit*. *Per* Ashurst, J.: "Here the intestate was by the terms of his contract to perform a given duty before he could call upon the defendant to pay him any thing; it was a condition precedent, without performing which the defendant is not liable. And it seems to me to conclude the question: the intestate did not perform the contract on his part; he was not indeed to blame for not doing it; but still as this was a condition precedent, and as he did not perform it, his representative is not entitled to recover."

Sumpter v. *Hedges* (1898): S agreed to erect certain buildings on H's land in consideration of a stipulated sum. When the buildings were only half finished, S ran out of money and could not complete them. H refused to pay S at all and S brought this action to recover on a *quantum meruit*. HELD by the Court of Appeal: the claim must fail. Where there is a contract to do certain work for a lump sum, the person who is to do the work cannot sue for the lump sum till he has completed that which he agreed to do. The plaintiff's claim to recover something on a *quantum meruit* fails because he showed no evidence of a fresh contract by which the defendant agreed to pay for the work that had been done.

4. Exceptions to the rule in Cutter v. Powell. The following exceptions exist to the rule that performance must be complete and total:

(*a*) *Divisible contracts:* Where the parties are deemed to have intended their contract to be divided into two or more separate contracts, then each separated contract is discharged separately, *e.g.* where there is a contract for the delivery of goods by instalments, payment is due from the buyer upon the delivery of each instalment. The buyer cannot defer payment until all instalments have been

XVII. DISCHARGE

delivered, unless there is a term of the contract to that effect: *Ebbw Vale Steel Co.* v. *Blaina Iron Co.* (1901).

NOTE: the question as to whether a contract is divisible or entire, depends upon the intention of the parties. Divisible contracts are sometimes called severable contracts.

(b) Substantial performance: According to the doctrine of substantial performance, a promisor who has substantially done what he promised to do can sue on the contract. His right to sue will be subject to a claim for damages by the promisee in respect of that part of the contract remaining unperformed.

H. Dakin & Co. v. *Lee* (1916): there was a contract by which a builder undertook to carry out substantial repairs to a building. He completed the entire contract work but some of it was carried out carelessly and with bad workmanship. The building owner refused to pay the balance due on the contract contending that there was no liability because the contractor's performance was not complete. The builder brought this action to recover the balance due. HELD by the Court of Appeal: the builders were entitled to recover the balance of the contract price, less the value of the defective work. *Per* Lord Cozens-Hardy, M.R.: "I regard the present case as one of negligence and bad workmanship, and not as a case where there has been an omission of any one of the items in the specification. The builders thought apparently, that they had done all that was intended to be done in reference to the contract; and I suppose the defects are due to carelessness on the part of some of the workmen or of the foremen: but the existence of these defects does not amount to a refusal by them to perform part of the contract; it simply showed negligence in the way in which they have done the work."

Hoenig v. *Isaacs* (1952): the plaintiff, an interior decorator and designer of furniture, entered into a contract to decorate and furnish a one-roomed flat belonging to the defendant. The agreed price was the sum of £750 to be paid "net cash, as the work proceeds, and balance on completion." While the work was in progress, the defendant paid two instalments of £150, and when the plaintiff claimed to have finished he asked for the balance of £450. At this point the defendant complained of faulty design and bad workmanship, paid a further instalment of £100 to the plaintiff and entered into occupation of the flat, using the furniture provided under the contract. The plaintiff sued for the balance of £350, and the Official Referee held that there was substantial compliance with the contract and that the defendant was liable to pay the sum due under the contract less the cost of remedying the defects. The defendant appealed from this decision. HELD, by the Court of Appeal: in a contract for work and labour for a lump sum payable on completion, the employer cannot repudiate liability on the ground that the work, when substantially performed, is in some respects not in accordance with the contract. In these circumstances the employer is liable for the balance due under the contract less the cost of making good the defects or omissions. And where the employer takes the benefit of the work by using chattels made under the contract, he cannot treat entire performance as a condition precedent to payment, for the condition is waived by his taking the benefit of the work. *Per* Denning, L.J.: "In determining this issue the first question is whether, on the true construction of the contract, entire performance was a condition precedent to payment. It was a lump sum contract, but that does not mean that entire performance was a condition precedent to payment. When a contract provides for a specific sum to be paid on completion of specified work, the Courts lean against a construction of the contract which would deprive the contractor of any payment at all simply because there are some defects or omissions. The promise to complete the work is therefore construed as a term of the contract, but not as a condition. It is not every breach of that term which absolves the employer from his promise to pay the price, but only a breach which goes to the root of the contract, such as an abandonment of the work when it is only half done. Unless the breach goes to the root of the matter, the employer cannot resist payment of the price. He must pay it and bring a cross claim for the defects and omissions, or, alternatively set them up in diminution of the price. The measure is the amount by which the work is worth less by reason of the defects and omissions and is usually calculated by the cost of making them good."

NOTE: in contracts of sale of goods which are governed by s. 13 of the *Sale of Goods Act*, 1893, the courts apply the maxim *de minimis non curat lex* (the law does not concern itself with trifles). Section 13 provides that where there is a contract for the sale of goods by description, there is an implied condition that the goods shall correspond with the description. Where goods do not correspond exactly with description there is a breach of this implied condition unless the discrepancy is minute. In *Wilensko* v. *Fenwick* (1938), a discrepancy of about 1% constituted a breach of the implied condition as to correspondence with description.

XVII. DISCHARGE 189

(c) *Prevention of performance:* where a party is prevented from completing his undertaking because of some act or omission of the other party, it would be unjust to apply the rule in *Cutter* v. *Powell*. In these circumstances, the party who has been prevented from performance may sue either for damages or on a *quantum meruit* (as much as he has earned).

5. Tender of performance. In an action for breach of contract, it is a good defence for the defendant to prove that he tendered performance, *i.e.* that he offered to perform his side of the bargain, and that the plaintiff refused to accept this. In these circumstances, the defendant is discharged from all liability under the contract.

But the following points should be noted:

(a) The tender of performance must be exactly in accordance with the terms of the contract.

(b) Where tender of performance took the form of an offer to make a money payment.

  (i) the amount tendered must have been the exact amount due, and in the form required by the *Coinage Act*, 1870, and the *Bank Notes Act*, 1928 (silver is legal tender up to £2, copper is legal tender up to one shilling, bank notes of any denomination are legal tender up to any amount) and

  (ii) the defence of tender must be accompanied by payment into court of the amout due.

DISCHARGE BY AGREEMENT

6. Discharge by agreement. On the principle that a thing may be destroyed in the same manner in which it is constituted, a contractual obligation may be discharged by agreement. Discharge by agreement may occur in either of two ways:

(a) A contractual obligation may be discharged by a subsequent binding contract between the parties.

(b) A contractual obligation may be discharged by the operation of one of the terms of the contract itself.

7. Discharge by subsequent binding contract. Discharge by subsequent agreement (which must be binding) may occur in any of the following ways:

(*a*) Where the contract is wholly executory, *i.e.* where neither party has completed his undertaking:

(i) *Waiver:* a contract may be discharged by mutual waiver. In effect, there is a new contract under which each party agrees to waive his rights under the old contract in consideration of being released from his obligations under the old contract.

(ii) *Waiver plus new rights and obligations:* a subsequent agreement between the parties may be to waive the old agreement and substitute an entirely new contract.

(*b*) Where the contract is partially executory, *i.e.* where one party only has completed his undertaking, and something remains to be done by the other party:

(i) *Release:* the party to whom the obligation is owed may release the other party by a subsequent agreement under seal. (N.B. Such a promise must be under seal because it is given for no consideration.)

(ii) *Accord and satisfaction:* the party to whom the obligation is owed may agree with the other party to accept something different in place of the former obligation. The subsequent agreement is the accord, and the new consideration is the satisfaction. Where there has been accord and satisfaction, the former obligation is discharged. But where the subsequent agreement by which one party consents to accept something different in place of the original obligation is under a threat that he will otherwise get nothing at all, there is no true accord and, consequently, the original obligation remains undischarged. The essential point is that unless there is a new consideration there can be no satisfaction, *i.e.* there can be no discharge of the previous agreement and no formation of an agreement in new terms. In *Pinnel's* Case (1602), "It was resolved by the whole Court that payment of a lesser sum on the day in satisfaction of a greater, cannot be any satisfaction for the whole, because it appears to the Judges that by no possibility, a lesser sum can be a satisfaction to the plaintiff for a greater sum: but the gift of a horse, hawk or robe, &c., in satisfaction is good. For it shall be intended that a horse, hawk or robe, &c., might be more beneficial to the plaintiff than the money, in respect of some circumstances, or otherwise the plaintiff would not have accepted of it in satisfaction."

D. & C. Builders, Ltd. v. *Rees* (1965): in July 1964 the defendant owed £482 13*s.* 1*d.* to the plaintiffs for work done by them as jobbing builders. In August and again in October the plaintiffs wrote to the defendant asking for payment. In November 1964 the defendant's wife telephoned the plaintiffs and said, "My husband will offer £300 in settlement. That is all you'll get. It is to be in satisfaction." The plaintiffs then discussed the problem between themselves. The company was a small one and it was in desperate financial straits: for this reason the plaintiffs decided to accept the £300. The plaintiffs then telephoned the defendant's wife, telling her that "£300 will not even clear our commitments on the job. We will accept £300 and give you a year to find the balance." She replied, "No, we will never have enough money to pay the balance. £300 is better than nothing." When she was told by the plaintiffs that they had no choice but to accept, she said, "Would you like the money by cash or by cheque. If it is cash, you can have it on Monday. If by cheque; you can have it tomorrow (Saturday)." The next day, the defendant's wife gave the plaintiffs a cheque for £300, asking for a receipt, and insisting on the words "in completion of account." So that the wording of the receipt was as follows: "Received the sum of £300 from Mr Rees in completion of the account. Paid, M. Casey." In evidence, Mr Casey explained why he gave a receipt in those terms: "If I did not have the £300 the company would have gone bankrupt. The only reason we took it was to save the company. She knew the position we were in." The plaintiffs brought this action to recover the balance of £182 13s. 1d. On a preliminary point whether there was accord and satisfaction, it was held by the County Court judge that the taking of the cheque for £300 did not discharge the debt of £482 13s. 1d. The defendant appealed. HELD by the Court of Appeal: there was no accord and satisfaction and the plaintiff was entitled to recover the balance. *Per* Danckwerts, L.J.: "The giving of a cheque of the debtor for a smaller amount than the sum due is very different from 'the gift of a horse, hawk, or robe &c.' mentioned in Pinnel's Case. I accept that the cheque of some other person than the debtor, in appropriate circumstances, may be the basis of an accord and satisfaction, but I cannot see how in the year 1965 the debtor's own cheque for a smaller sum can be better than payment of the whole amount of the debt in cash. The cheque is only conditional payment, it may be difficult to cash, or it may be returned by the bank with the letters 'R.D.' on it. ... I agree also that, in the circumstances of the present case, there was no true accord. Mr and Mrs Rees really behaved very badly. They knew the plaintiffs' financial difficulties and used their awkward situation to intimidate them."

8. Discharge by the operation of a term in the contract.

There is no reason why a contract should not contain a term providing for the discharge of obligations arising from the contract. Such a term may be either a condition precedent or a condition subsequent, or it may be a term giving one or both parties the right to end the agreement by giving notice to the other party.

(a) A condition precedent is a condition which must be satisfied before a contract becomes binding. Where a condition precedent is not fulfilled, there is no true discharge because the rights and obligations under the contract were contingent upon an event which did not occur, *i.e.* the rights and obligations never came into existence: *Pym* v. *Campbell* (1856).

(b) A condition subsequent is a term providing for the discharge of obligations outstanding under the contract, in the event of a specified occurrence: *Head* v. *Tattersall* (1871).

(c) A party's right to end the agreement. A contract may contain a term providing that one or both parties may bring the agreement to an end by giving notice to that effect. This provision is quite usual in contracts of employment.

There is no presumption that a commercial contract with no express power of determination is intended to be perpetual. In appropriate cases the Court will imply a term to empower a party to determine the contract on giving reasonable notice to the other party: *see Beverley Corporation* v. *Richard Hodgson & Sons* (1972).

DISCHARGE BY ACCEPTANCE OF BREACH

9. Breach of contract. Breach of contract occurs where a party fails to perform his contractual obligations, or where he repudiates his obligations, expressly or impliedly, without justification. A party not in breach always has an action for damages against the party in breach and, in certain circumstances, he may treat the contract as repudiated by the party in breach and refuse further performance. That is to say, breach by one party may enable the other party to become discharged from further liability. *See* V, **19**.

XVII. DISCHARGE

10. Breach does not always cause a contract to become discharged. A contract is not discharged by breach unless the innocent party elects to treat the breach as a repudiation of the contract. In *Howard* v. *Pickford Tool Co.* (1951), Asquith, L.J., said that "An unaccepted repudiation is a thing writ in water and of no value to anybody: it confers no legal rights of any sort or kind." However, repudiation takes place only where the breach goes to the root of the contract. Where the breach does not go to the root of the contract the party not in breach is not entitled to treat the contract as repudiated, his remedy sounds in damages only.

The party not in breach may, if he wishes, give the other party an opportunity to change his mind and perform his contractual obligations: *see, e.g. White & Carter* v. *McGregor* (1962). In these circumstances, the right to treat the contract as repudiated by breach will be lost if the contract is discharged in some other manner: *Avery* v. *Bowden* (1855).

Where the consequences of a breach is an event which would have frustrated the contract if it had occurred without the fault of either party then the innocent party must be treated as having accepted the breach as a repudiation of the contract. In these circumstances there is no need for an election, the contract being discharged automatically: *Harbutt's Plasticine* v. *Wayne Tank Co.* (1970), *see* V, **10**.

White and Carter (Councils), Ltd. v. *McGregor* (1962): a Scottish appeal. The appellant company's business was the supply of litter bins to local authorities in urban areas. It was the company's practice to attach advertisement plates to the bins, for which the advertisers would pay according to the terms of a standard form of contract. The respondent, who carried on a garage business, entered into a contract through his sales manager by which the company undertook to prepare and exhibit plates advertising McGregor's business for a period of three years. The contract form was headed by a notice that it was not to be cancelled by the advertiser and one of the express conditions provided to the same effect. Immediately after this contract was signed, the following letter was sent to the company: "We regret that our Mr Ward signed an order today continuing the lamp post advertisements for a further period of three years. He was unaware that our proprietor Mr McGregor does not wish to continue this form of advertisement. Please therefore cancel the order." The appellant company did not accept the attempted cancellation and displayed the advertisements during the ensuring three years. The respondents refused to pay and the appellant sought to recover the sum due under the contract. HELD by the House of Lords: the contract remained unaffected by the unaccepted repudiation and the appellant company was entitled to recover the sums due under the contract. *Per* Lord Hodson: "It is settled as a fundamental rule of the law of contract, that repudiation by one of the parties to a contract does not itself discharge it. . . . It follows that, if, as here, there was no acceptance [of the breach], the contract remains alive for the benefit of both parties and the party who has repudiated can change his mind but it does not follow that the party at the receiving end of the proffered repudiation is bound to accept it before the time for performance and is left to his remedy in damages for breach."

Ellen v. *Topp*, (1851): T was apprenticed to E to learn three trades, *viz.*, auctioneer, appraiser, and corn factor. During the contract period, E gave up trading as a corn factor. T refused further performances. HELD: T was discharged from further liability on the contract of apprenticeship because E's act had rendered the real purpose of the contract unattainable.

Hong Kong Fir Shipping Co., Ltd. v. *Kawasaki Kisen Kaisha, Ltd.* (1962): the owners of a ship undertook by charterparty to let it to the charterers for a period of twenty-four months. They undertook that the ship was fitted in every way for ordinary cargo service and that they would maintain her in a thoroughly efficient state in both hull and machinery. It was agreed that no payment should become due for time lost exceeding twenty-four hours in carrying out repairs to the vessel and that such off-hire periods might, at the option of the charterers, be added to the charter time. The charterers took delivery of the vessel at Liverpool on 13th February 1957, when she sailed in ballast for Newport News, U.S.A., where it was intended that she should pick up a cargo of coal and then proceed to Osaka via the Panama Canal. Between Liverpool and Osaka, the ship was at sea for eight and a half weeks, and for five weeks she was off-hire for repairs. When the ship arrived at Osaka on 15th May, it was discovered that her engines were in bad condition and that major repairs were necessary. The bad state of the engines on arrival at Osaka was due in part to the incompetence of the engine-room staff. On 15th September, the ship was once more ready to put to sea and the engine-room staff was by then adequate and efficient. In the meantime, the charterers wrote to the owners on 6th June, 27th July and 11th September, repudiating the charterparty and claiming for breach of contract. On each occasion, the owners replied that they would treat the contract as wrongfully repudiated and that they would claim damages accordingly. On 13th September, the owners formally accepted the charterers' repudiation and subsequently brought this action for damages for wrongful repudiation of the charterparty. The charterers counter-claimed for damages for breach of the charterparty. The owners succeeded before Salmon, J., and the charterers appealed. HELD by the Court of Appeal: neither the unseaworthiness by itself nor the delay caused by the owners' breach of contract entitled the charterers to repudiate the charterparty.

General Billposting Co. Ltd. v. *Atkinson* (1909): the defendant, a billposter, entered into a contract of employment with the plaintiff company, the contract being subject to termination by either party giving twelve months notice in writing. By the contract, the defendant undertook that he would not, within two years of leaving the plaintiff company's employment, engage as a billposter within a radius of fifty miles of the company's registered office. The company dismissed him without giving the agreed twelve months' notice. He then set himself up as a billposter within fifty miles of the company's registered office. The company brought this action against him, claiming damages and an injunction to restrain him from working as a billposter within the range of fifty miles as agreed in the contract of employment. The action came before Neville, J., who gave judgment for the plaintiff company. The defendant appealed and it was held by the Court of Appeal that the company, by dismissing the employee without the agreed period of notice had completely and totally repudiated the contract of employment and that, accordingly, the employee was entitled to accept the repudiation and regard himself as no longer bound by any of its terms. The company appealed to the House of Lords. HELD by the House of Lords: the employers dismissed the defendant in deliberate disregard of the terms of the contract, and the defendant was thereupon justified in rescinding the contract and treating himself as resolved from further performance of it on his part. *Per* Lord Robertson: "The respondent's position in entering into the contract is a very intelligible one. He says: 'I am a billposter, and I desire occupation, either on my own account or in the service of others. If I enter the employment of others, I am willing to give up the right to trade on my own account to the extent specified in this agreement. I do not desire to have it both ways.' The claim of the appellants, on the other hand, as now put forward, is that taking him at his word, as expressed in the contract, and getting his services, they are to be entitled both to deprive him (against the contract) of the right to serve them and also of the right to serve himself. It seems to me that the covenant not to set up business is not only germane but ancillary to the contract of service, and that, once the contract of service is rescinded, the other falls with it."

11. Contracts of sale of goods. Where there has been a breach of *condition* by the seller of goods, the buyer may treat the contract as repudiated and refuse further performance. But the buyer may elect, or be compelled, to treat the breach of condition as a breach of warranty giving rise to an action for damages only. Where a condition sinks to the level of a warranty in this way, the breach is known as a breach of warranty *ex post facto*. These rules apply equally to express conditions and to implied conditions.

The *Sale of Goods Act*, 1893, *s*. 11 (1), provides that:

"(*a*) Where a contract of sale is subject to any condition to be fulfilled by the seller, the buyer may waive the condition or may elect to treat the breach of such condition as a breach of warranty, and not as a ground for treating the contract as repudiated:

"(*b*) Whether a stipulation in a contract of sale is a condition, the breach of which may give rise to a right to treat the contract as repudiated, or a warranty, the breach of which may give rise to a claim for damages but not to a right to reject the goods and treat the contract as repudiated, depends in each case on the construction of the contract. A stipulation may be a condition, though called a warranty in the contract:

"(*c*) Where a contract of sale is not severable, and the buyer has accepted the goods, or part thereof, or where the contract is for specific goods, the property in which has passed to the buyer, the breach of any condition to be fulfilled by the seller can only be treated as a breach of warranty, and not as a ground for rejecting the goods and treating the contract as repudiated, unless there be a term of the contract, express or implied, to that effect."

DISCHARGE BY FRUSTRATION

12. Supervening impossiblity. It is a basic common law rule that a party is *not* discharged from his contractual obligations merely because performance has become more onerous or impossible owing to some unforeseen event. The general rule is that a contractual obligation is absolute, and if a party wishes to protect himself against subsequent difficulties in performance, he should stipulate for that protection. The doctrine of frustration has, however, developed a number of exceptions to this general rule of absolute contractual liability.

Paradine v. *Jane* (1648): the plaintiff brought this action to recover rent due under a lease and was met with the defence "that a certain German prince, by name Prince Rupert, an alien born, enemy to the King and kingdom, had invaded the realm with an hostile army of men; and with the same force did enter upon the defendant's possession, and him expelled, and held out of possession from the 19 of July 18 Car. till the Feast of the Annunciation, 21 Car. whereby he could not take the profits; ..."

The Court held that "when the party by his own contract creates a duty notwithstanding any accident by inevitable necessity, because he might have provided against it by his contract.... Now the rent is a duty created by the parties upon the reservation, and had there been a covenant to pay it, there had been no question but the lessee must have made it good, notwithstanding the interruption by enemies, for the law would not protect him beyond his own agreement, no more than in the case of reparations; this reservation then being a covenant in law, and whereupon an action of covenant hath been maintained (as Roll said) it is all one as if there had been an actual covenant. Another reason was added, that as the lessee is to have the advantage of casual profits, so he must run the hazard of casual losses, and not lay the whole burthen of them upon his lessor; and ... that though the land be surrounded, or gained by the sea, or made barren by wildfire, yet the lessor shall have his whole rent: and judgement was given for the plaintiff."

13. The doctrine of frustration. Under the doctrine of frustration, a contract will be discharged and the parties released from further obligation where the following conditions are satisfied:

(*a*) That the contract does not contain an absolute undertaking, express or implied. Where a party has bound himself to perform his side of the contract in any event, the doctrine of frustration does not apply: *Blackburn Bobbin Co., Ltd.* v. *T. W. Allen* (1918).

(*b*) That due to some event, the fundamental purpose of the contract became frustrated, or rendered impossible of performance; so that any attempted performance would amount to something quite different from what must have been contemplated by the parties when they entered the contract. It is not sufficient that an event makes an obligation more onerous: *Tsakiroglou & Co. Ltd.* v. *Noblee Thorl G.m.b.H.* (1962); *Davis Contractors* v. *Fareham U.D.C.* (1956).

(c) That the event causing the frustration was not one which the parties could be deemed to have contemplated at the time of making the contract.

(d) That the event causing the frustration was not induced by one of the parties: *Maritime National Fish, Ltd.* v. *Ocean Trawlers, Ltd.* (1935). But where it is alleged that the event causing frustration was induced by one of the parties, the burden of proof is on the party alleging it.

Joseph Constantine Steamship Line, Ltd. v. *Imperial Smelting Corporation, Ltd.* (1942): a ship was chartered to load a cargo at Port Pirie in South Australia and to carry it to Europe. While the vessel was anchored in the roads off Pirie and before she became an "arrived ship," there was a violent explosion near her auxiliary boiler, causing damage and making it impossible to perform the charterparty. The charterers claimed damages, alleging that the owners had broken the charterparty by their failure to load the cargo. The owners contended that the contract was frustrated by the destructive consequences of the explosion. There was no evidence that the explosion was due to the fault of the owners. It was held by the Court of Appeal that the defence raised by the owners, that the charter was frustrated, must fail unless the owners could prove affirmatively that the frustration occurred without their default. The owners appealed. HELD by the House of Lords: the onus of proving default lies upon the party denying the frustration. Since there was no evidence that the explosion was attributable to the fault of the owners, the contract was frustrated.

14. The basis of the doctrine of frustration. In the *Joseph Constantine* Case, Viscount Simon said: "[I]t is well to emphasise that, when 'frustration' in the legal sense occurs, it does not merely provide one party with a defence in an action brought by the other. It kills the contract itself and discharges both parties automatically. The plaintiff sues for breach at a past date and the defendant pleads that at that date no contract existed. In this situation, the plaintiff could only succeed if it were shown that the determination of the contract were due to the defendant's 'default,' and it would be a strange result if the party alleging this were not the party required to prove it. The doctrine of discharge from liability by frustration has been explained in various ways, sometimes by speaking of the disappearance of a foundation which the parties assumed to be the basis of their contract, sometimes as deduced from a rule arising from impossibility of performance, and sometimes as flowing from the inference of an implied term. Whichever way it is put, the legal consequence is the same. The most satisfactory basis, I think, upon which the doctrine can be put is that it depends on an implied term in the contract of the parties. It has the advantage of bringing out the distinction that there can be no discharge by supervening impossibility if the expressed terms of the contract bind the parties to performance notwithstanding that the supervening event may occur. Every case in this branch of the law can be stated as turning on the question of whether, from the express terms of the particular contract, a further term should be implied which, when its conditions are fulfilled, puts an end to the contract. If the matter is to be regarded in this way, the question therefore, is as to the construction of the contract, taking into consideration its express and implied terms." The implied condition theory of the basis of the doctrine of frustration is merely an extension of the more general doctrine of the implied term, *i.e.* that the law will imply a term where necessary to give effect to the unexpressed but presumed intentions of the parties. In *Taylor* v. *Caldwell* (1863), which may, perhaps, be regarded as the origin of the doctrine of frustration, the subject-matter of the contract was destroyed: in holding that the parties were discharged, Blackburn, J., said that the contract was "subject to an implied condition that the party shall be excused in case, before breach, performance becomes impossible from the perishing of the thing without default of the contractor."

The most recent theory of the basis of the doctrine of frustration is that the courts have a power to impose a solution on the parties. In other words, that the courts have a power to impose a condition which will discharge the contract. In a 1944 House of Lords case, in which the parties were in dispute as to whether frustration had occurred, Lord Wright said, "The Data for decision are on the one hand the terms and construction of the contract, read in the light of the then existing circumstances, and on the other hand the events which have occurred. It is the court which has to decide what is the true position between the parties": *Denny, Mott & Dickson, Ltd.* v. *Fraser & Co., Ltd.* (1944).

15. Factual circumstances in which a contract may be frustrated. Decisions show that the doctrine of frustration may be invoked in circumstances such as the following:

(*a*) Where there is a total or partial destruction of some object necessary to the performance of the contract: *Taylor* v. *Caldwell* (1863).

(*b*) Where a change in the law or State intervention renders any attempted performance illegal. For example, in *Baily* v. *De Crespigny* (1869), statutory powers conferred on a railway company frustrated the performance of a covenant in a lease.

(*c*) Where death or illness prevents a party from performing an obligation of a personal nature: *Robinson* v. *Davison* (1871).

(*d*) Where an event which is fundamental to the contract does not occur: *Krell* v. *Henry* (1903). But there must be an absolute non-occurrence: *Herne Bay Steamboat Co.* v. *Hutton* (1903).

Taylor v. *Caldwell* (1863): the defendants agreed to let the plaintiffs have the use of the Surrey Gardens and Music Hall on four specific days for the purpose of giving a series of four concerts and day and night fetes. After the making of this agreement and before the date fixed for the first concert, the Hall was destroyed by fire. The contract contained no express stipulation with reference to fire. The plaintiffs, who had spent money on advertisements and otherwise in preparing for the concerts, brought this action to recover damages. It was contended that, according to the rule in *Paradine* v. *Jane*, the destruction of the premises by fire did not exonerate the defendants from performing their part of the agreement. HELD: both parties were excused from performance of the contract.

Robinson v. *Davidson* (1871): the plaintiff was a professor of music and a giver of musical entertainments, and the defendant was the husband of a celebrated pianist. The plaintiff entered into a contract with the defendant's wife (as her husband's agent) to perform at a concert he had arranged

XVII. DISCHARGE

for a specified evening. A few hours before the concert was due to begin the plaintiff received a letter from the defendant's wife informing him that on account of her illness she could not perform at the concert. The plaintiff brought this action for breach of contract. HELD: the contract was conditional upon the defendant's wife being well enough to perform and, consequently, the defendant was excused. *Per* Bramwell, B.: "This is a contract to perform a service which no deputy could perform and which, in case of death, could not be performed by the executors of the deceased; and I am of the opinion that by virtue of the terms of the original bargain incapacity either of body or mind in the performer, without default on his or her part, is an excuse for non performance. Of course the parties might expressly contract that incapacity should not excuse, and thus preclude the condition of health from being annexed to their agreement. Here they have not done so; and as they have been silent on that point, the contract must in my judgment be taken to have been conditional, and not absolute."

Krell v. *Henry* (1903): by a written contract, the defendant agreed to hire from the plaintiff a third-floor flat in Pall Mall for 26th and 27th June 1902. The defendant's purpose was to view the coronation processions which had been proclaimed to pass along the street below on those dates, but there was no express mention of this in the contract. The agreed price was £75, of which £25 was advanced to the plaintiff at the time the contract was made. The King fell ill and processions did not take place on the days appointed, and the defendant refused to pay the balance of £50 according to the agreement. The plaintiff brought this action to recover it. The defendant denied liability and counter claimed for the recovery of £25, the amount paid by way of deposit. Darling, J., following *Taylor* v. *Caldwell*, gave judgment for the defendant on the claim and on the counter-claim. The plaintiff appealed and the defendant abandoned his counter-claim. HELD by the Court of Appeal: there was a necessary inference from the circumstances, recognised by both parties, that the coronation procession and the relative position of the rooms was the foundation of the contract; the express terms of the contract to pay for the use of the flat on the days named, though unconditional, were not used with reference to the possibility of the cancellation of the procession, and consequently, the plaintiff was not entitled to recover the balance of £50, the contract being discharged. *Per* Vaughan Williams, L.J.: "I think that the coronation procession was the foundation of this contract, and that the non-happening of it prevented the performance of the contract and, secondly I think that the non-happening of the procession, to use the words of Sir James Hannen in *Baily* v. *De Crespigny*, was an event 'of such a character that it cannot reasonably be supposed to have been in the contemplation of the contracting party when the contract was made, and that they are not to be held bound by general words which, though large enough to include, were not used with reference to the possibility of the particular contingency which afterwards happened.'"

Herne Bay Steamboat Co. v. *Hutton* (1903): the plaintiff steamship company contracted to place their steamboat *Cynthia* at the disposal of the defendant on 28th June 1902, "for the purpose of viewing the Naval Review and for a day's cruise round the fleet; also on Sunday June 29th 1902, for a similar purpose." The *Cynthia* was fitted out for this trip but on 25th June the postponement of the review was announced. On 26th June the plaintiffs telegraphed the defendant: "What about *Cynthia*? She is ready to start at six tomorrow. Waiting cash." There was no reply from the defendant. The plaintiff brought this action for damages for breach of contract. Grantham, J., gave judgment for the defendant on the claim and on the counter-claim. The plaintiff appealed. HELD by the Court of Appeal: the defendant was not discharged from his obligations under the contract by the postponement of the Naval Review because (i) the object in hiring the vessel was the defendant's alone and of no concern to the plaintiff and (ii) the holding of the Naval Review was not the foundation of the contract.

16. Payment, retention and recovery of money after frustration.

Where a contract is terminated by frustration the parties are under no liability for obligations which would otherwise have accrued after the frustrating event took place. The contract is terminated at that point in time. It is not, however, rendered void by the frustration. Accordingly, at common law, obligations which accrued before the frustrating event are not affected. And money paid before the frustrating event can be recovered in quasi-contract where there has been a complete failure of consideration.

Fibrosa v. *Fairbairn* (1943), H.L.: the parties entered a contract in July 1939 by which the vendors undertook to manufacture and deliver certain machinery c.i.f. Gdynia. By the terms of the contract (i) if dispatch was hindered by any cause beyond the vendor's reasonable control, a reasonable extension of time should be granted, and (ii) one third of the purchase price was payable at the time of the order being given.

One third of the purchase price was £1600, and, of this £1000 only was paid in July 1939. In September 1939 Gdynia was occupied by the enemy, rendering impossible the lawful delivery of the machinery there. The London agents of the purchasers brought this action to recover the £1000 paid in advance, contending that the contract was frustrated notwithstanding the provision for reasonable extension. HELD by the House of Lords: the stipulation providing for a reasonable extension referred only to a temporary impossibility and not to the prolonged period of impossibility occasioned by the outbreak of war, and that the contract was, accordingly, frustrated: the buyer was entitled to the recovery of the £1000 paid in advance as money paid upon a consideration which had wholly failed.

In the *Fibrosa* case Viscount Simon, L.C., said of the decision: "While this result obviates the harshness with which the previous view in some instances treated the party who had made a prepayment, it cannot be regarded as dealing fairly between the parties in all cases, and must sometimes have the result of leaving the recipient who has to return the money at a grave disadvantage. He may have incurred expenses in connection with the partial carrying out of the contract which are equivalent, or more than equivalent, to the money which he prudently stipulated should be prepaid, but which he now has to return for reasons which are no fault of his. He may have to repay the money, although he has executed almost the whole of the contractual work, which will be left on his hands. These results follow from the fact that the English common law does not undertake to apportion a prepaid sum in such circumstances. It must be for the legislature to decide whether provision should be made for an equitable apportionment of prepaid moneys which have to be returned by the recipient in view of the frustration of the contract in respect of which they were paid." The legislation envisaged by Viscount Simon was passed very shortly after the *Fibrosa* decision in the form of the *Law Reform (Frustrated Contracts) Act*, 1943. Sections 2 and 3 of the Act give the court a statutory power to order payment, retention or recovery of money as it thinks just, having regard to the circumstances of each case.

NOTE

(i) Section 2 of the *Law Reform (Frustrated Contracts) Act*, 1943, provides that: "All sums paid or payable to any party in pursuance of the [frustrated] contract ... shall, in the case of sums paid, be recoverable from him as money received by him to the use of the party by whom the sums were paid, and, in the case of the sums payable, cease to be so payable: Provided that, if the party to whom the sums were so paid or payable incurred expenses before the time of discharge in, or for the purpose of, the performance of the contract, the court may, if it considers it just to do so having regard to all the circumstances of the case, allow him to retain or, as the case may be, recover the whole or any part of the sums so paid or payable, not being an amount in excess of the expenses so incurred." Section 3 provides further that: "Where any party to the contract has, by reason of anything done by any other party thereto in, or for the purpose of, the performance of the contract, obtained a valuable benefit . . . before the time of discharge, there shall be recoverable from him by the said other party such sum . . . not exceeding the value of the said benefit to the party obtaining it, as the court considers just, having regard to all the circumstances of the case. . . ."

(ii) The Act does not apply to voyage charterparties, insurance contracts, or to contracts to which the *Sale of Goods Act*, 1893, *s*. 7 applies (*s*. 7 of the *S.G.A.* provides that where there is an agreement to sell specific goods, and subsequently the goods, without any fault on the part of the seller or buyer, perish before risk passes to the buyer, the agreement is thereby avoided).

PROGRESS TEST 17

1. In what ways may a contract be discharged?

2. Explain the rule in *Cutter* v. *Powell*.

3. What exceptions are there to the rule in *Cutter* v. *Powell*?

4. "In an action for breach of contract, it is a good defence for the defendant to prove that he tendered performance." Comment on this statement.

5. Explain how a contract may be discharged by agreement.

6. In what circumstances may a contracting party treat a breach by the other party as a repudiation of the contract?

7. "It is a basic common law rule that a party is not discharged from his contractual obligations merely because performance has become more onerous or impossible owing to some unforeseen event." Explain the doctrine of frustration as an exception to this rule.

8. Outline the provisions of *s*. 2 of the *Law Reform (Frustrated Contracts) Act*, 1943.

9. What do you consider to be the theoretical basis of the doctrine of frustration?

10. A, an American exporter, contracted to sell to B, a British

importer, 5000 tins of cooked ham, to be packed in cases of 50 tins. When the ham was tendered to B, he discovered that about a third of the cases contained only 25 tins, but the total consignment was 5000 tins. B thereupon refused to take delivery of the ham. A wished to know whether he can claim against B. Advise him.

11. C agrees to coach D for an examination. Shortly before the date of the first lesson, C falls seriously ill, and is unable to give any lessons at all. D cannot find another tutor, and he fails the examination. Consider the legal position.

12. E, a British manufacturer, contracts to make certain machinery for F, a Ruritanian importer. F pays to E the sum of £1500 by way of deposition. E prepares his factory for the manufacture of the machinery at a cost of £1100, but before he can begin production, it becomes illegal to export machinery to Ruritania. F now seeks to recover his deposit of £1500. Do you think he will succeed?

13. What is the connection between anticipatory breach, repudiation, and fundamental breach?

CHAPTER XVIII

REMEDIES FOR BREACH OF CONTRACT

REMEDIES

1. Ubi jus ibi remedium (where there is a right, there is a remedy). A right would be of little value if there were no remedy available in the event of an infringement. A remedy is the means given by law for the enforcement of a right, or for the recovery of pecuniary compensation in lieu of performance. A breach of contract by one party necessarily causes an infringement of the contractual rights of the other party. A breach of contract usually, but not always, causes a loss: in any event, there is a right of action against the contract-breaker.

2. Breach of contract. There is a breach of contract where a party fails to perform his contractual obligations, or where he repudiates his obligations, expressly or by implication.

3. Repudiation before performance is due. Where a party repudiates his contractual obligations before the time for performance, a right of action will immediately accrue to the other contracting party. Repudiation before performance is due is known as anticipatory breach. Notice that, in theory, there is no breach, for the time for performance has not arrived, yet a right of action exists as if there were a breach. An anticipatory breach may arise from an express or an implied repudiation of the contractual obligation. For example, if A has contracted to sell Blackacre to B, and he (A) subsequently contracts to sell the same land to C, there is an implied repudiation of A's obligation to B: but if A had said to B, "I shall not convey Blackacre to you according to our agreement," there would be an express repudiation.

Where there is a wrongful repudiation by one party which is not accepted by the other party, the contract survives and the rights of the innocent party are preserved. There is no duty on the innocent party to vary the terms of the contract and he can, accordingly, carry out his own obligations under the contract after the wrongful repudiation, and then sue on the contract for the other party's breach: *White & Carter, Ltd.* v. *McGregor* (1961) H.L.

Where a contract has been repudiated by an anticipatory breach and the contract-breaker subsequently becomes entitled under the contract to cancel the contract, the damages awarded will be nominal only.

Maredelanto Compania Naviera S.A. v. *Bergbau-Handel G.m.b.H.* (1970): It was provided by a charterparty dated 25 May 1965 that the *Mihalis Angelos* "now trading and expected ready to load under this charter about 1st July 1965" would proceed to Haiphong and there load a cargo of apatite. The charterparty also provided that, "Should the vessel not be ready to load . . . on or before the 20th July 65 Charterers have the option of cancelling this contract." The ship arrived at Hong Kong on 23 June and discharged its cargo by 23 July. She then underwent a special survey lasting two days. On 17 July the charterers purported to cancel the charterparty on grounds of *force majeure*. The owners accepted the cancellation as a repudiation of the charter and on 29 July they contracted to sell the vessel. On arbitration, it was found that there was no frustration of the charterparty before 17 July, (ii) that on 25 May the owners could not reasonably have estimated that the vessel would arrive at Haiphong "about 1st July 1965," and (iii) that, had the vessel ultimately proceeded to Haiphong, the charterers would have exercised their contractual right to cancel on grounds of delay. HELD by the Court of Appeal: (i) the expected readiness clause was a condition of the contract meaning that the owner honestly expected the vessel to be ready to load on 1 July; there was a breach of this condition and, accordingly, the charterers were entitled to terminate the charter forthwith. (ii) The charters could not have relied on the cancellation clause to justify their cancellation on 17 July because the right to cancel was not exercisable before 20 July. (iii) The owners were entitled to nominal damages only for the wrongful repudiation of the charterers because the charterers could have cancelled as of right on 20 July.

4. Remedies for breach of contract. There are various remedies for breach of contract. The appropriate remedy in any case will depend on the subject-matter of the contract and the nature of the breach. In certain circumstances there may be a plurality of remedies available, either together or in the alternative. In all cases the plaintiff must state in his pleadings the remedy (or remedies) that he desires: he may

(a) sue for unliquidated damages;
(b) sue for liquidated damages;
(c) sue for damages by way of recovery of a specific sum of money owed under a contract, *e.g.* for the agreed price of goods, or for the agreed remuneration for services;
(d) sue on a *quantum meruit*;
(e) sue for a reasonable price for goods where the price is not determined in accordance with *s.* 8 (1) of the *S.G.A.*;
(f) sue for a decree of specific performance;
(g) sue for an injunction to restrain the breach of a negative term.

These various remedies should each be considered separately.

NOTE: Where a person has entered into a contract after an innocent misrepresentation has been made to him, and the misrepresentation has become a term of the contract, he may be entitled to the equitable remedy of rescission as an alternative to his remedy for breach of contract. *See* VIII, 12.

UNLIQUIDATED DAMAGES

5. Compensation, not punishment, is the object. Where a plaintiff claims damages for breach of contract, it is the function of the court to assess the money value of the loss suffered, and to award this sum as *damages*. In effect, this is an order to the party in breach to pay the sum fixed by the court as compensation to the other party. Notice that damage is a remedy to the injured party: punishment of the contract-breaker is *not* the object of damages. Unliquidated damages may be:

(a) *substantial damages, i.e.* pecuniary compensation intended to put the plaintiff in the position he would have enjoyed had the contract been performed; or
(b) *nominal damages, i.e.* a small token award where there has been an infringement of a contractual right, but no actual loss has been suffered; or
(c) *exemplary damages, i.e.* the sum awarded is far greater than the pecuniary loss suffered by the plaintiff. It seems

that exemplary damages are awarded only where a banker wrongfully dishonours a trader's cheque. Exemplary damages are not awarded for wrongful dismissal: *Addis* v. *Gramophone Co.* (1909).

6. The measure of damages. In its endeavours to assess the loss suffered by the injured party for which damages should be awarded, the court will consider the following questions:

(a) Was the loss caused by the breach?

(b) Is any part of this loss too remote (in terms of causation) from the breach to be the proper subject of compensation?

(c) Could the loss have been mitigated in any way by any reasonable act on the part of the injured party?

7. The rule(s) in Hadley v. Baxendale. The foundations of the modern approach to the related problems of causation of loss and remoteness of loss, were laid in *Hadley* v. *Baxendale* (1854). In that case, Baron Alderson said, "Where two parties have made a contract which one of them has broken, the damages which the other party ought to receive in respect of such breach of contract should be such as may fairly and reasonably be considered either:

arising naturally, *i.e.* according to the usual course of things, from such breach of contract itself, or

such as may reasonably be supposed to have been in the contemplation of both parties, at the time they made the contract, as the probable result of the breach of it."

The "either" and the "or" produce, in effect, two distinct rules.

Hadley v. *Baxendale* (1854): the plaintiffs were millers in Gloucester and the defendants were common carriers of goods. The crankshaft of the plaintiffs' steam-engine was broken with the result that work in their mill had come to a halt. They had ordered a new shaft from an engineer in Greenwich and arranged with the defendants to carry the broken shaft from Gloucester to Greenwich to be used by the engineer as a model for the new shaft which had been ordered. The defendants did not know that the plaintiffs had no spare shaft and that the mill could not operate until the new shaft was installed. The defendants delayed the delivery of the broken shaft to the engineer for several days, with the result that the plaintiffs were prevented from working their steam-mills and grinding corn, and were unable to supply their customers with flour during that period. The plaintiffs claimed damages from the defendants. On the question of measure of damages, HELD by the Court of Exchequer: where two parties have made a contract which one of them has broken the damages which the other party ought to receive in respect of such breach of contract should be such as may fairly and reasonably be considered as either arising naturally, *i.e.* according to the usual course of things, from such breach of contract itself, or such as may reasonably be supposed to have been in the contemplation of both parties at the time they made the contract as the probable result of the breach of it. If special circumstances under which the contract was actually made were communicated by the plaintiffs to the defendants, and thus known to both parties, the damages resulting from the breach of such a contract which they would reasonably contemplate would be the amount of injury which would ordinarily follow from a breach of contract under the special circumstances so known and communicated. But, on the other hand, if these special circumstances were wholly unknown to the party breaking the contract, he, at the most, could only be supposed to have had in his contemplation the amount of injury which would arise generally, and in the great multitude of cases not affected by any special circumstances, from such a breach of contract. For, had the special circumstances been known, the parties might have specially provided for the breach of contract by special terms as to the damages in that case; and of this advantage it would be very unjust to deprive them. In the present case, the only circumstances here communicated by the plaintiffs to the defendants at the time the contract was made were that the article to be carried was the broken shaft of a mill and that the plaintiffs were the millers of that mill. Accordingly, the loss of profits could not reasonably be considered such a breach of contract as could have been fairly and reasonably contemplated by both the parties when they made the contract. Such a loss would neither have flowed naturally from the breach in the great multitude of such cases occurring under ordinary circumstances, nor were the special circumstances, which, perhaps, would have made it a reasonable and natural consequence of such breach of contract, communicated to or known by the defendants.

8. A restatement. The rule in *Hadley* v. *Baxendale*, refined in the light of later authorities, were restated in *Victoria*

Laundry, Ltd v. *Newman Industries, Ltd.* (1949). In that case there was a single judgment which contained a summary of the law relating to causation and remoteness of loss.

Victoria Landry, Ltd. v. *Newman Industries, Ltd.* (1949): the plaintiffs, who were launderers and dyers, decided to extend their business, and with this end in view, purchased a large boiler from the defendants. The defendants knew at the time of the contract that the plaintiffs were laundrymen and dyers and that they required the boiler for the purposes of their business. They also were aware that the plaintiffs wanted the boiler for immediate use. But the defendants did not know at the time the contract was made exactly how the plaintiffs planned to use the boiler in their business. They did not know whether (as the fact was) it was to function as a substitute for a smaller boiler already in operation, or as a replacement of an existing boiler of equal capacity, or as an extra unit to be operated in addition to any boilers already in use. The defendants, in breach of contract, delayed delivery of the boiler for five months. The plaintiffs brought this action for damages. The defendants disputed that the plaintiffs were entitled to damages for the loss of profits they would have earned if the boiler had been delivered on time. The plaintiffs contended that they could have taken on a large number of new customers in the course of their laundry business and that they could and would have accepted a number of highly lucrative dyeing contracts for the Ministry of Supply. Streathfield, J., awarded £110 damages under certain minor heads but no damages in respect of loss of profits on the grounds that this was too remote. The plaintiffs appealed. HELD by the Court of Appeal: there were ample means of knowledge on the part of the defendants that business loss of some sort would be likely to result to the plaintiffs from the defendants' default in performing their contract; the appeal should, therefore, be allowed and the issue referred to an official referee as to what damage, if any, is recoverable in addition to the £110 awarded by the trial judge.

The importance of *Victoria Laundry* v. *Newman Industries*, is that it gave to the Court of Appeal the opportunity to review and restate the principles governing measure of damages. After reviewing the authorities, Asquith, L.J., who read the judgment of the Court, said: "What propositions applicable to the present case emerge from the authorities as a whole, including those analysed above? We think they include the following: (i) It is well settled that the governing purpose of damages is to put the party whose rights have been violated in the same position, so far as money can do so, as if his rights had been observed. This purpose, if relentlessly pursued, would provide him with a complete indemnity for all loss *de facto* resulting from a particular breach, however improbable, however unpredictable. This, in contract at least, is recognised as too harsh a rule. Hence, (ii): In cases of breach of contract the aggrieved party is only entitled to recover such part of the loss actually resulting as was at the time of the contract reasonably foreseeable as liable to result from the breach. (iii) What was at that time reasonably foreseeable depends on the knowledge then possessed by the parties, or, at all events, by the party who later commits the breach. (iv) For this purpose knowledge 'possessed' is of two kinds—one imputed, the other actual. Everyone, as a reasonable person, is taken to know the 'ordinary course of things' and consequently what loss is liable to result from a breach of that ordinary course. This is the subject matter of the 'first rule' in *Hadley* v. *Baxendale*, but to this knowledge, which the contract-breaker is assumed to possess whether he actually possesses it or not, there may have to be added in a particular case knowledge which he actually possesses of special circumstances outside the 'ordinary course of things' of such a kind that a breach in those special circumstances would be liable to cause more loss. Such a case attracts the operation of the 'second rule' so as to make additional loss also recoverable. (v) In order to make the contract-breaker liable under either rule it is not necessary that he should actually have asked himself what loss is liable to result from a breach. As has often been pointed out, parties at the time of contracting contemplate, not the breach of the contract but its performance. It suffices that, if he had considered the question, he would as a resonable man have concluded that the loss in question was liable to result. (vi) Nor, finally, to make a particular loss recoverable, need it be proved that on a given state of knowledge the defendant could, as a reasonable man, foresee that a breach must necessarily result in that loss. It is enough if he could foresee it was likely so to result."

The following cases are examples of the application of these principles. See also *Harbutt's Plasticine* v. *Wayne Tank Co* (1970) and *Maredelanto Compania Naviera* v. *Bergbau-Handel* (1970).

Heskell v. *Continental Express, Ltd.* (1950): H had contracted to sell goods to X, an importer in Persia. There was a breach of this contract by H, owing to failure of the carriers, C.E., to deliver the goods. Accordingly, H paid £1319 damages to X, the amount being the assessment of X's loss of profits. H now sought to recover damages from C.E. HELD: the measure of damages was £175, being the loss of profit on a sub-sale at the wholesale level of trade. Knowledge of the abnormally high retail prices obtaining temporarily in Persia could not be imputed to the carrier, C.E.

Diamond v. *Campbell-Jones* (1960): C-J contracted to sell certain land, well-known to be ripe for development, to D, a property dealer. C-J wrongfully repudiated the contract and D claimed damages. HELD: the measure of damages was the difference between the market value of the property at the date of the breach and the contract price. The profit which D could have made by developing the property was too remote a loss, because knowledge that D intended to use the property in a particular manner could not be imputed to C-J.

9. A further refinement of the principles.

In 1967 the House of Lords had occasion to consider the principles enunciated in *Hadley* v. *Baxendale* and *Victoria Laundry* v. *Newman Industries*, when the appeal was heard in the case of the *Heron II*. In that case, Lord Upjohn said: "Asquith, L.J., in the *Victoria Laundry* case used the words 'likely to result' and he treated that as synonymous with a serious possibility or a real danger. He went on to equate that with the expression 'on the cards,' but like all your lordships I deprecate the use of that phrase, which is far too imprecise and to my mind is capable of denoting a most improbable or unlikely event, such as winning a prize on a premium bond on any given drawing. It is clear that on the one hand the test of foreseeability as laid down in the case of tort is not the test for breach of contract; nor on the other hand must the loser establish that the loss was a near certainty or an odds-on probability. I am content to adopt as the test a 'real danger' or a 'serious possibility.' There may be a shade of difference between these two phrases, but the assessment of damages is not an exact science and what to one judge or jury will appear a real danger may appear to another judge or jury to be a serious possibility. I do not think that the application of that test would have led to a different result in *Hadley* v. *Baxendale*. I cannot see why [the carrier] in the absence of express mention should have contemplated as a real danger or serious possibility that work at the factory would be brought to a halt while the shaft was away."

The Heron II. Koufos v. *Czarnikow* (1967), H.L.: the respondents chartered the appellant's vessel, *Heron II*, to sail to Constanza, and there to load a cargo of sugar and to carry this to Basrah or to Jeddah at the charterer's option. The option was not exercised and the vessel arrived at Basrah with a delay of nine days due to deviations made in breach of contract. The respondents had intended to sell the sugar promptly after arrival at Basrah but the appellant did not know this, although he was aware that there existed a sugar market at Basrah. Shortly before the sugar was sold at Basrah, the market price fell partly by reason of the arrival of another cargo of sugar. If the appellant's vessel had not been in delay by nine days, the sugar would have fetched £32 10s. per ton. The price realised on the market was £31 2s. 9d. per ton. The respondent charterers brought this action to recover the difference as damages for breach of contract. The appellant shipowner, while admitting liability to pay interest for nine days on the value of the sugar, denied that the fall in market value should be taken into account in assessing damages. It was held by the Court of Appeal that the loss due to the fall in market price was not too remote and could be recovered as damages. The shipowner appealed to the House of Lords. HELD by the House of Lords: the case fell within the first branch of the rule in *Hadley* v. *Baxendale* and that the difference was recoverable as damages for breach of contract. *Per* Lord Morris: "The present case is one in which no special information was given to the carrier as to what the charterers intended to do with the goods after they arrived at Basrah. In those circumstances in deciding what damages would fairly and reasonably be regarded as arising, if the delivery of the goods was delayed, I think that the reasonable contemplation of a reasonable shipowner at the time of making the charterparty must be considered. I think that such a shipowner must reasonably have contemplated that, if he delivered the sugar at Basrah some nine or ten days later than he could and should have delivered it, then a loss by reason of a fall in the market price for sugar at Basrah was one that was liable to result or at least was not unlikely to result. This results from the facts of this case. It is a question of what the parties contemplated. Even without notice of special circumstances or special considerations there may be situations where it is plain that there was a common contemplation."

XVIII. REMEDIES FOR BREACH OF CONTRACT

10. Damages for mental distress. The nineteenth-century authorities indicate that damages will not be awarded for mental distress. These authorities now appear to be outdated in the light of the decision of the Court of Appeal in *Jarvis* v. *Swan Tours, Ltd.* (1972). In this case, Lord Denning said: "In a proper case damages for mental distress can be recovered in contract, just as damages for shock can be recovered in tort. One such case is a contract for a holiday, or any other contract to provide entertainment and enjoyment. If the contracting party breaks his contract, damages can be given for the disappointment, the distress, the upset and frustration caused by the breach. I know that it is difficult to assess in terms of money, but it is no more difficult than the assessment which the courts have to make every day in personal injury cases for loss of amenities."

Jarvis v. *Swan Tours, Ltd.* (1972): the plaintiff booked a winter sports holiday described in a brochure issued by the defendants. During his stay at the holiday resort, the plaintiff found that the holiday provided was very much inferior to that described in the brochure. The plaintiff brought this action for damages for breach of contract. At first instance, the judge took as the measure of damages the difference between what the plaintiff had paid for the holiday (£63.45) and what he actually got, and on this footing awarded damages of £31.72. The plaintiff appealed. HELD by the Court of Appeal: this was a proper case in which damages for mental stress could be awarded. The measure of damages was the sum required to compensate the plaintiff for the loss of entertainment and enjoyment which he had been promised by the defendants and did not get. In arriving at this sum, his vexation and disappointment could be taken into account. Damages increased to £125.

11. The duty to mitigate the loss. Where one party has suffered loss resulting from the other party's breach of contract, the injured party should take reasonable steps to minimise the effect of the breach. Any failure to mitigate the loss will be taken into account by the court in its assessment of damages, and the injured party will be penalised to that extent.

The principle of mitigation was explained by Viscount Haldane, L.C., in *British Westinghouse Electric Co., Ltd.* v. *Underground Electric Co., Ltd.* (1912) as follows: "I think that there are certain broad principles, which are quite well settled.

The first is that, as far as possible, he who has proved a breach of a bargain to supply what he contracted to get is to be placed as far as money can do it, in as good a situation as if the contract had been performed. The fundamental basis is thus compensation for pecuniary loss naturally flowing from the breach; but this first principle is qualified by a second, which imposes on a plaintiff the duty of taking all reasonable steps to mitigate the loss consequent on the breach, and debars him from claiming in respect of any part of the damage which is due to his neglect to take such steps. In the words of James L.J., in *Dunkirk Colliery Co.* v. *Lever* (1878): 'The person who has broken the contract is not to be exposed to additional cost by reason of the plaintiffs not having done what they ought to have done as reasonable men, and the plaintiffs not being under any obligation to do anything otherwise than in the ordinary course of business.' As James, L.J., indicates, this second principle does not impose on the plaintiff an obligation to take any step which a reasonable and prudent man would not ordinarily take in the course of his business. But when, in the course of his business, he has taken action arising out of the transaction, which action has diminished his loss, the effect in actual diminution of the loss which he has suffered may be taken into account, even though there was no duty on him to act."

But the duty to mitigate does not preclude a party from going to the expense of performing his side of the contract after the other party has wrongfully repudiated the contract: *White & Carter, Ltd.* v. *McGregor* (1961).

12. Measure of damages in sale of goods. Where the buyer refuses to accept, or the seller refuses to deliver the goods under a contract of sale, the measure of damages is *prima facie* the difference between the contract price and the market price of the goods at the time when they ought to have been accepted or delivered: *Sale of Goods Act*, 1893, *ss.* 50 and 51.

LIQUIDATED DAMAGES

13. Pre-assessment of loss. Where contracting parties make a genuine pre-assessment of the loss that would flow from any particular breach, and stipulate accordingly in their contract that this sum shall be payable in the event of a breach, the sum payable is *liquidated damages*.

Where the sum inserted in the clause is intended as a punishment on the contract-breaker and is not connected with the amount of loss which could be contemplated by the parties at the time of contracting, the sum is a penalty. Liquidated damages clauses and penalty clauses must be distinguished carefully.

14. Effect of liquidated damages and penalties compared.

(*a*) A liquidated damages clause is binding on the parties. In the event of a breach, the sum fixed and no more and no less can be claimed. No action for unliquidated damages is allowed.

(*b*) A penalty clause is void. In the event of a breach, the injured party may bring an action for unliquidated damages. The penalty clause is disregarded.

15. Penalty or liquidated damages? It occasionally happens that contracting parties are in dispute as to whether a sum stipulated is a penalty or liquidated damages. In these circumstances it is the duty of the court to decide the issue in the light of the rules given by Lord Dunedin in *Dunlop Tyre Co.* v. *New Garage Co.* (1914), a House of Lords case. The rules consist of the following propositions:

(*a*) The use by the parties of the words "penalty" or "liquidated damages" is not conclusive.

(*b*) The essence of a penalty is a payment stipulated as *in terrorem* of the offending party: the essence of liquidated damages is a genuine pre-estimate of loss.

(*c*) The issue is one of construction of each particular contract, judged at the time of making the contract and not at the time of the breach. In construing the contract, the following tests may be used:

(i) If the sum stipulated is extravagant or unconscionable in amount compared with the greatest loss which could conceivably be proved to have followed from the breach, it is a penalty.

(ii) If the breach consists only of the non-payment of money, and the sum stipulated is greater, it is a penalty.

(iii) Where a single lump sum is payable on the occurrence

of one or more of several events, some of which may occasion serious and others but trifling loss, there is a *presumption* that it is a penalty.

(iv) It is no obstacle to the sum stipulated being a genuine pre-estimate of loss that the consequences of the breach are such as to make precise pre-estimation almost an impossibility.

In construing the contract, the court will take into account all the circumstances at the time the contract was made. For example, where the hirer of a juke box under a hire-purchase contract terminated the agreement and returned the juke box a reasonable sum stipulated to be payable by way of depreciation was held to be liquidated damages: *Phonographic Equipment, Ltd.* v. *Muslu* (1961). But where a depreciation clause in a hire-purchase contract of a motor car bore no relation to the actual depreciation in value of the car, but was intended only to ensure a certain financial return to the owner, the clause was held to be a penalty clause: *Bridge* v. *Campbell Discount Co., Ltd.* (1962).

Dunlop Pneumatic Tyre Co., Ltd. v. *New Garage Co., Ltd.* (1914) H.L.: Dunlop, through an agent, entered into a contract with New Garage Co., by which they supplied them with their goods, consisting mainly of motor car tyres, covers, and tubes. By this contract, New Garage Co. undertook not to do a number of things, including the following: not to tamper with the manufacturer's marks; not to sell to any customer at prices less than the current list prices; not to supply to persons whose supplies Dunlop had decided to suspend; not to exhibit or to export without Dunlop's assent. The agreement contained the following clause: "We agree to pay to the Dunlop company the sum of £5 for each and every tyre, cover or tube sold or offered in breach of this agreement, as and by way of liquidated damages and not as a penalty." The New Garage Co. sold covers and tubes at prices below the list prices and Dunlop brought this action for liquidated damages. On the question whether the £5 stipulated in the agreement was penalty or liquidated damages, HELD by the House of Lords: the stipulation was one for liquidated damages and the New Garage Co. was liable to pay the sum specified in respect of each and every breach of the contract.

CLAIM FOR A SPECIFIC SUM AS DAMAGES

16. Non-payment as a breach of contract. Where one party is under a contractual obligation to pay a specific sum of money to the other party, and there is a total or partial failure to pay according to the contract, there is a breach of contract.

17. Liquidated demands. In a case of breach by non-payment of a specific sum of money, it is advantageous to the plaintiff to make a liquidated demand rather than to claim unliquidated damages. A liquidated demand is a claim that the defendant owes the plaintiff a certain sum of money.

NOTE: Under Order 14 of the Rules of the Supreme Court, an expeditious procedure is available for the recovery of a specific sum of money under a liquidated demand.

18. Actions for the price of goods. The *Sale of Goods Act* 1893, *s.* 49, provides that where, under a contract of sale, the buyer wrongfully neglects or refuses to pay for the goods according to the terms of the contract, the seller may maintain an action against him for the price of the goods. Section 8 (1) of the Act provides that the price in a contract of sale may be fixed by the contract, or may be fixed in a manner thereby agreed, or may be determined by a course of dealing between the parties. An action for the price of goods where the price is determined in accordance with *s.* 8 (1) will take the form of a liquidated demand.

19. Damages in addition to a liquidated demand. Where a plaintiff has suffered some loss in addition to the non-payment of money, he may also claim for unliquidated damages. Damages may be claimed in the same action as the liquidated demand, or in an action subsequently brought: *Yeoman Credit, Ltd.* v. *Waragowski* (1961); *Overstone* v. *Shipway* (1962).

Overstone, Ltd. v. *Shipway* (1962): the plaintiff finance company had entered a contract of hire-purchase of a motor car with S, the defendant. S fell into arrears with his hire instalments and the company took the car from him and recovered the arrears of instalments on a liquidated demand. In the present action, the company claimed damages with respect to the loss incurred on the re-sale of the car. HELD by the Court of Appeal: the claim for damages should succeed as it was quite distinct from the liquidated demand in the earlier action. *Per* Holroyd Pearce, L.J., "In my judgment, it is impossible to hold that a claim for sums due under the hiring is the same cause of action as a claim for damages for breach."

QUANTUM MERUIT AS A REMEDY FOR BREACH

20. The quantum meruit claim. Where a plaintiff sues to recover an *unliquidated* sum by way of payment for services rendered, he is said to claim on a *quantum meruit* (as much as he has earned). The distinction between a *quantum meruit* claim and a claim for damages is that the former is a claim for reasonable remuneration, while the latter is a claim for compensation for a loss. Both are claims for an unliquidated sum. It is usually a matter of procedural tactics whether a plaintiff claims on a *quantum meruit* in preference to a claim for damages.

21. Circumstances where a quantum meruit is appropriate.

(*a*) Where there is an express or implied contract to render services, but no agreement as to remuneration, reasonable remuneration is payable. The court decides what is reasonable. The reasonable remuneration is the *quantum meruit*.

Upton R.D.C. v. *Powell* (1942): there was an implied contract between P and the Upton fire brigade for the services of the brigade. HELD by the Court of Appeal: reasonable remuneration was payable by P for the services he had received.

(*b*) Where, from the circumstances of the case and the conduct of the parties, a new contract is implied, taking the place of their original contract, an action on a *quantum meruit* is available to a party who has performed his obligations under the fresh implied contract.

Steven v. *Bromley* (1919): there was a contract between S, a ship-owner, and B, a charterer, for the carriage of a certain consignment of steel, at an agreed rate of freight. The goods actually delivered to S for shipment consisted partly of steel and partly of general merchandise, for which the freight rates were higher than for steel. S accepted the goods entirely and

XVIII. REMEDIES FOR BREACH OF CONTRACT

they were stowed on the ship. S claimed freight in excess of that agreed under the contract. HELD: a new contract could be implied from the facts, and the higher freight could be claimed as reasonable remuneration, *i.e.* on a *quantum meruit*.

But where no new contract can be implied, the plaintiff cannot succeed in a claim on a *quantum meruit*: see *Sumpter* v. *Hedges* (1898), XVII, **3**.

(c) Where a contracting party has elected to treat the contract as discharged by the breach by the other party, he may bring an action on a *quantum meruit*. Similarly, where one party prevents the other party from performing his obligations under a contract, that other party may sue on a *quantum meruit*.

De Bernady v. *Harding* (1853): a principal wrongfully revoked his agent's authority before the agent had completed his duties. HELD: the agent could recover on a *quantum meruit* for the work that he had done and the expenses he had incurred in the course of his duties.

See also *Planché* v. *Colburn* (1831).

NOTE: (*a*), (*b*), and (*c*) above are examples of *quantum meruit* as a remedy for breach of contract. The remedy is also available in certain circumstances where there has been no breach of contract. These circumstances are outside the scope of this chapter and are dealt with in Chapter XIX.

RECOVERY OF A REASONABLE PRICE FOR GOODS

22. The price of goods. Where, under a contract of sale, the buyer wrongfully neglects or refuses to pay for the goods according to the terms of the contract, the seller may maintain an action against him for the price of the goods: *Sale of Goods Act*, 1893, *s.* 49. Where the price is ascertainable in a manner provided in *s.* 8 (1) of the Act, the appropriate claim is a liquidated demand: the remedy is the award of the liquidated sum. But where the price is not determined in accordance with *s.* 8 (1), the buyer must pay a *reasonable price*. What is a reasonable price is a question of fact dependent on the circumstances of each particular case: *s.* 8 (2). (As to *s.* 8 (1), *see* para. **18** *above*.)

23. The action for a reasonable price. The action for a reasonable price for goods is a claim for an unliquidated sum. The remedy is the award of whatever sum the court (or the jury, if there is one) consider reasonable in the circumstances.

24. Quantum valebant. Before 1894, when the *Sale of Goods Act* came into operation, an action for the reasonable price of goods under a contract of sale took the form of a claim on a *quantum valebant* (as much as they are worth). This common law action is comparable to the *quantum meruit* in the case of services rendered. A claim on a *quantum valebant* may still be available today in cases where there has been no breach of contract. Such a claim would arise *quasi ex contractu*.

SPECIFIC PERFORMANCE

25. An equitable remedy. A decree of specific performance is issued by the court to the defendant, requiring him to carry out his undertaking exactly according to the terms of the contract. Specific performance is an equitable remedy and is available only where there is no adequate remedy at common law or under a statute. Generally, this means that specific performance is available only where the payment of a sum of money would not be an adequate remedy. Specific performance, is, therefore, an appropriate remedy in cases of breach of a contract for the sale or lease of land, or of breach of contract for the sale of something which is not available on the market, *e.g.* a rare book.

26. A discretionary remedy. The granting or withholding of a decree of specific performance is in the discretion of the court. The discretion is, however, exercised on certain well-established principles:

(*a*) Specific performance will never be granted where damages or a liquidated demand is appropriate and adequate.

(*b*) The court will take into account the conduct of the plaintiff, for he who comes to equity must come with clean hands.

(*c*) The action must be brought with reasonable promptness, for delay defeats the equities. Undue delay sufficient

XVIII. REMEDIES FOR BREACH OF CONTRACT 223

to cause the court to withhold an equitable remedy is known as laches. *See* **32** below.

(*d*) Specific performance will not be awarded where it would cause undue hardship on the defendant.

(*e*) A promise given for no consideration is not specifically enforceable, even if made under seal.

(*f*) Specific performance will not be awarded for breach of a contract of personal services.

(*g*) Specific performance will not be awarded for breach of an obligation to perform a series of acts which would need the constant supervision of the court. Thus building contracts are specifically enforceable only in certain special circumstances.

(*h*) Specific performance will not be awarded for breach of a contract wanting in mutuality, *i.e.* a contract which is not binding on both parties. Thus where a contract is voidable at the option of one party, he will not get specific performance against the other. This rule is of particular importance in connection with infants' voidable contracts.

INJUNCTION

27. Breach of a negative term. The Court has a discretionary power to grant an injunction to restrain the breach of a negative term of a contract even though the positive part of the contract is not specifically enforceable, *e.g.* in the case of a contract of personal service.

Lumley v. *Wagner* (1852): Joanna Wagner entered into a written contract with the plaintiff to sing in operas to be performed in his theatre during a period of three months. As part of this contract, Mademoiselle Wagner undertook "not to use her talents at any other theatre, nor in any concert or re-union, public or private, without the written authorisation of Mr. Lumley." In breach of her agreement, Mademoiselle Wagner engaged herself to sing at another theatre. The plaintiff brought this action for an injunction to restrain the breach of this negative term. HELD: the court had jurisdiction to grant an injunction to restrain the defendant from performing at any theatre other than the defendant's; it is no objection to the exercise of this jurisdiction that the plaintiff may have a right to recover damages at common law.

The rationale of the jurisdiction to grant an injunction to restrain a breach of contract was explained by Lord St.

Leonards, L.C., in *Lumley* v. *Wagner*: "Wherever this court has not proper jurisdiction to enforce specific performance, it operates to bind men's consciences, so far as they can be bound, to a true and literal performance of their agreements; and it will not suffer them to depart from their contracts at their pleasure, leaving the party with whom they have contracted to the mere chance of any damages which a jury may give. The exercise of this jurisdiction has, I believe, had a wholesome tendency towards the maintenance of that good faith which exists in this country to a much greater degree perhaps than in any other; and although the jurisdiction is not to be extended, yet a judge would desert his duty who did not act up to what his predecessors have handed down as the rule for his guidance in the administration of such an equity."

28. The equitable nature of the remedy. Where a contract of personal service contains a negative term, the enforcement of which would amount either to a decree of specific performance of the positive part of the contract or to a decree under which the defendant would have to choose between complying with the positive terms or remaining idle, the Court will not grant an injunction.

Ehrman v. *Bartholomew* (1898): an employee contracted to serve his employer for ten years and during that period not to engage in any other business. The employee left his employment in breach of the positive term and obtained other employment in breach of the negative term. HELD: an injunction would not be granted to restrain the breach of the negative term because, in the circumstances of the case, it would inflict undue hardship on the defendant (*i.e.* an injunction would force the defendant to choose between starvation or returning to his former employer).

Since an injunction is a discretionary remedy, the Court may limit it to what the Court considers reasonable in all the circumstances of the case. For example, where a negative term forbad the defendant to engage in "any trade, business, or calling, either relating to goods of any description sold or manufactured by the [plaintiff] or in any other business whatsoever" the Court severed the negative term. An injunction was granted, not to restrain the defendant from engaging in "any other business whatsoever," but framed so as to give the plaintiff a reasonable protection and no more: *William Robinson & Co., Ltd.* v. *Heuer* (1898).

Warner Bros. v. *Nelson* (1937): the defendant, a prominent film actress, entered into a contract with the plaintiffs by which she undertook not to render any services for or in any other photographic or stage or motion-picture production or business of any other person or engage in any other occupation during the term of employment without the written consent of the plaintiffs. The defendant, in breach of this agreement, made arrangements to work for another film company. The plaintiffs brought this action for an injunction. HELD: (*i*) the case was one in which it would be proper to grant an injunction unless to do so would be tantamount to specific performance or to remain idle; (*ii*) it would be impossible, therefore, to grant an injunction covering all the negative covenants in the contract; (*iii*) injunction granted in restricted terms, namely, in terms forbidding the defendant, without the consent of the plaintiffs, to render any services for or in any motion-picture or stage production for anyone other than the plaintiffs; (*iv*) the injunction to remain in force during the continuance of the contract or for three years, whichever is the shorter.

LIMITATION OF ACTIONS

29. The Limitation Act, 1939. The procedural right to bring an action for breach of contract may be extinguished by the passage of time under the provisions of the *Limitation Act, 1939*. Section 2 (1) of the Act provides that an action founded on a simple contract or in tort cannot be brought after the expiration of six years from the date on which the cause of action accrued. The legal right to an account, *e.g.* the right of a principal as against his agent, (*see* XVI, **16**) is governed by *s.* 2 (2) which provides that an action for an account shall not be brought in respect of any matter which arose more than six years before the commencement of the action. Section 2 (3) provides that an action upon a specialty, *i.e.* a promise given under seal, cannot be brought after the expiration of twelve years from the date on which the cause of action accrued.

In the case of simple contracts and specialties, the statutory periods of six years and twelve years, respectively, are expressed to run from the date on which the cause of action accrued. Time begins to run from the date on which the breach of contract was committed. Thus, in the event of an anticipatory breach, time will begin to run from the date of the breach and not from the date when performance became due.

30. The effect of fraud or mistake. It is provided by *s*. 26 of the *Limitation Act*, 1939, that where (*a*) the action is based upon the fraud of the defendant or his agent, or (*b*) the right of action is concealed by fraud, or (*c*) the action is for relief from the consequences of mistake, the statutory period of limitation does not begin to run until the plaintiff has discovered the fraud or mistake or could with reasonable diligence have discovered it.

Section 26 contains a proviso to the effect that nothing in the section enables any action to be brought to recover, or enforce any charge against, or set aside any transaction affecting any property which (i) in the case of fraud, has been purchased for valuable consideration by a person who was not a party to the fraud and did not at the time of the purchase know or have reason to believe that any fraud had been committed, or (ii) in the case of mistake, has been purchased for valuable consideration, subsequently to the transaction in which the mistake was made, by a person who did not know or have reason to believe that the mistake had been made.

31. The effect of disability. Section 22 of the *Limitation Act*, 1939, makes special provision for the extension of the statutory period of limitation in cases where the plaintiff is under a disability, *e.g.* on the grounds of infancy or of unsoundness of mind. The section provides that where a right of action accrues to a person who is under a disability, the action may be brought at any time before the expiration of six years from the date when the person ceased to be under the disability or has died, whichever event occurred first.

32. Fresh accrual of the right of action. It must be emphasised that the statutory rules limiting the right of action are procedural in nature. The rules set limits to a plaintiff's right to bring an action before the courts: it is the procedural right to bring an action which may be extinguished: the plaintiff's substantive rights remain unaffected yet he cannot seek a remedy in the courts. His substantive rights are said to be statute-barred. But where there is a fresh acknowledgment or part-payment of a debt or other liquidated pecuniary claim, the right of action is deemed for the purposes of the *Limitation Act*, 1939, to have accrued on and not before the date of the acknowledgment or last payment: *s.* 23. Accordingly, even where a right of action appears to be statute-barred, an acknowledgment or part payment of the debt will cause the right of action to be revived. The period of limitation will then run from the date of the acknowledgment or part payment.

33. Limitation of equitable claims. The *Limitation Act*, 1939, does not in general apply to claims for equitable relief. Claims for specific performance or injunctions or other equitable relief are excluded by *s.* 2 (7) of the Act, except in so far as any provision of *s.* 2 may be applied by analogy. Accordingly, where a claim in equity corresponds with an action at law for which statutory provision for limitation has been made, the court, in its equitable jurisdiction, adopts the statute as its own rule of procedure: *Knox* v. *Gye* (1872). Thus, for example, where a trustee by mistake of fact overpays one beneficiary to the detriment of another beneficiary, a claim by that beneficiary against the other for the recovery of his share will be barred six years after the accrual of the cause of action. Because the trustee's mistake is one of fact, the action is treated as analogous to the common law action of money had and received: *Re Robinson, McLaren* v. *Public Trustee* (1911). Similarly, an equitable claim to an account is regarded as analogous to a legal claim to an account, and is, accordingly, governed by *s.* 2 (2). *See* **28** above.

Apart from the exceptional cases where an equitable claim is regarded as analogous to one at law, the doctrine of laches applies to claims for equitable relief. The maxim is: *Delay defeats the equities.* But no rigid rule can be postulated as to the period of time in which an equitable claim must be brought. The court decides in each case as a matter of discretion whether the delay on the part of the plaintiff in bringing his action is sufficiently long to bar his claim. Examples of the application of the doctrine of laches may be found in the two cases set out below and also in *Leaf* v. *International Galleries* (1950), VIII, **13**.

Pollard v. *Clayton* (1855): the defendant undertook to extract and sell to the plaintiff all the coal in a specified mine. For a time the defendant sold this coal to the plaintiff, but he subsequently made deliveries to a third person, refusing to sell any more to the plaintiff. When the plaintiff discovered the defendant's breach, he communicated his objection but with no effect. The defendant continued in his refusal to sell the coal. Eleven months after making his objection, the plaintiff brought this action claiming specific performance of the contract. HELD: in the circumstances, the delay of eleven months was sufficient to bar the claim for specific performance.

Williams v. *Greatrex* (1956): by the terms of a written contract, a builder agreed to buy an area of land to be laid out in building plots. The contract provided that the purchaser was to be entitled to enter on each plot in order to build on it, the vendor being bound to convey each plot on payment of the balance of its price. The contract further provided that the purchase of all plots was to be completed within two years. The purchaser paid a deposit on plots 3 and 4 and began to build on them, but soon had to discontinue the work because of the antagonistic attitude of the vendor and the difficulty of obtaining building licences. Nine years after beginning to build, the purchaser attempted to complete the work but the vendor contracted to sell the plots to a third party. In the following year, the purchaser brought this action for specific performance of the contract of sale. HELD by the Court of Appeal: the purchaser was entitled to specific performance notwithstanding the delay of ten years. He was not barred by the doctrine of laches because he had an equitable title to plots 3 and 4 as a result of the contract of sale, and he had entered into possession.

PROGRESS TEST 18

1. What is an anticipatory breach of contract?
2. Outline the various remedies available for breach of contract.
3. What are:

    (a) substantial damages;
    (b) nominal damages; and
    (c) exemplary damages?

4. What questions will the court consider in its endeavours to assess the measure of damages?
5. Explain how the rule in *Hadley* v. *Baxendale* was refined and restated in *Victoria Laundry* v. *Newman*.
6. "Where one party is in breach of contract, there is a duty

XVIII. REMEDIES FOR BREACH OF CONTRACT 229

on the other to mitigate the loss occasioned by the breach." Explain this statement.

7. What is a penalty clause? How does a penalty differ from liquidated damages?

8. "In a case of breach by non-payment of a specific sum of money, it is advantageous to the plaintiff to make a liquidated demand rather than to claim unliquidated damages." Explain this statement.

9. Distinguish between a *quantum meruit* claim and a claim for damages. In what circumstances is a *quantum meruit* claim appropriate?

10. In what circumstances does an unpaid seller bring an action for a *reasonable price* for goods?

11. Compare *quantum meruit* with *quantum valebant*.

12. Explain how the *Limitation Act*, 1939, fixes the period within which an action must be brought.

13. What is specific performance? Explain the principles on which the court awards or withholds the remedy.

14. In what circumstances is an injunction the appropriate remedy for breach of contract?

15. A enters a contract with B, a portrait painter, to have his portrait painted for £250. After the first sitting, B tells A that he does not wish to complete the painting, and that he (A) need not bother to attend further sittings. Nevertheless, A persists in his attempts to get B to finish the painting, until the day B is killed in a motor accident. Consider the legal position.

16. A large education authority invited tenders for the supply of school furniture as and when required. The tender submitted by C, a furniture manufacturer, was accepted. The first order from the authority was for 200 desks to be delivered during August. Owing to a breach of contract on the part of C's timber supplier, D, it was not possible for C to deliver the desks until mid-September. The education authority accepted delivery of the desks, but C received a letter from the authority informing him that no further orders would be placed with him, since he could not be relied upon to deliver promptly. C now intends to bring an action against D for breach of contract. Consider the factors the court will take into account when assessing damages.

17. E, a jam manufacturer, orders a consignment of strawberries from a grower, F. The price agreed on by the parties is £460. F sends the consignment to E according to the contract, but E refuses to accept delivery, and the strawberries are returned to F. The carrier's charges for this consignment amount to £8, which F pays. F sells the strawberries to another buyer for £420. If F brings an action against E for breach of contract, how much do you think he is likely to recover by way of damages?

THE LAW OF CONTRACT

18. G enters a written agreement with H under which G promises to deliver certain goods to H on a specified date. The contract contains a term providing that liquidated damages of £60 will be payable by G to H in the event of any of the following breaches:

(a) If the goods are not of the stipulated quality;
(b) If the goods are not delivered on the contract date;
(c) If less than the stipulated quantity is delivered.

G delivers the goods of the right quality, and the right quantity, but one day after the stipulated date. H accepts the goods. H now intends to bring an action against G for breach of contract. Advise him as to whether he can claim £60 as liquidated damages. Assume that the breach caused H no actual loss.

19. There is an agreement between J and K, a house painter, by which K undertakes to paint the interior of J's house. The parties made no mention of remuneration during their negotiations. K completes the job satisfactorily, and then sends a bill to J. J refused to pay, saying that K's charges are unreasonable. Advise K.

20. L, a ship-owner, enters a contract with M, for the carriage of a certain consignment of sheet steel, at an agreed rate of freight. The goods actually delivered to L for shipment consist partly of sheet steel, and partly of general merchandise, for which higher freight rates obtain. L accepted the goods entirely and they were stowed on his ship. Advise L as to whether he can claim from M the higher rate of freight.

21. N has agreed to sell O a rare postage stamp for £500. N subsequently discovers that P is prepared to pay £750 for the stamp. If N neglects to deliver the stamp to O, what remedy would you advise O to seek?

22. Q, an actor, has entered a contract with a television company to appear in a series of television plays, to take place weekly over a period of one year. The contract provides that Q shall not, during the contract period, engage in any other work without the consent of the television company. Q has now entered another contract, this time with a film company, under which he is to act in a film to be made during the television contract period. The television company seek your advice as to whether Q can be restrained from acting for the film company. Advise.

CHAPTER XIX

QUASI-CONTRACT

THE MEANING OF QUASI-CONTRACT

1. The circumstances generally. Where, in all justice, one person should be held accountable to another for a sum of money, and no action lies for its recovery in contract or in tort, the law will, in certain circumstances, allow an action in so-called quasi-contract. Also, an action in quasi-contract will sometimes lie as an alternative to damages for breach of contract.

2. The characteristics of quasi-contract. Although this part of the law is called quasi-contract, there is a sharp division of opinion as to whether it has any real connection with contract at all. The characteristics of a quasi-contractual right are:

(*a*) It is always a right to claim a sum of money: usually, but not always, a liquidated claim.

(*b*) Unlike a contractual right, a quasi-contractual right does not stem from agreement; quasi-contractual rights and obligations are, as in tort, imposed by the general law.

(*c*) Quasi-contractual rights and obligations exist between specific persons, as in contract: in tort, on the other hand, rights exist against the whole world.

3. The basis of quasi-contract. There is no generally accepted juridical theory of quasi-contract into which all the cases can be neatly fitted. There are two conflicting theories to be considered:

(*a*) That quasi-contract is a form of implied contract, and that a quasi-contractual right will exist only according to usual rules of implied terms in contracts: *Re Diplock* (1948).

(*b*) That the courts have a jurisdiction, quite apart from implied contract, to recognise claims where one person should, in justice, account to another for a sum of money. That is to say, a claim may be made in any case of unjust enrichment. There is considerable judicial support for this theory: *The Fibrosa Case* (1943); *Nelson* v. *Larholt* (1948).

ACTIONS IN QUASI-CONTRACT

4. The particular circumstances. An action in quasi-contract may be allowed in any of the following circumstances:

(a) Where the plaintiff has paid money to a third person to the defendant's use.

(b) Where the plaintiff has paid money to the defendant under a mistake of fact.

(c) Where the plaintiff has paid money to the defendant and the consideration moving from the defendant has totally failed.

(d) Where the plaintiff claims on an account stated with the defendant.

(e) Where the plaintiff claims on a *quantum meruit* not based on a contract with the defendant.

5. Money paid to the defendant's use. The plaintiff has a quasi-contractual claim where he has paid a sum of money to a third person to the use of the defendant. This may happen in one of two ways:

(a) Where the defendant expressly requests or allows the plaintiff to make a payment or incur an obligation on his behalf. It seems here that the basis of the action is the implied promise by the defendant to re-imburse the plaintiff, *e.g.* the implied indemnity given by a principal debtor to a guarantor.

(b) Where the plaintiff is compelled by law to make a payment to a third party, and the payment discharges the defendant's obligation to that third party.

Brooks Wharf v. *Goodman Bros.* (1937): the defendant stored a consignment of imported skins, on which he was liable to pay customs duty, in the plaintiff's bonded warehouse. The skins were stolen before the defendants had paid the duty. The plaintiff was, consequently, under a statutory obligation to pay the customs duty to the authorities. The plaintiff paid the duty and then, in this action, claimed the amount from the defendants. HELD: the sum paid was recoverable.

6. Money paid under a mistake of fact. Where the plaintiff was induced to pay money to the defendant by a mistake of fact (not law), the sum paid is recoverable.

Larner v. *L.C.C.* (1949): L, who was in the employment of the L.C.C., was called up for military service. Now the L.C.C. had resolved to pay its employees who went on military service the difference between their service pay and their former civilian pay. In order to benefit from this resolution, employees had to undertake to notify the L.C.C. of any change in their service pay. L did not notify the L.C.C. of his increase in service pay, and, in consequence, he was overpaid by the council. HELD: the amount overpaid was recoverable.
NOTE: But where overpayment is made on a misconstruction of regulations, and the payee does not know of the mistake, the mistake is regarded as one of law, and recovery is not permitted: *Holt* v. *Markham* (1923).

7. Money paid on a total failure of consideration. Where the plaintiff has paid money to the defendant under a valid contract, and the defendant totally fails to perform his contractual duty, the plaintiff may elect to bring his action in contract or quasi-contract. In quasi-contract, the amount recoverable is limited to the sum paid: in contract, the rules relating to the measure of damages apply. It is a matter of procedural tactics whether a plaintiff, having this choice, will prefer to claim in quasi-contract or contract. In *Wilkinson* v. *Lloyd* (1845), a plaintiff succeeded in his action to recover money paid to the defendant who had totally failed in his promise under the contract. The plaintiff could have brought an action for damages, thus regarding the contract as still alive, but he preferred to regard the contract as discharged and to sue in quasi-contract.

8. Account stated. Where there has been a series of transactions between the parties, followed by an agreed balance payable by one party to the other, the agreed balance is known as an account stated. It may be regarded as an admission of indebtedness by the party owing. Thus if X sells to Y £300 worth of goods; then Y sells to X £100 worth of goods; then Y supplies to X £50 worth of services; then the parties agree in writing that, on balance, Y owes X £150, that is an account stated. Where an action is brought on an account stated, it is not necessary to prove the series of transactions: the plaintiff must prove the account stated only. But it is open to the defendant to rebut the evidence of an account stated. Accordingly, it may be preferable to regard account stated as a principle of procedure, and not one of quasi-contract: *Camillo Tank Co.* v. *Alexandria Engineering Works* (1921).

9. Quantum meruit. The *quantum meruit* claim as a remedy for breach of contract has already been considered. The claim is also available where there is no contract between the parties, and yet, in justice, reasonable remuneration should be paid. These circumstances may arise where work has been done under a void contract, or where the courts cannot infer a contract between the parties.

Craven-Ellis v. *Canons, Ltd.* (1936): C-E rendered services to the company as managing director. The contract under which he was appointed was void. C-E sought to recover remuneration (i) by way of damages on a liquidated demand, and (ii) in the alternative, on a *quantum meruit*. HELD: (i) the claim for damages failed because the contract was void *ab initio*; (ii) the claim on the *quantum meruit* should succeed.

William Lacey, Ltd. v. *Davis* (1957): the plaintiff, a builder, performed certain services for the defendant in circumstances giving rise to an inference that there was a mutual understanding that a certain building was to be reconstructed and that the plaintiff would get the contract. The services were given in connection with a tender for the construction work, but amounted to more than normally given gratuitously by a builder submitting a tender. The plaintiff claimed (i) damages and (ii) in the alternative, on *quantum meruit*. HELD: (i) a contract between the parties could not be implied, therefore no damages could be awarded; (ii) reasonable remuneration was recoverable on the *quantum meruit*.

PROGRESS TEST 19

1. What are the characteristics of a quasi-contractual right?
2. Consider the two main theories of the basis of quasi-contract. Which theory do you prefer?
3. Can you find a relationship between the theories of the basis of frustration and those of the basis of quasi-contract?

XIX. QUASI-CONTRACT

4. In what circumstances will the court allow an action in quasi-contract? Give examples.

5. A took a lease of B's house. C took a sub-lease from A. A has fallen into arrears with rent payable to B, who is threatening to re-enter the property. C, therefore, pays A's arrears of rent to B. C now brings an action against A to recover the sum paid. Will he succeed? Give reasons for your answer.

6. D has worked for the XYZ Company as a factory manager for three months. He has just been informed that his appointment was void as it was not made in a manner required by the Memorandum of Association. D has not yet received any remuneration from the XYZ Company. On what grounds can he claim payment?

APPENDIX I

EXAMINATION TECHNIQUE

1. Two types of question. The student preparing for an elementary law examination must train himself to answer two kinds of examination question:

(a) *Text-book questions*, i.e. requiring the exposition of discussion of a particular topic.

(b) *Problems*, i.e. requiring the application of legal principles to a given situation.

2. Text-book questions. These are designed to test the student's knowledge and understanding of the subject. Such questions require the statement, criticism, or discussion of principles. Here are some points for guidance:

(a) *Read the question very carefully.* In any examination, there are always students who fail to do this. Underline any parts of the question which seem to you to be significant. Notice particularly what you are told to do.

(b) *Make an outline plan of your answer.* In order to do this, you must try to see exactly what the examiner wants. If the question is widely drawn, you will need a widely drawn plan. If the question is narrowly drawn, you will need a narrowly drawn plan. Make sure that the aim and scope of your plan exactly satisfy the question. It is at this stage that you must discard irrelevancies. It is at this stage that you must settle what goes into the answer. Your outline plan will probably consist of four or five key sentences arranged in logical sequence. (Each of these key sentences will probably develop into a paragraph of your final answer.) Jot down the names of cases and statutes you wish to cite.

(c) *Write an answer based on the plan.* Stick to the plan and try to set out the answer in an attractive way. Let the plan "show through" the answer so that your work has an obvious shape to it. If you think that subheadings will help to underline the form of your answer, then use them.

(d) *Express yourself with clarity and precision.* Your style of writing is personal, but in law examinations it is usually best to aim at simplicity. Never use a long sentence when a shorter one will do. Never use a long sentence when the ideas contained in it can be more simply expressed in two or three short sentences. Keep close to the line of argument in your outline plan. Above all, do not "waffle": the examiner will always recognise this for what it is, and it will gain you no marks.

3. Problems. These are designed to discover whether the student can (i) recognise the legal principles which are applicable to any given situation, and (ii) apply these principles. Here are some points for guidance:

(a) *Read the problem very carefully.* Be sure that you have considered all the facts stated. Do not bother how these facts could be proved: just accept them as facts. Notice what the instructions are. You may be required, *e.g.* to advise X, or to comment on the legal position, or to say whether you think A and B are contractually bound. In your answer, you should carry out these instructions exactly.

(b) *Decide what principles should be applied.*

(c) *Make an outline plan of your answer.* The plan should consist of the principles briefly stated. The sequence should be such as to allow you to bring out the relationship between these principles, *e.g.* where you need to apply a rule which is an exception to the general rule, state the general rule and follow it with the exception; also, where two conflicting rules seem to apply, state both rules. Jot down the names of cases to be cited. Complete your plan by making a brief note of the result when relevant principles are applied to the case in question.

(d) *Write an answer based on the plan.* Aim at a *concise* statement of the rules applicable to the problem. Give an authority for each rule stated. The name of a case is usually sufficient. Do not launch out on a long rigmarole about the facts of cited cases. The examiner is looking for an ability to solve legal problems, he is not trying to test your memory. When your brief statement of the law is complete, come immediately to the solution of the problem. It may be necessary to compare the facts in the problem with the facts of decided cases. Mention only those facts which are relevant to the point under discussion. Do not succumb to the temptation to display the detailed knowledge you have of all the irrelevant details. The examiner is interested to know whether you are able to identify and isolate the facts which are of legal significance. These are the only facts with which you should concern yourself. Where the answer to the problem depends upon a fact which has been deliberately omitted, you should say so. In this event, you will have to supply the alternative facts yourself, and model the rest of the answer accordingly. This may mean that the final solution of the problem will branch out into two limbs as alternatives.

4. Sitting the examination.
If you have prepared yourself thoroughly, you should be able to enter the examination room with confidence. If you have disciplined yourself beforehand to write good answers, you should have nothing to worry about. Here are some hints which may help you to get the best out of yourself:

(a) *Read the paper through several times.* Mark the questions which you know you can answer well.

(b) *Make outline plans of all the questions to be attempted.* Time spent on this is not wasted. In fact, few students can write good answers without doing this planning. In a three-hour examination, it is worth spending 20–30 minutes in studying the questions and making the plans. (Do not be put off by other candidates around you who may be writing answers from the moment they sit down.) Divide the remaining time *equally* between the questions to be attempted, so that you know exactly how long you have for each answer.

(c) *Write your answers.* Begin with the questions which you can answer well. Stick to your time schedule or you will be rushed at the end. If you do not finish an answer within the time you planned, *leave it and go on to the next question.* Leave a space so that you can come back to it if there is time at the end.

(d) *Read your work.* Try to leave five or ten minutes at the end of the examination for reading and checking for small mistakes of spelling, punctuation, etc.

APPENDIX II

EXAMINATION QUESTIONS

OFFER AND ACCEPTANCE

1. On 1 June Jack posts a letter to Jill offering to sell his car to her for £500. Discuss if, and when, a contract is formed between them in each of the following situations.

(a) Jill receives the letter on 2 June. On 4 June she posts a reply accepting the offer. This reply reaches Jack on June 5 but he had sold the car to Bill on 3 June.

(b) Jill receives the letter on 2 June and posts a reply on that day, saying "£500 is too much, but I will give you £450 for the car." Jack receives this letter on 3 June.

(c) Jill receives the letter on 2 June and posts a reply accepting the offer on that day. This reply goes astray in the post, and does not reach Jack until 10 June. On 8 June Jack had decided that he would not sell the car but would keep it for his own use.
Intermediate Laws.

2. Advise the parties as to their legal position in the following cases:

(a) A signs a memorandum in which he acknowledges that he has agreed to take a lease of B's house for seven years from 1 October at a rent of £500 per annum "subject to the terms of a formal lease to be hereafter executed."

(b) C, while window-shopping after shop hours, sees in the window of a general store a colour television set marked, "Special offer—demonstration colour set £150." He immediately goes home, writes a letter addressed to the manager of the store stating that he accepts the offer and catches the 8 p.m. post that night. The next morning he attends at the store but although the manager admits receipt of the letter, he refuses to sell the set to C. *Intermediate Laws.*

3. Lulabelle, having lost her jewel-encrusted gold cigarette case, puts a notice on a tree near her house which reads as follows:

"Thirty pounds reward to the first honest person who enables me to recover my lost gold cigarette case. All communications should be made in writing and sent to the address given below."

Alonzo, a rogue, having seen the reward notice, finds the cigarette case two months later. Alonzo keeps the cigarette case for a fortnight but then decides to return it and claim the reward. Alonzo takes the case to Lulabelle's place of business and leaves it there together with a note as to his name and address. Unknown to Alonzo, Lulabelle has earlier inserted a very small notice in the columns of the local newspaper stating that the reward notice has been withdrawn. Discuss the rights and liabilities, if any, of Lulabelle and Alonzo. *Intermediate Laws.*

4. On 1 January D wrote to C offering to sell him his motor car for £500. On 1 June C replied saying, "I accept your offer, but I consider that £450 is enough." D had in fact sold the car to X on 1 May.

C consults you as to his rights: advise him. *C.I.S.*

5. L wrote to M offering him 10 tons of groundnuts. The offer was posted on 1 January. Due to abnormal conditions there was post delay and L's letter did not reach M until 10 January when M at once replied, accepting L's offer.

M's letter was also delayed and it did not reach L until 15 January. L, having expected a reply in normal course of post not later than 5 January at latest, had sold the groundnuts to N on 14 January, having by then assumed that M was not interested in the offer.

M, having agreed to re-sell the groundnuts to O at a profit, seeks your advice. Advise him. *C.I.S.*

6. Discuss with reasons whether the offers in the following cases have been validly accepted.

(a) P, a poet, sends his latest volume of poetry to B with a covering letter in which P informs B that unless the volume is returned to P within a week, B will be deemed to have accepted P's offer to sell the book to him for £1. B wraps up the book with a view to returning it, but forgets to do so.

(b) S, a student, has lost his lecture notes. He advertises his loss in a daily newspaper and offers to pay the finder £2 provided he (the finder) inserts a reply in the "Lost and Found" columns of the newspaper giving his address. F, who has found the notes, does so, but X refuses to pay the reward to him, having in the meantime secured another set of notes.

(c) Q offers to S £2000 for S's country cottage. S writes to Q saying "I take it that you will pay separately for the furniture in the cottage." Q replies to the effect that he had intended to pay £2000 for the cottage including its furnishings. S now accepts Q's offer, but Q denies the existence of a contract claiming that S had tried to attach conditions to his acceptance.

(d) O offers to sell to M for £20 his (O's) set of Shakespeare's collected works. M rings up O to tell him that he accepts his offer, but O is unable to hear what M says since there is some interference on the line. O has now sold the books to Z.

C.I.S.

7. (a) Describe the general rules of the law of contract concerning the acceptance of an offer.

(b) X has enquired at the Seaview Hotel in Newtown about holiday accommodation for himself and his family. The hotel manager replies, giving the necessary information, and adds: "Since this is the only room left for the fortnight in question I must ask you to reply by return by first-class mail if you wish to accept my offer." X receives the manager's letter on Friday. What would be the legal position if the manager refuses to accept X's booking and X has

  (i) travelled to Newtown on Saturday and has handed in a note at the hotel accepting the offer;
  (ii) accepted the manager's offer by telegram sent on Friday;
  (iii) accepted the manager's offer by second-class mail posting this letter on Friday. The letter reaches the hotel on the following Tuesday;
  (iv) accepted the manager's offer by first-class mail on Friday, but his letter was misdirected and did not reach the hotel until Wednesday of the following week? *A.E.B.*

8. (a) What is the position in law where the terms of an offer are not certain? In what ways could vague terms in an offer be made certain?

(b) A had agreed to supply B in 1968 with fixed monthly quantities of fuel oil for B's central heating installation at an agreed price. The contract gave B an option to purchase further quantities of oil in 1969, but nothing was said about price or frequency of delivery. When, in 1969, B wished to exercise his option A claimed that it was not legally binding on him since nothing had been said in the original contract about the terms on which the oil was to be supplied in 1969. Advise the parties. *A.E.B.*

9. (a) How far do the rules concerning the acceptance of an offer by post differ from those concerning other modes of acceptance? Illustrate your answer by reference to decided cases.

(b) A, by letter, offers to sell his house to B for £5000. What will be the legal position in the following cases?

(i) B replies by return of post accepting the offer. As soon, however, as he has posted his letter of acceptance he has second thoughts on the matter and sends a telegram to A withdrawing his acceptance. A receives the telegram before the letter of acceptance.

(ii) B is an invalid and cannot get out of the house. He writes a letter accepting the offer made by A and hands the letter to a postman who promises to post it. Through an oversight the postman does not post the letter until two days later and in the meantime B has received a further letter from A revoking the earlier offer. *A.E.B.*

10. (a) In what circumstances will an offeror not be able to withdraw his offer?

(b) S, by letter, has offered on 1 January to sell his grand piano to P for £50 and has given P until 8 January to reply. If P accepts the offer will a binding contract come into existence if:

(i) P accepted on 10 January;

(ii) P accepted the offer on 6 January without knowing that a letter of revocation written by S was in the post at that time;

(iii) P accepted the offer on 6 January while away from home not knowing that S's letter of revocation was awaiting him there;

(iv) P accepted the offer on 6 January after having been told the previous day by T, a third party, that he (T) had bought the piano from S? *A.E.B.*

11. (a) "An offer must be firm." What does this mean? Explain.

(b) A wrote to B: "I am prepared to offer my Jaguar car to you for £1000. You may have the car examined by a skilled engineer if you wish." B replied: "I accept your offer and enclose my cheque for £1000. There is no need for me to have your Jaguar tested as I know its performance well." A now refuses to deliver the car to B. State with reasons whether a valid contract has come into existence. *A.E.B.*

12. (a) What is meant by a tender? In what circumstances will a tender constitute a valid offer? Illustrate your answer by suitable examples.

(b) The governors of a school invite tenders for the supply of coke for the school boilers. X submits a tender for the supply of coke at a stated price "in such quantities and at such times as the governors may require." The governors accept X's tender. What would be the legal position if:

(i) the governors decide to convert the school boilers to oil firing and order no coke at all;

(ii) the governors order a quantity of coke in the middle of a cold spell and X, who has run out of stock, is unable to supply the coke at once;

(iii) the market price of coke has risen and X refuses to supply a quantity of coke ordered by the governors unless he is offered a better price. *A.E.B.*

13. (*a*) "A vague offer is no offer." Discuss and explain what is meant by vagueness in this context.

(*b*) A sold to B a painting for £1000 "on the usual credit terms." Consider the validity of this contract if:

(i) there were no "usual" credit terms in the trade;

(ii) there existed "usual" credit terms in the trade but B, a newcomer to the trade, did not know what they were;

(iii) there existed in the trade two different sets of credit terms, one of which was favourable to the seller while the other was favourable to the buyer. *A.E.B.*

14. (*a*) Explain what is meant by (i) lapse of an offer and (ii) a counter-offer.

(*b*) X, a prominent citizen in Seaport, advertised in a local newspaper that he would give £100 to any resident of Seaport who swam across a local lake on Christmas Day, 1970. Y accepted this challenge by X, but X revoked his offer when Y was only half way across the lake.

What is the legal liability (if any) of X to Y? *Bankers.*

15. (*a*) Generally an offer can be accepted by the offeree unless and until it is revoked. Explain how this rule operates where a letter of acceptance by the offeree and a letter of revocation by the offeror are posted simultaneously.

(*b*) Albert in Cumberland posts to Bertram in Cornwall a letter accepting an offer made by Bertram to Albert. An hour later Albert sends Bertram a telegram which reaches Bertram before the letter. What is the legal position:

(i) if the telegram states "I refuse your offer";

(ii) if it states "Please treat my letter of acceptance as cancelled"? *Bankers.*

16. (*a*) Mrs L loses her handbag. She puts an advertisement in a shop window offering £10 for its return. M finds it and returns it to her. Later on M sees the advertisement. Is M entitled to the £10 reward?

(*b*) On Monday Frank offers to sell his motor scooter to Gregory for £40, the offer to remain open until noon on Thursday. On Wednesday Frank sells it to Henry for £45. On Thursday morning at 10 a.m. Gregory posts a letter to Frank accepting his offer but the letter does not reach him until Friday. Indicate the legal position. *Bankers.*

17. On 1 January 1971, Albert gave Brown, in writing, the option to buy Albert's car for £725 during the next seven days. Between 2 p.m. and 3 p.m. on 2 January, Albert wrote to Brown revoking the offer. At 5 p.m. the same afternoon, Brown posted a letter accepting the offer and, at 9.30 p.m. the same evening, he received Albert's revocation of the offer. At 10 a.m. on 3 January, Albert received Brown's acceptance through the post.

What is the legal position? *Bankers.*

INTENTION TO CREATE LEGAL RELATIONS

1. Horatio, an employee of Triflerings (Cochlea) Ltd., is head of "The Bauble Dippers and Dimplers Union," all of whose members are employees of the company. Acting on behalf of the Union, Horatio enters into an agreement with the Company whereby, in consideration of the Company giving all its employees a 50p a week rise, the Union will cease to arrange token strikes which coincide with mid-week soccer matches. The Company, finding Horatio a nuisance, send him a letter which states "as and when you may wish to tender your written resignation the Company will make you an *ex gratia* payment of £5000."

Horatio, who has trouble with his wife, tells her that he will pay her £35 per week if she will go back to her mother in Scotland for two years. His wife goes the next day taking the car with her and as a result Horatio has to arrange to be given a lift to and from work in a car owned by Manuel. In return for this service it becomes customary for Horatio to fill up the car's petrol tank once a week.

On Friday 13 August Horatio is forced to declare a token strike in order that his Union members may see Cochlea United play Mabbleswick in a pre-season "friendly." The same day Horatio hears that his wife is claiming twelve weeks arrears of money and that Manuel is threatening to sue him for £15 on the basis that Horatio has not put any petrol in the car for six weeks. Horatio would like to tender his written resignation, claim the £5000, and retire to Islington but wishes first to be advised as to the legal position in respect of all the above matters. Advise him.

Intermediate Laws.

2. (a) How far is it true to say that every agreement of a commercial nature is in law binding as a contract?

(b) XY Ltd. have entered into the undermentioned agreements. State with reasons whether these agreements will be legally binding on the company.

(i) A service agreement for five years with the company secretary, S, which provdes that at the end of the five-year period the company will "favourably consider" an application by S for a renewal of his contract.

(ii) An agreement with E Inc., an American company, by which XY Ltd. were appointed sole agents in the United Kingdom for E's products. The agreement provides that "it is not entered into as a formal or legal agreement and that it will not be subject to the jurisdiction of the courts of law."

C.I.S.

3. (a) "The common law does not require any positive intention to create a legal obligation as an element of contract." Discuss.

(b) John, when visiting the house of Fred, notices that Fred's wife throws away the labels from a type of tinned food. He asks whether he may have the labels since he wants to enter the competition for which the labels serve as entrance coupons. Fred's wife says: "You may have them, provided you will give me half of your winnings, if any." John agrees, enters the competition and wins a prize of £1000. Consider whether Fred's wife will be entitled to claim £500 from John. *A.E.B.*

4. (a) X agreed to donate £500 to the Y charity but he now refuses to pay. Can the charity compel him to do so?

(b) Jack promised to buy his wife, Jill, a new coat, but he now refuses to do so. Can he be compelled to do so?

(c) A, B, and C decided to enter for a competition advertised in a newspaper. The prize was to be £1000 and the entry fee 15p. They agreed that the entry form should be in the name of A only, that the fee be paid equally by them and that, if A won, the prize money be shared equally. A has been declared the winner and has received £1000. He now refuses to share it with B and C. Can he be compelled to do so? *Bankers.*

CONSIDERATION

1. (a) Arthur, a wine dealer, regularly supplies wine to Freda who pays him every month. At the end of May Freda pays her bill and tells Arthur that, due to financial difficulties, she will not be able to afford any more wine. David, a friend of Freda, knows of

her financial difficulties and, early in June, he tells Arthur to supply Freda with wine every week and he, David, will pay the bills every two months. Arthur supplies wine to Freda during June and July but David refuses to pay the bill when Arthur presents it to him on 1 August. Advise Arthur as to his remedies, if any.

(b) Henry offers a reward of ten pounds for information leading to the recovery of his watch which has been stolen. Some days later P.C. Dixon arrests Joe for housebreaking and discovers Henry's watch in Joe's possession. Advise Dixon whether he is entitled to the ten pounds reward. *Intermediate Laws.*

2. (a) Distinguish between executory, executed, and past consideration. Are there any, and if so what, exceptions to the rule that past consideration is no consideration?

(b) James, who operates a petrol-filling station, promises his pump-attendants a bonus of 10 per cent of the profits for the year ending 31 December next. On the strength of this promise, the pump-attendants do their best to increase trade by giving polite and efficient service. Advise James whether he can, with impunity, revoke his promise. *Intermediate Laws.*

3. (a) Talad, a part-time fireman, is walking home when he hears Jones shouting that his house is on fire. As Talad is helping to put out the blaze Jones calls out that his daughter is trapped on the second floor and that he will give £1000 to anyone who will rescue her. Talad rushes into the blazing house and rescues the daughter. When Talad later claims the £1000 Jones refuses to pay. Advise Talad.

(b) In March 1970 Wilhelm agrees to hire his amphibious car to McNab for the months of July and August for £100. In April Isaac offers to buy the car from Wilhelm for £2000 but Wilhelm explains that he cannot sell at that time due to his agreement with McNab. Isaac tells Wilhelm that he is not to worry about the agreement as he, Isaac, will see that McNab gets the car as agreed. On this assurance Wilhelm sells the car to Isaac. In June Isaac decides that the car is just the thing for his own fishing holiday and he writes to McNab telling him that he will not be able to have the car as arranged.

Discuss the rights and liabilities, if any, of McNab, Wilhelm, and Isaac. *Intermediate Laws.*

4. X agreed to repair Y's garden fence for £5. Z owned an adjoining garden and wanted to plant some climbing roses to screen his side of the fence and, since it was late in the year, he wanted the fence mended quickly. Z therefore approached X and

said "Do the job for Y and I will give you £2." "Right," said X; and he did the job.

X has now demanded the £2 from Z who has refused to pay: "You've already been paid for the work by Y," he said. Advise X.

C.I.S.

5. "Past consideration is no consideration." Discuss.

B, a shopkeeper, wanted to take a holiday; so he asked A, a friend, to take care of the shop during the ten days of his absence. A agreed to do this. B went on holiday and A did keep shop for him. A week after B had returned from his holiday he said to A "I will give you £50 by way of reward for your help in the shop."

A now claims the £50 from B, but B has refused to pay it. Advise A.

C.I.S.

6. (a) Discuss the principle of equitable (promissory) estoppel in relation to the doctrine of consideration.

(b) C is buying paraffin regularly from D, a dealer, who charges C's current account with the cost of the orders. From time to time C sends D a cheque to clear his account. In March of this year C sent a cheque for £30, this being the amount he believed he owed D. D informs him, however, that his debt stands at £12 only. C is delighted to hear this and he at once orders from D a new paraffin heater for £18 to make up the balance of his cheque. In April D informs C that through an unfortunate error some of C's supplies had been charged to another customer and that therefore C's March account had in fact been £30. D claims the balance of £18. Discuss whether he will succeed.

A.E.B.

7. (a) How far is the *sufficiency* of consideration necessary for the formation of a valid contract?

(b) Tom, a young man about town, has been living above his means for many years and is now facing bankruptcy. His aunt Agatha who is keen to see him settle down at last has introduced him to a young lady with a view to marriage. In order to give Tom a decent start in his married life, Agatha would like to see all his debts cleared. She writes to all of Tom's creditors and offers to pay half his outstanding debts on condition that the creditors accept this payment in full settlement of the debts. All the creditors agree and are duly paid by Agatha. Tom, who has married the young lady, a wealthy heiress, is now presented with a demand from John, one of his former creditors, for the balance of the original debt. John has read somewhere about the rule in *Pinnel's case* and believes that he would succeed in a court action. Advise Tom.

A.E.B.

8. (a) Explain what is meant by the principle in the *High Trees* case (1947).

(b) Jim, a cyclist, is knocked down by a car driven by Peter and sustains injuries. Peter, who is a prospective Parliamentary candidate, fears that if he were to be the defendant in a running down action his political career might be imperilled. On his own initiative, Peter offers Jim by way of settlement, £500 at once and another £1000 payable in four years' time. Jim is satisfied with this offer and does not bring an action against Peter. Four years later when the second payment falls due, Peter refuses to pay, having in the meantime given up his political ambitions. State with reasons whether Jim would be successful if he were to sue Peter for the £1000. *A.E.B.*

9. (a) What is meant by past consideration? In what circumstances, if at all, will it be treated as valuable consideration?

(b) Green, a wealthy man of eighty, has just lost his wife. His five children agree that they must provide a home for their father and Helen, an unmarried daughter, agrees to give up her job as a nurse and move into the old man's house and look after him. When Green dies five years later, his estate is divided equally among his children and the four who have not looked after their father jointly agree to pay Helen £5000 for the interruption in her career and the consequent loss of earnings. Subsequently, however, they refuse to pay. Discuss whether Helen is entitled to the promised £5000. *A.E.B.*

10. (a) What is "valuable" consideration? Explain the circumstances in which consideration will not be deemed to be "valuable."

(b) X is the manager of a café owned by the Y Co. Ltd. There have been complaints from customers about cleanliness and the quality of service and the managing director of Y Co. Ltd. has decided to visit the café for an inspection. X, who is afraid that he might lose his job, offers to the staff of the café £1 per head if they all turn up on time on the day of the visit and clean the café properly before the managing director arrives. The visit has passed off successfully, but X now refuses to honour his promise to the staff. State, with reasons, whether he is bound to so do.
A.E.B.

11. Can the following promises be enforced by law:

(a) a promise by A to B that, if C paints A's house, A will pay B £100;

(b) promise by P to Q, a policeman, that if Q recovers some goods which have been stolen from P, then P will pay Q £100;

(c) promise by X to Z that, if Y will accept 50p in the £ in full settlement of a debt which Z owes Y, X will similarly accept 50p in the £ in full settlement of a debt which Z owes X?

Bankers.

THE TERMS OF A CONTRACT

1. "I do not think that what is a fundamental term has ever been closely defined. It must be something, I think, narrower than a condition of the contract, for it would be limiting the exceptions too much to say that they applied only to breaches of warranty. It is, I think, something which underlies the whole contract so that, if it is not complied with, the performance becomes something totally different from that which the contract contemplates."— Devlin, J. in *Smeaton Hanscomb* v. *Sassoon Setty* (1953).

Discuss this statement in the light of the House of Lords decision in the Suisse Atlantique case (1966).

Intermediate Laws.

2. "When a company inserts in printed conditions an exemption clause purporting to exempt them from all and every breach, that is not readily to be contrued or considered as exempting them from liability for a fundamental breach; for the good reason that it is only intended to avail them when they are carrying out the contract in substance; and not when they are breaking it in a manner which goes to the very root of the contract." Discuss.

Intermediate Laws.

3. Fred books a ticket on the *s.s. Malaise* for a "ten day common market cruise." The front of the ticket states in bold type that it is issued "subject to the conditions on page 7." Page 7 contains the following: "The company accepts no responsibility for any personal injury or loss of life or any other form of inconvenience suffered by passengers whilst on board this ship." This statement is in small italic type and Fred is unable to read it as he has very poor eye-sight.

When joining the ship Fred leaves two cases in the port "Left Luggage Office" and receives a receipt which declares, "Whilst every possible care is taken of luggage deposited at this office, the port authority is in no way to be held liable for its loss or damage." Early in the voyage Fred upsets Baschein, a steward, by refusing to tip him on every occasion his services are required. Baschein places a bar of soap outside Fred's cabin door and as a result of slipping on the soap Fred suffers a broken arm and two broken ribs.

Due to trouble at several of the ports of call the cruise is called off after only seven days. When calling to collect his cases Fred discovers that they have been given to someone else, although a notice outside the Luggage Office clearly states that luggage will only be given to persons producing the proper receipt, a warning which appears on the receipt itself. Advise Fred to his legal rights, if any. *Intermediate Laws.*

4. In order for terms to be implied in a contract such terms must be necessary to give effect to what must be considered to have been the intentions of the parties or otherwise to be required by statute. Discuss. *Intermediate Laws.*

5. To what extent is it true to say in relation to the sale of goods that the law applies the maxim *caveat emptor*—"let the buyer look after himself"? *C.I.S.*

6. J bought a ticket for a world cruise from the agents of K & Co., a shipping line. J was allergic to a certain type of deodorant; so, after he had paid the agent for the ticket and put it away in his wallet, he asked the agents' clerk whether this deodorant was in use on the ship. The clerk said that it was not. There was a statement on the ticket that "The company accept no responsibility for any illness or other physical loss occasioned to passengers as a result of the state of the ship or of the use of any preparations or appliances thereon."

The deodorant in question was in fact in use on the ship. J went on the cruise and became ill as a direct consequence of inhaling it. Advise J. *C.I.S.*

7. (a) Distinguish carefully between conditions and warranties as terms of a contract. How will the court decide whether a contractual term is a condition or a warranty?

(b) A, who wishes to take his family on a holiday, rents from B a villa for the month of August at an agreed rent. The agreement signed by A and B states *inter alia* that the villa is two hundred yards from the beach and that it has been recently redecorated. What action may A take if he discovers in July that the villa is a good mile from the beach? Would your answer differ if the bungalow was in fact only two hundred yards from the beach but had not been decorated for five years? Give reasons for your answer. *C.I.S.*

8. (a) In what circumstances will conditions attached to an offer not be binding on an offeree who has accepted the offer?

(b) Mrs H, before leaving on a cruise to Australia, wishes to deposit her mink coat with a furrier. She visits the premises of Cat, a furrier, pays for six months' storage and is given a receipt for the coat and the fee. The receipt refers in small, but legible, print to the existence of conditions which Mrs H does not read. When she comes to reclaim her coat she discovers that it has been damaged by moths. Cat relies on one of the conditions by which he is not to be responsible for this kind of damage to fur coats deposited with him. Discuss whether Mrs H will be able to secure damages from Cat. *A.E.B.*

9. (*a*) Consider the importance of terms in a contract providing for the time of performance, distinguishing between the position at common law and in equity.

(*b*) Pickwick has been invited as guest of honour at the local Dickensian Society's annual dinner and is informed that guests are expected to wear evening dress. Since Pickwick does not own the necessary outfit, he arranges to hire it from Messrs Knicker, Bocker & Co., men's outfitters. It is agreed that he should collect the suit on 15 February. When he calls on that day he is informed that the suit would not be ready until the following day which is, however, too late for Pickwick, since his dinner takes place in the evening of 15 February. He misses his dinner and is also asked to pay for the hire of the suit. Discuss the legal position.

A.E.B.

MISTAKE

1. (*a*) What types of mistake on the part of a person intending to enter into a contract render the contract (i) void (ii) voidable?

(*b*) Last year, Smith bought a secondhand caravan. Six months ago, he offered to hire it to Jones for two years at £3 a week. He told Jones that although he could not be certain, he thought the caravan was a 1965 model. Jones inspected the caravan and decided it was worth £3 a week and he entered into a two-year agreement with Smith. Jones has now discovered that it is, in fact, a 1962 model and, in consequence, is only worth £2 a week. Advise him. *Intermediate Laws.*

2. Orlando has hanging in his Art Gallery a painting described as "early Welsh—artist unknown" priced at £40. Pierre sees the painting and recognises it to be a genuine "Sirebnall," worth at least £15,000, and he immediately offers Orlando the £40. Orlando, having had his suspicions aroused by Pierre's behaviour, refuses to sell. Pierre therefore misinforms Orlando that he is Owen Ap-Ap, world famous art connoisseur, and that this painting is just what he requires to complete his collection of unknown Welsh

painters, and in order to do so he is prepared to pay £100. Orlando, aware of the prestige that could attach to him through such a sale, agrees to sell at this price. Two weeks later Orlando sees a photograph of the same painting in "Art World" together with a notice which states that the painting is a genuine "Sirebnall" and is to be sold that very day at the auction rooms of Messrs Esquire, Close and Smoothly. Orlando rushes to the auction rooms and arrives just in time to seize the auctioneer's hammer as he prepares to knock down the painting to Hiram T. Urgle. Advise Orlando as to his legal position. *Intermediate Laws.*

3. In what circumstances will the court make available the equitable remedy of rectification in relation to a contract?
Intermediate Laws.

4. What are the requirements for establishing a defence of *non est factum* to a contractual claim? *C.I.S.*

5. (a) "The mere fact that one of the parties to a contract acted under a mistake does not, as a general rule, affect the validity of the contract." When will a mistake by one of the parties affect the validity of the contract?

(b) B, a builder, submits an estimate to H, a householder, for the erection of a garage. H, who is satisfied with the price quoted, asks B to do the work. While building is still in progress B discovers that he made a mistake in his calculations on which the estimate was based and he asks your advice as to whether he is bound by his estimate which formed the basis of the contract with H. *C.I.S.*

6. (a) "A signature implies assent to the document signed." What then is the position where the signer (i) does not know what kind of document he has signed or (ii) does not fully understand the terms of the contract he has signed although he appreciates what type of contract is involved?

(b) S, the secretary of XY Ltd, is signing his correspondence while engaged in an important telephone conversation. B, the office boy, who is passing the letters to S for his signature notices that S is signing them without reading them properly. B, who has been gambling unsuccessfully, is in urgent need of money to pay off his bookmaker. He has arranged to borrow the money from a moneylender who requires however a guarantee before advancing any money to B. B had intended to ask S to act as guarantor but he now sees an opportunity of being able to avoid a possible refusal. He slips a guarantee form among the correspondence and S signs it unread. B hands the guarantee form to M, the money-

lender, who advances some money to him. B has failed to repay
the loan and M demands payment from S. You may assume that
B was of full age. Advise S. *C.I.S.*

7. (a) What are the equitable remedies for a mistake made in
the formation of a contract?

(b) X has heard a rumour that shares in an Australian gold
mining company called Theseus are about to rise in value. X
approaches his stockbroker, Y, who tells him that he has never
heard of Theseus and that X must be thinking of a company called
Perseus. X buys from Y 1000 Perseus shares at £1 each. Three
months later, when these shares have fallen in value to 50p, X
finds out that the company whose shares he wanted to buy was
called Thespis. Explain whether X will be entitled to avoid his
contract with Y. *A.E.B.*

8. (a) In what circumstances, if at all, will a mistake concerning
the subject matter invalidate a contract?

(b) X sees in the antique shop of Y a painting which X believes
to be an early Picasso. He asks for the price and a price is quoted
by Y which though high would be fairly reasonable for an early
Picasso. No statement about the authorship of the painting is
made by either party. X buys the painting. State with reasons
whether X will be able to avoid the contract and recover back the
purchase price if the painting turns out to be the work of a less
well known painter and

    (i) Y believed it to be a Picasso, although he did not openly
claim so;
    (ii) Y knew that the painting was not by Picasso, but failed to
mention this fact to X;
    (iii) Y knew that the painting was not by Picasso, and also
knew that X believed it to be the work of this painter, but failed
to inform him of the true facts. *A.E.B.*

9. (a) In what circumstances will a mistake as to the identity of
the other party avoid a contract?

(b) Crook, pretending to be Wheel, a famous racing driver, buys
and obtains immediate possession of a car from Spanner, a car
dealer. Crook gave Spanner a cheque drawn on Wheel's account,
which was dishonoured by Wheel's bank since the signature was
not that of Wheel. Crook drove the car at once to Birmingham and
sold it there to Bull, another dealer, who bought the car in good
faith. Spanner now claims from Bull the return of the car or its
value. State with reasons whether he is likely to succeed.
A.E.B.

10. (a) "As a general rule a person is bound by his signature to a document whether he reads or understands it or not." What are the exceptions to this general rule?

(b) Jones has signed a contract note by which he agreed to buy Sharp's Rolls Royce car for £3000. Will Jones be bound by the contract if he:

(i) did not know that he was buying a car, having signed the form without enquiring as to its nature;

(ii) knew that he was buying the car but believed that the price was £2000;

(iii) believed that he was witnessing Sharp's will?

Give reasons for your answer. *A.E.B.*

11. (a) In what circumstances will a mistake as to the identity of the subject-matter of the contract avoid the contract? Illustrate your answer by reference to decided cases.

(b) Joe Bloggs wishes to engage a private secretary. He interviews Miss Type and engages her. Will the contract be treated as binding if Bloggs discovers subsequently that

(i) Miss Type's real name is Snodgrass and that she is a married woman with three children;

(ii) the Miss Type who works for him is not the girl he interviewed but her twin sister;

(iii) Miss Type cannot spell.

Give reasons for your answers. *A.E.B.*

MISREPRESENTATION

1. Distinguish between innocent and fraudulent misrepresentation inducing a contract and explain the legal consequences of and remedies available for each of such forms of misrepresentation.
Intermediate Laws.

2. P owned a private "zoo." It was stocked with harmless animals. Intending to enlarge the zoo and to introduce dangerous animals, P approached the Q Insurance Company asking them for cover against loss arising from damage or injury caused to third parties by the escape of his animals. Knowing of P's plans, the company sent him a proposal form. This form contained the question, "Do you keep poisonous reptiles?" P wrote "No"; and this was, of course, true.

The Q Co. accepted P's proposal. P effected his enlargements and brought in dangerous animals. A cobra has now escaped from the zoo, has bitten R, and R is claiming against P. P wishes

APPENDIX II 255

to know whether he can claim under his policy against Q & Co. Advise P. *C.I.S.*

3. (*a*) In what circumstances will the court grant rescission of a contract on the grounds of misrepresentation? When will rescission not be granted?

(*b*) X, by producing forged references and a forged set of accounts, obtains from Y an agency for the sale of Y's products. When Y, four years later, discovers the fraud he asks the court to rescind the agency agreement. X claims that, as a condition for rescission, Y should return to him the four annual payments which X had to make to Y in consideration of the agency. Advise the parties. *A.E.B.*

4. (*a*) What is meant by innocent and by fraudulent misrepresentation? What are the legal remedies available to the party misled (a) at common law and (b) under the *Misrepresentation Act*, 1967?

(*b*) E wishes to buy a caravan trailer to use on a touring holiday. F, a dealer, tells him that model X would be most suitable for his needs and could easily be pulled by E's existing car. E buys the trailer but discovers after a week's trial run that the trailer is too heavy for his car and would damage it if used for any length of time. What redress, if any, will E have against F? What difference would it make to your answer if the contract specifically excluded liability for misrepresentation? Give reasons. *A.E.B.*

5. (*a*) "A misrepresentation is an untrue *statement of fact* which has *induced* a party to enter into a contract." Explain and illustrate the meaning of the italicised words.

(*b*) P is looking for shop premises in which to open a grocer's business. V tells him that he (V) thinks that a certain shop is just ideal for P's needs. P buys the shop from V. What redress, if any, will P have against V if P subsequently discovers that all the surrounding area is scheduled for demolition? *A.E.B.*

6. (*a*) What is a contract of utmost good faith (*uberrimae fidei*)? How does it differ from other contracts?

(*b*) L wants to buy a country cottage. He is offered a cottage called Mon Repos by M and after inspecting the cottage buys it for £2000. Will L have any redress against M if L finds out after signing the contract but before the cottage has been conveyed to him that M had failed to inform him that

(i) all the rafters of the cottage are infested by woodworm;
(ii) the water supply to the cottage operates only for one hour per day;
(iii) M had only a seven-year lease of the cottage? *A.E.B.*

7. Harold, a chemist when negotiating for the sale of his business, stated in his offer to sell to Ian that his customers included all the nursing homes within five miles of his shop. Since he made that offer the largest nursing home within that area informed Harold that they had formed their own dispensary and regretted that they would cease to deal with him.

Ian bought the business, but became aware of this development only after completing the purchase. He wishes to sue Harold for damages, for Harold had not informed him of this change in the terms of the offer.

What legal advice would you give Ian? *Bankers.*

8. (a) What is meant by a contract *uberrimae fidei*?

(b) In 1971 Lionel sent to an insurance company a proposal for fire insurance of his house. In answer to the question "Has this or any other insurance of yours been declined by any other company?" he replied "No," and a policy was issued to him. It later appeared that in 1970 another insurance company had declined to issue a policy to cover Lionel in respect of his motor car insurance. In 1972 Lionel's house was destroyed by fire. Can the insurance company repudiate liability? *Bankers.*

DURESS AND UNDUE INFLUENCE

1. (a) Explain the notion of undue influence and its effects upon the making of contracts.

(b) Gordon, aged 40, takes out a policy of a life assurance with the Improvident Assurance Co. to secure a loan received from a friend. On the application form, Gordon in good faith writes "No," in answer to the question, "Have you at any time undergone an operation?" In fact Gordon had had his adenoids removed when he was six. Gordon is killed in an air crash 18 months after the policy was issued. Advise the Improvident Assurance Co.
Intermediate Laws.

2. (a) Explain the difference between duress and undue influence. How far do they respectively affect the validity of a contract?

(b) M has agreed to sell his house to N for less than its market value. Will this contract be binding on M if he was induced to sell his house by:

(i) N's threat to start bankruptcy proceedings against M for some unpaid judgment debts;

(ii) N's threat to refuse to allow his daughter to marry M's son;

(iii) N's threat to prosecute M's son, whom he had employed and who had embezzled some funds belonging to N?

Give reasons for your answers. *A.E.B.*

3. (*a*) Lydia has just attained 21, and on her 21st birthday her father induced her to execute a deed by which she settled on her father for life a substantial legacy which she had received. She now wishes that she had not executed the deed. Advise her.

(*b*) Jonathan obtained a bank overdraft while an infant by pretending that he was over 21. The bank has informed his father that, unless the overdraft is repaid, they will prosecute Jonathan for obtaining credit by fraud. In great distress, Jonathan's father executes a deed by which he promises to repay the overdraft himself. Is he liable on the deed? *Bankers.*

4. (*a*) "Equity will give relief where an agreement has been obtained by certain forms of improper pressure not amounting to duress." Discuss.

(*b*) To what extent may one party to a contract attempt to safeguard his own interests by imposing unilateral restraint on the future free trading of the other party? *Intermediate Laws.*

CAPACITY

1. (*a*) Outline the circumstances in which a loan to an infant can be recovered.

(*b*) Describe the circumstances under which an agreement made by a person of unsound mind is legally binding.

Intermediate Laws.

2. James, a trainee salesman, entered into the following contracts when he was seventeen:

(*a*) A contract to purchase a second-hand motor car costing £70, payable within one month. Two weeks after taking delivery it is badly damaged in an accident and James refuses to pay the purchase price;

(*b*) A hire-purchase agreement in respect of an ice-cream making machine which he requires for use in his own part-time business. After paying off £200 of the £500 total hire-purchase price, James refuses to pay any further instalments;

(*c*) A contract whereby he agrees to take Clarissa on a camping holiday in Austria, in consideration for which Clarissa agrees to buy and provide the tents. After attaining his eighteenth birthday, James continues to discuss the holiday with Clarissa and they spend several days going over the best routes to take and the places they wish to see. A little later James tells Clarissa to go ahead and buy the tents which she does. Two weeks after Clarissa buys the tents James tells her that he has changed his mind about Austria and that he is going instead to a football festival at Southend with some friends.

Advise James as to his legal position in each case.

Intermediate Laws.

3. H, aged 16 years, went to G's antique shop and ordered a valuable chair. G, suspecting that H was a minor, asked him his age. He answered "21." G thereupon accepted a cheque in payment and has now delivered the chair.

H's cheque (which did not belong to him) having been dishonoured, G seeks your advice. Advise G. *C.I.S.*

4. (a) Certain contracts made by infants are treated as "void," while others are said to be "voidable." Name the contracts falling into the two categories and explain the meaning of "void" and "voidable" in this context.

(b) M, an infant, bought an electric guitar for £40, paying £10 at the time of purchase and promising to pay the balance in six monthly instalments of £5 each. What would be the legal position if:

(i) M fails to pay any of the instalments and refuses to return the guitar;

(ii) M, who has failed to pay any of the instalments, sells the guitar to his friend Bingo (who is over 21) and delivers the guitar to him;

(iii) M finds that he cannot play the guitar and wants to return it and reclaim the £10 that he has already paid? *A.E.B.*

5. (a) Laura has just attained the age of 18. On her 18th birthday, her father persuaded her to execute a deed by which she gave him a substantial interest in a trust fund she had inherited recently. She now regrets making that deed.

What is her legal position?

(b) John obtained a bank overdraft, while an infant, by pretending that he was over 18. The bank has informed his father that, unless the overdraft is repaid, they will prosecute John for obtaining money by deception. In great distress his father executes a deed by which he promises to repay the overdraft himself.

Must he pay this money? *Bankers.*

ILLEGAL CONTRACTS

1. (a) George asks Sam to lend him £50 to be repaid within a month. Sam asks George what he needs the money for and George replies that he wants £40 to pay household bills and £10 to pay a gambling debt. Sam lends George the £50. When, over a month later, Sam asks for repayment of the £50, George refuses to do so. Advise Sam as to his legal remedies, if any.

(b) Bert goes to a car-hire firm owned by Dereck and arranges to hire a car for two days during the following week. Bert intends to use the car for carrying drugs from London to Torquay, but he does not tell this to Dereck. The next day Dereck is told by another person in the car-hire business that Bert wanted a car to take drugs to Torquay. Dereck says "Well, I've agreed that he can hire one of my cars and I'm not bothered what he uses it for."

The next week Bert collects the car, paying £5 with the balance of £15 to be paid at the end of the hire period. Two days later Bert duly returns the car but refuses to pay the £15 he owes Dereck. Discuss whether Dereck can recover the £15 by any legal action. *Intermediate Laws.*

2. (a) Under current regulations, the period for payments under a hire-purchase agreement or credit sale transaction must not exceed 24 months. At the request of Smart, Boycott, a car dealer, delivered a Spanking car to Smart under a hire-purchase agreement which provided for payment by 36 monthly instalments and stated that the property in the car should remain in Boycott until payment of the final instalment. After paying two instalments, Smart refuses to make any further payments or to return the car to Boycott. Advise Boycott.

(b) In what ways, if any, would your answer to the above question be different if, instead of entering into a hire-purchase agreement with Boycott, Smart had borrowed the money to buy the car from Mrs Boycott, the loan to be repaid by 36 monthly instalments, and had then entered into a direct purchase of the car from Boycott? *Intermediate Laws.*

3. In December 1969 Quaint decided to go to Hamburg for his Christmas holidays. He discovered, however, that the Exchange Regulations then in force did not permit him to change sufficient English money into German currency in order that he might holiday in the fashion to which he was accustomed. Quaint approached Muckle with his problem and Muckle agreed to ensure that plenty of German currency would be available in Hamburg for Quaint when he got there. Quaint agreed to reimburse Muckle whatever money he used on his return and further to pay Muckle

£100 for his services. It was further agreed that as security for repayment Muckle should take possession of Quaint's pair of Purdey shotguns (valued at £1750) to be returned to Quaint at the time of his making full payment to Muckle. During his holiday Quaint became stricken with conscience at what he had intended to do and he decided to live frugally and thus be able to manage on the money permitted him by the Currency Regulations. On his return home Quaint went to Muckle and told of his change of heart and asked Muckle to return the shotguns to him. Muckle refused to return the guns unless he was paid the £100 and still refuses to return them. Advise Quaint on his remedies, if any.

Intermediate Laws.

4. (a) Which contracts are illegal at common law? What are the effects of this illegality?

(b) State with reasons which, if any, of the following contracts would be illegal:

    (i) Mr and Mrs X agree to live apart and for Mr X to pay his wife a monthly allowance of £100.

    (ii) Mr and Mrs X agree to part in five years' time when their children will have grown up. The financial arrangements are as under (i).

    (iii) Utopia imposes for political reasons a surcharge on import duty on goods which have originated in Ruritania. A British exporter handling products originating in Ruritania agrees with an importer in Utopia that the goods should be invoiced as British products in order to avoid payment of the surcharge.

A.E.B.

5. (a) What are the legal consequences where a contract has been made which was illegal from the outset?

(b) X has supplied to Y a set of tools which Y to X's knowledge intends to use for housebreaking purposes. X was promised a share in the proceeds of the housebreaking. If Y has now decided to abandon his housebreaking attempt, will X be entitled to recover the tools from him? Would the position be different if Y had sold the tools to Z, a joiner, and had retained the proceeds of the sale? Give reasons for your answer. *A.E.B.*

6. (a) "*In pari delicto potior est conditio defendentis* (Where the parties are equally at fault the position of the defendant is the stronger one)." Explain the meaning of this principle as applied to illegal contracts and account for the exceptions to it.

(b) S offers to pay £1000 to M if M will kill S's mother-in-law. S gives M an advance of £100. Before M can put his plans of murder into effect S changes his mind since his mother-in-law has decided to pay him an annual allowance. He now asks M not to proceed with the plan and to return the £100. M refuses to return the money. Would S be entitled to recover back the money? What difference, if any, would it make to your answer if S's request had been caused by the fact that his mother-in-law had died from natural causes? Give reasons for your answer ignoring any implications of this transaction regarding criminal law. *A.E.B.*

VOID CONTRACTS

1. Carter owns a garage and car salesroom in the city of Newtown. His main speciality is the sale and maintenance of "Supersport" sports cars, though he does deal with other types of sports car. Production of the "Super-sport" ceased in 1930 and only a dozen or so garages in England specialise in their maintenance.

In 1964 Keen began to work for Carter as a motor mechanic. Keen had already been trained in this work but he had no knowledge of the "Super-sport" car. Under Carter's supervision Keen developed great expertise in repairing and maintaining the "Supersport" car. He also became fully conversant with all knowledge relevant to the sale of these cars.

The contract of employment between Carter and Keen contained the following passage:

"If the employee leaves the employment of Mr Carter he shall not

(*a*) within the city of Newtown engage in the commercial sale, repair or maintenance of any sports cars for a period of five years; nor

(*b*) within fifty miles of the city of Newtown engage in the commercial sale, repair or maintenance of 'Super-sport' cars for a period of twenty years."

In 1968 Keen leaves the employ of Carter and seeks your advice as to whether he may open a garage specialising in sports cars in general and "Super-sport" cars in particular. He wants to open this garage in Newtown. Advise him. *Intermediate Laws.*

2. Cad incurs losses of £1000 on bets on horses placed with Tosh, a bookmaker. Consider Cad's liability, if any, in each of the following alternative sets of circumstances:

(*a*) He gives Tosh a cheque for £1000 which Tosh indorses to Winn in payment of successful bets placed by Winn.

(*b*) He borrows £1000 from Mugg and pays Tosh but later refuses to repay Mugg.

(*c*) In consequence of threats by Tosh to post him (Cad) as a welsher, Cad promises to transfer shares worth £1000 to Tosh but fails to do so. *Intermediate Laws.*

3. L owned a garage. M was a garage hand. L had invented a special process for mending motor tyres more quickly than is usual, and he instructed M in this method. At the time he took M into his employment L obtained an agreement from him that when he left his service he would not, upon leaving it, "work for any other garage in our Town." The Town was a small one.

M has now left L's service and has joined another garage, a mile away, at the far end of the town. L has discovered also that during his service M revealed the mending process to N, the owner of the other garage, and that N has reaped much benefit thereby. Advise L. *C.I.S.*

4. B made two bets with A. By the first he backed a horse which was running in a race, by the second he backed an oarsman who was rowing the Atlantic to reach New York by a certain date. B lost both bets and he paid A by means of two cheques: A indorsed the first cheque (in respect of the horse) to C in return for a golf club, and the second (in respect of the oarsman) to D in return for a lamp. C and D were both aware of the bets. They now seek to claim against B upon their respective cheques. Advise them.
C.I.S.

5. (a) Compare and contrast gaming and wagering contracts. With respect to these contracts explain the legal position concerning (i) the recovery from a loser of money staked by him; (ii) the recovery of money lent by a third party to a loser which he has used to settle his gaming or wagering debts.

(b) On a by-election night a party is being held at Q's house. The twenty people present agree to £10 each into a pool, to be held by Q, the pool to be paid out in its entirety to the person who has produced the nearest correct forecast of the number of votes cast for candidate C. X is the lucky person and Q, who has not yet collected all the contributions from the participants, pays out £200 to him. S, one of the participants, refuses now to pay his £10 to Q. Discuss whether Q is likely to be successful in an action against S for the unpaid £10. (Your answer should be based on the common law rules and no account need be taken of the *Betting, Gaming, and Lotteries Act*, 1963.) *A.E.B.*

6. Which agreements have to be registered under the *Restrictive Trade Practices Act*, 1956? Describe the further procedure after registration. What are the consequences of failure to register an agreement which should have been registered? *A.E.B.*

7. (a) What will the plaintiff have to prove in order to induce the court to enforce an agreement in restraint of trade against the defendant?

(b) Scissors has been employed as a barber in the "hair culture salon" of Alphonse in the centre of Toad-in-the-Hole an industrial town in the county of Yorkshire. In his contract of employment Scissors had agreed that if he were to leave Alphonse's service he would not set up as, or be employed by, a gentlemen's hairdresser anywhere in Yorkshire and the neighbouring counties of Durham and Northumberland for a period of three years. Scissors has now left Alphonse and has set up his own hairdressing business a quarter of a mile from Alphonse's salon. Alphonse seeks your advice whether he could obtain an injunction against Scissors. Advise him. *A.E.B.*

8. (a) How would you distinguish between a contract of gaming and one of wagering? Explain, with reasons, whether an agreement between a football pool company and a member of the public who has completed one of their coupons is legally binding on the parties.

(b) Bob owes £10 to Tom as a debt arising out of a card game. Bob refuses to pay and Tom threatens to tell Bob's wife that Bob has been playing cards when she assumed him to be at work. Bob, who is frightened of his wife's reaction, promises to settle the debt if Tom will keep quiet. Will this promise be legally binding on Bob? Give reasons. *A.E.B.*

9. To what extent is a promise not to carry on a competing business enforceable:

(a) if given by an employee to his employer as one of the terms of his employment; and

(b) if given by a seller of a business to the purchaser?

Bankers.

UNENFORCEABLE CONTRACTS

1. Jones orally agreed to purchase an acre of land from Smith for £5000. Before the agreement, Smith told Jones that there would be no difficulty obtaining planning permission to build a house on the land. Smith in fact believed this to be the case since he had been informed by a friend, who was an official of the local planning authority, that there would be no difficulty in obtaining such planning permission. After the agreement, Jones applied for planning permission but this was refused on the ground that the land was in an area zoned as green belt. Jones then wrote to

Smith as follows: "Dear Smith, since the local planning authority has refused to grant permission for the building of a house on your acre of land, I shall not now be proceeding with the purchase although if you would reduce the price from £5000 to £1000 I would then be prepared to go ahead. Signed, Jones." Advise Smith.
Intermediate Laws.

2. (*a*) In what circumstances is special evidence required in the case of a contract to answer for the debt of another person? What is the nature of this evidence? What is the legal position if it is not provided?

(*b*) H has agreed to sell J a case of wine, but still has it in his possession and has not been paid for it. J has resold the wine to K, who needs it urgently. K telephones H and tells him that he will guarantee J's payment to H if H will allow him (K) to collect the case from him. K does collect the case. J having refused to pay H, H now seeks to claim against K. Advise him. *C.I.S.*

3. (*a*) Some contracts have to be evidenced in writing but need not necessarily be made in writing. Give *two* examples of these contracts and indicate the nature of the written evidence that has to be available.

(*b*) P has agreed to buy V's house for £5000, vacant possession to be granted on 1 June 1972. P has paid a deposit of £500 by cheque made payable to the estate agents who acted for V. V has signed a receipt for the £500 giving full particulars of the transaction. If P now refuses to complete the transaction will V be able to enforce the contract against him? Give reasons for your answer. *A.E.B.*

4. (*a*) How far is writing an essential requirement for the validity and enforceability of a contract?

(*b*) George Smith orally agreed to sell his house to William Robertson for £6000. Smith subsequently sent a letter through the post to Robertson which read as follows:

Dear Sir, 1st March 1968.
    I confirm that we have agreed today on the sale of my house Greenacre to you at a price of £6000. Completion of the contract and payment of the purchase price are due to take place on November 1st, 1968.

                                  Yours faithfully,
                                  George Smith.

Smith subsequently refuses to complete the contract. Consider carefully the circumstances in which Robertson may be able to enforce it against him. *A.E.B.*

5. (a) Distinguish carefully between contracts which have to be made in writing and those which have to be evidenced in writing. Give two examples of each and indicate the legal consequences of failure to comply with the requirements concerning form in these two cases.

(b) Green, a car dealer, agreed orally with Red that he would pay Red a fixed commission for every customer introduced by Red, provided Red guaranteed the solvency of the clients introduced by him. Red introduces Brown, who buys a second-hand Jaguar from Green. After having paid a few instalments Brown becomes insolvent leaving a debt of £200 which Green now claims from Red. State the reasons whether Green will succeed. *A.E.B.*

6. (a) Distinguish between a contract of guarantee and a contract of indemnity.

(b) What formal requirements does the law impose in respect of such contracts? *Bankers.*

7. Kenneth paid £5000 to Lionel who, in return, orally agreed to sell to Kenneth his house for that sum. Lionel is now refusing to sell the house.

Advise Kenneth of his rights, if any:
   (a) under statute law;
   (b) in equity. *Bankers.*

PRIVITY OF CONTRACT

1. Consider the doctrine of privity of contract and give an account of any exceptions to the doctrine. *Intermediate Laws.*

2. In the light of recent pronouncements by the courts, do you consider that the doctrine of privity of contract is fundamental and irrevocably embedded in the law of contract? Give reasons for your view. *Intermediate Laws.*

3. Define what is meant by the doctrine of privity of contract. How far, in your opinion, does it require modification at the present day? *Intermediate Laws.*

4. (a) How far is it possible for a person to be bound by the terms of a contract to which he was not a party?

(b) A agreed to sell his houseboat on the Thames to B on condition that he might have the use of it, free of charge, for his annual week's holiday in August. B later sold the houseboat to C subject to this right in favour of A. C now refuses to allow A to use the houseboat for this purpose. Advise A.

Intermediate Laws.

5. (a) "The doctrine of privity, evolved by the common law in a simpler age, has proved inadequate for modern needs." Discuss.

(b) In March of this year, George agreed to hire out a motor cruiser to Henry for the last two weeks in September at a total hiring fee of £100 which Henry paid to George. On 1 September, George sold the motor cruiser to Albert subject to the hiring agreement but Albert has now informed Henry that the boat will not be available to Henry as he, Albert, intends using it himself throughout the month of September. Advise Henry as to his legal rights. *Intermediate Laws.*

6. X, a television star, agreed to do a series of performances for the H. television network free of charge, in return for their agreeing to pay £5000 *per annum* to Miss J (X's secretary) for three years after his death. X did perform, as agreed. In order to ensure that she would get the money Miss J telephoned K, the manager of the H. network, and asked him to guarantee the payment. "Yes, I will," K replied.

X has now died and both the H. network and K refuse to make any payment to Miss J. Advise Miss J. *C.I.S.*

7. "No one can claim the benefit of a contract unless he is a party to it."
Consider this statement. *C.I.S.*

ASSIGNMENT

1. (a) How far may rights under a contract be assigned? How may such an assignment be carried out?

(b) Distinguish carefully between a legal and an equitable assignment. *A.E.B.*

2. Distinguish between (a) legal assignment and (b) equitable assignment of rights under a contract.

K agreed with F, who was financing K, that the purchase price of all furniture sold by K should be paid to F by the customer. K sold furniture to D; and F gave notice to D to pay the price to F; but D disregarded the notice and paid K.
Is D liable to pay F? *C.I.S.*

3. (a) How far is it possible to assign contractual rights?

(b) Brick, a builder, needs ready cash to buy additional supplies and to meet his wage bills. He borrows £5000 from the A bank and the same amount from C bank. Both banks require security for their loans. Brick therefore assigns to the A bank a debt of

£7000 owing to him by the Mudville Borough Council on the understanding that the debt would be reassigned to Brick when he had repaid the loan made to him by the A bank.

To the C bank Brick assigns absolutely £7000 out of a debt of £10,000 owing to him from the Giant Manufacturing Co. Ltd.

Discuss whether the above assignments are valid. *A.E.B.*

4. (*a*) Define and distinguish carefully between assignability and negotiability.

(*b*) How far is it possible to assign contractual liabilities?

A.E.B.

AGENCY

1. Outline the obligations owed by an agent to his principal.

H employed J to sell cloth on his behalf, and it was agreed that J should receive a commission of £2 for every bale he sold. J told every buyer that if he (the buyer) would pay J £1 in respect of each bale bought he (J) would do his best to ensure quick delivery: and J in fact did his best to do this. Having paid J £100 in respect of the sale of 50 bales, H has now discovered that J has received the extra £50 from the customers. Advise H. *C.I.S.*

2. Discuss briefly the doctrine of the undisclosed principal in relation to agency. *C.I.S.*

3. U was a wealthy man. He had an aged aunt living with him at his home. While U was abroad on holiday the aunt died. Being unable to get in touch with U, V, a friend of U's, arranged a sumptuous funeral for the aunt and paid for a huge statue of her to be erected. On U's return, V has demanded that U should repay him his outlay on the funeral and on the statue. Advise U.

C.I.S.

4. Examine the rights and duties of all parties concerned where an agent acts for an undisclosed principal. *C.I.S.*

5. (*a*) Describe with examples what is meant by an "agency by necessity."

(*b*) P, a university professor at a South American University, has asked A, a London bookseller, to acquire for him a library of scientific books due to be sold by public auction and has made funds available for this purpose. A secures the books but is unable to ship them to P because a revolution has broken out in P's country and all shipping is stopped. A finds that he has difficulties in storing the books and he sells them to C, a *bona fide* buyer, at a price 10 per cent higher than that paid for them at the auction sale. P now seeks your advice concerning his legal rights against A and C. *C.I.S.*

6. (a) What in the law of agency is meant by warranty of authority? Who provides the warranty and for whose benefit? What is the measure of damages in the event of breach of warranty of authority?

(b) G, a resident of Glasgow, is planning to visit London with his family. On Wednesday G sends a telegram to his friend J, who lives in London, reading as follows: "Please book five stall seats for Saturday matinee of *Murder Most Vicious*" (*Murder Most Vicious* is a play shown in one of the London theatres). J telephones the theatre and books five seats for the Saturday matinee of that week. G had in fact been thinking of the following Saturday. The tickets remain uncollected and unsold. State, with reasons, whether the theatre management may claim payment from G or from J. *C.I.S.*

DISCHARGE

1. "The law recognises that performance (of a contract) short of precise and exact performance will in certain circumstances preclude the promisee from treating the contract as discharged by breach." Discuss. *Intermediate Laws.*

2. "Under the doctrine of frustration a contract may be discharged if after its formation events occur making its performance illegal, impossible, or commercially sterile." Discuss this statement in the light of decided cases. *Intermediate Laws.*

3. His Imperial Highness, the Emperor of Ruritania, was due to visit Stonehenge on 1 June 1971. F & Co. advertised a conducted tour to Stonehenge by motor coach from London on that day to coincide with "His Imperial Highness' visit." On 30 May it was announced that the Emperor would be unable to make the visit.

On 31 May, E, who had paid for a ticket to go on the tour, sought to cancel his booking on account of the Emperor's absence. F & Co. refused a refund. Advise E. *C.I.S.*

4. Give a *brief* account of the law relating to frustration of contract.

N (a theatrical producer) has taken from O a three year lease of a theatre at an agreed rent. After the lease has run for one year lightning strikes the theatre and the fire which develops is so serious that it is estimated that it will take one year to rebuild the theatre, so as to make it again usable for the plays which N promotes. N now claims to be absolved from his obligations under the lease. O claims to be entitled to full rent according to its terms.

Consider the legal position in this case. *C.I.S.*

5. (a) When could a party to a contract rely on the doctrine of frustration to avoid liability on the contract?

(b) S had sold a quantity of cotton material to B which was to be shipped in a named month. S had arranged that the consignment should be carried on the S.S. *Perseus*. Before the ship could start loading it was severely damaged in a collision and was thus unable to sail. State with reasons whether S's contract with B will be treated as frustrated. How far, if at all, would your answer differ if the contract between S and B had specified that the goods were to be carried on S.S. *Perseus*? *C.I.S.*

6. (a) When will a party to a contract be able to claim payment under it although he has not fully performed his own part of it?

(b) (i) T, a tailor, agrees to make a suit for C at a price of £30. After completing the trousers, T goes out of business and the jacket is never made. T now claims from C £10, this being the estimated cost of labour and materials for the trousers which have been accepted by C.

(ii) B, a builder, agrees with C to pull down C's garage and rebuild it at a total cost of £250. After having pulled down the existing building, B becomes bankrupt and his trustee in bankruptcy claims from C £50, this being the labour cost of demolishing the garage.

State with reasons whether T and B's trustee in bankruptcy are likely to succeed. *A.E.B.*

7. (a) In what circumstances will a contract be discharged by breach?

(b) R, a former member of the secret service, had agreed with P, a publisher, that P should publish R's memoirs. The manuscript was to be delivered to P in July 1968. In March 1968 R informs P that he has received a better offer from another publisher and will therefore let this firm handle his book. What alternatives are open to P in this situation? How would the position be affected if in May 1968 an Act were passed prohibiting the publication of material on the secret service? *A.E.B.*

8. (a) What is meant by the discharge of a contract by accord and satisfaction? Illustrate your answer by suitable examples and indicate how this form of discharge differs from one by novation.

(b) S had contracted to buy some shares from T at an agreed price. T discovered that he would find difficulty in supplying the shares and he therefore offered S £1000 to be released from his contractual promise. S accepted this offer. Before T had paid the £1000 the shares suddenly rose in value and S regretted having surrendered his rights to them. He refuses to accept the £1000 and brings an action against T for the shares or their current value and claims that the agreement whereby he surrendered his right to the shares is not binding on him since he has not actually received the £1000. Advise the parties. *A.E.B.*

9. (a) In what circumstances will a person who has not fully performed his promises under a contract be entitled to claim payment for what he has done?

(b) Jones agreed for £300 to install a central heating system in Smith's house. After laying some of the pipes, Jones fell ill and was unable to complete the job. Consider whether he is entitled to claim payment for the work done. *A.E.B.*

10. (a) Explain and illustrate the doctrine of frustration as applied to contracts.

(b) Mr Brown booked for himself and his family a package holiday in Morocco with the X travel agency. The booklet published by the travel agency stated that the best available aircraft would be used for conveying its passengers and that the approximate duration of the flight would be 4 hours. A fortnight before Brown is due to leave he receives a letter from the travel agency stating that because of Government restrictions they are unable to use the aircraft they had intended to use and that the duration of the flight would now be seven to eight hours. Mr Brown who is inclined to suffer from air sickness seeks your advice whether he may treat his contract with the agency as frustrated and recover back the deposit which he had paid. Give reasons for your advice. *A.E.B.*

11. (a) What is meant by a breach of contract? How far is it true to say that a contract is discharged by its breach?

(b) Jill, a singer, agrees to appear in George's night club for one week commencing 1 January 1971. In October 1970 George reads in his paper that Jill has left for Hollywood to appear in a film, the shooting of which will take six months. George writes to Jill reminding her of her contract and receives a reply from Jill's secretary that Jill has no intention of honouring it. George who was once engaged to Jill still hopes that she will not let him down and takes no immediate action. On Boxing Day 1970 Jill falls down a flight of stairs and sustains serious injuries. George who now realises at last that Jill will not be coming to his night club, brings an action against her for breach of contract. Discuss his chances of success. *A.E.B.*

12. (*a*) Where a contract has become discharged by frustration, how will the financial consequences be settled?

(*b*) A wants to show the annual Lord Mayor's Procession in London to his American cousins who are on a visit to this country. He arranges with B to rent B's office which overlooks the route of the procession for the Saturday in question for a payment of £25, £10 of which is payable at once and is handed in fact to B. B agrees as part of the arrangement to supply not only the office accommodation but also to provide A and his visitors with a champagne luncheon. The procession is cancelled because of an influenza epidemic. A demands from B the return of the £10 and B, whose champagne luncheon has been wasted, counter claims for the balance of £15. Advise the parties. *A.E.B.*

13. (*a*) In what circumstances will a contract be treated as discharged by frustration?

(*b*) In return for an annual payment of £25, F has agreed with H that he (F) will tend H's father's grave and remove all weeds. A year later H visits the churchyard and finds his father's grave covered by weeds. When challenged, F claims that he was unable to undertake weeding because the vicar did not allow him to enter the cemetery. State, with reasons, whether F is liable for breach of contract. *A.E.B.*

REMEDIES FOR BREACH OF CONTRACT

1. "The classic judgment in *Hadley* v. *Baxendale* (1854) has continuously been recognised as enshrining and formulating the guiding rules which are to be followed in deciding whether damage which has been the result of a breach of contract should be paid for by the contract breaker."—Lord Morris in *The Herron II* (1967).

Describe the "guiding rules" referred to in this statement and discuss the way in which they have been applied by the courts.
Intermediate Laws.

2. (*a*) In what circumstances will the remedy of specific performance be granted by the courts?

(*b*) In the holiday town of Seabay there are two theatres, one owned by Magnum and the other by Swank. Magnum engages Conrad, a well-known singer, to perform nightly at his theatre throughout the summer season, at £500 per week. Three days before the start of the season Conrad tells Magnum that he will not be appearing at his theatre but will be appearing at Swank's theatre throughout the season. It is too late for Magnum to engage any other artist of Conrad's calibre. Advise Magnum.

Intermediate Laws.

3. (*a*) What remedy or remedies, if any, are available to one party to a contract where the contract provides for performance by a certain specified date and the other party fails to perform by that date?

(*b*) In October last year, Francis ordered from Black & Co. a new XJ6 car, it being understood that delivery would be made in the following February. In February, Black & Co. informed Francis that delivery would be delayed until March, and in March they further informed Francis that delivery would be further delayed until May but that "there would be no question of it being further delayed." The car was not delivered in May and Francis thereupon placed an order for a similar car with Grey & Co. who effected delivery in July. In August, Black & Co. informed Francis that the car was now awaiting collection by him. Advise Francis (who does not wish to take the car) as to his position in relation to Black & Co. *Intermediate Laws.*

4. (*a*) Poor, a builder, agreed to build a house and garage for Jock on Jock's land at a total contract price of £10,000 payable on completion. When the house had been erected, it was discovered that due to Poor having inaccurately marked the boundaries of Jock's land, there was no room to build a garage without encroaching on adjoining land. Jock has refused to pay any sum to Poor. Advise Poor.

(*b*) Swift & Co. ordered from Ballyhigh & Co., a firm of aircraft dealers in England, an American executive jet aircraft costing £300,000. On being informed that the aircraft was ready for collection, Swift & Co. cancelled the order. At that time, Ballyhigh & Co. could not have obtained, on the open market, more than £275,000 for the aircraft but, before re-selling, import duty on aircraft was increased and in consequence Ballyhigh & Co. were able to re-sell the aircraft for £310,000. Advise Ballyhigh & Co. what measure of damages, if any, they could recover from Swift & Co. for breach of contract. *Intermediate Laws.*

5. (*a*) While on a motoring holiday in Lancashire Sybil sees a genuine 1900 "Burnmeister Blitz" motor car of which there are only about five left in the world. Sybil immediately seeks out the owner, one O'Shady, and offers to buy the car. After a great deal of haggling O'Shady agrees to sell the car to Sybil for £7000. Two days later Sybil turns up to collect the car and tenders the £7000,

but O'Shady refuses to take the money and tells her that he has changed his mind as a rich Peruvian has offered him twice as much for the car. Advise Sybil as to her remedies, if any.

(b) Gareth, a clothes manufacturer in Cardiff, agrees to sell 3000 silk veils to Salome, a Go-Go dancer, for £2000. Under the terms of the contract it is agreed that in the event of breach of contract by either party, the party in default is to pay £500 damages to the other party. Gareth sends the veils to Salome but she refuses to accept delivery and they are re-delivered to Gareth. Gareth demands the £500 damages agreed under the contract but Salome refuses to pay this sum on the ground that Gareth's actual loss will only be about £50 since there is a steady market in silk veils. Advise Salome. *Intermediate Laws.*

6. (a) Distinguish between "penalty" and "liquidated damages" in relation to provision in a contract for the payment of money in specified events.

(b) Spaztours, a firm of holiday tour operators, issue a brochure containing particulars of different holidays in various countries. Included in the particulars of each holiday are details of the hotel accommodation and the price—inclusive of air travel and hotel accommodation. On the first page of the brochure, printed in prominent characters, the following statement appears: "Spaztours GUARANTEE that your hotel accommodation will be at least as good as that described in the particulars and if, for a single day of your holiday, your hotel accommodation falls short of this standard, Spaztours will refund the full cost of your holiday." Sparks books a fifteen-day holiday in Lloret at the Hotel Brava, the bedrooms in which are described in the brochure as all having their own bathroom and balcony. On arrival at the hotel, Sparks was, for the first day, given a room without a bathroom or balcony but the following day was given a room with a bathroom and balcony in which he spent the remainder of the holiday. Sparks now wishes to recover the full cost of the holiday (£60) from Spaztours. Advise him. *Intermediate Laws.*

7. C, who owned a riverside quay, let out motor boats on hire. Wishing to have a new boat made he wrote to D & Co., a boat-making firm, and they sent a representative to C's office adjoining the quay. C ordered a boat from D & Co. and told the representative that it must be ready by "1st May certain." Nothing was said about the use to which the boat would be put.

The boating season ran from 1 May to 1 October. D & Co. failed to deliver the boat until August. C thus lost profit on the hire of the boat from 1 May to August.

Advise C. *C.I.S.*

8. What is meant by "anticipatory breach" of a contract?

On 1 January A agreed to employ B at a large fee to drive his (A's) car in an international motor rally which was to start on 1 June. On 1 March A wrote to B telling him that he had changed his mind and that B's services would not be required. B replied that he intended to hold A to his contract and that if he refused to allow him (B) to drive the car on 1 June he (B) would sue. On 1 May, due to a dispute among the promoters of the rally, the rally was cancelled.

It is now 1 June and B wishes to sue A for the fee. Advise B.
C.I.S.

9. (*a*) What is meant by an anticipatory breach of contract? What steps may be taken in this event by the innocent party?

(*b*) N has engaged T to tutor N's son for a forthcoming examination, T to take up his appointment on 1 January. On 1 December T informs N that because of the illness of his (T's) mother he will be unable to accept the appointment. N at once engages Q to take T's place as from 1 January. On 15 December T writes to N to say that his mother has now recovered and that he is ready to take up his post on 1 January. When N informs T that he is no longer interested in using his services, T brings an action for breach of contract. Discuss whether T is likely to succeed. *A.E.B.*

10. (*a*) "English law holds that the object of awarding damages for breach of contract is to put the victim so far as money can do it in the same position as if the contract had been performed." Explain and illustrate how this principle is being implemented by our law.

(*b*) X has been shortlisted for a teaching appointment and has been asked to attend an interview on 3 June at 10 a.m. X contracts with a taxi driver to take him to the interview, informing the taxi driver of the time and place and the importance of the occasion. Through the taxi driver's fault X does not arrive for the interview until noon and by that time another candidate has been appointed. Discuss whether X is likely to succeed in an action against the taxi driver claiming damages for the lost chance of securing the teaching appointment. *A.E.B.*

11. (*a*) In what circumstances will the court award an order of specific performance or an injunction for breach of contract?

(*b*) W is the works manager of C Co. Ltd. and he is employed under a five year contract which provides that he should devote his entire working time to his employers. After two years, when the contract has still three years to run, W decides to leave since he has received a better offer from one of his employers' competitors. Will C Co. Ltd. be likely to secure:

(i) an order for specific performance to compel W to serve out the full term of his contract;

(ii) an order for an injunction to stop him from working for C Co.'s competitors;

(iii) damages for breach of contract?

Give reasons for your answers. *A.E.B.*

12. (*a*) State the main rules of our law concerning the distinction between liquidated damages and penalties.

(*b*) F, a professional footballer, agreed in his service contract that during the football season he would be in bed daily by 10 p.m., would neither smoke nor drink and would not pursue his hobby of motor racing. The contract further provided that for every infringement of any one of these stipulations the club could deduct £5 from F's weekly wage of £70. State with reasons whether these deductions would be treated as penalties or as liquidated damages.

A.E.B.

13. (*a*) What principles will the court follow in assessing the measure (*quantum*) of damages for breach of contract?

(*b*) Harry is employed by Charles as his accountant on a three year contract at an annual salary of £2000. After one year Harry is dismissed without any good reason. Charles accepts the fact that he will have to pay damages to Harry for breach of contract but the amount of the damages payable is in dispute. What factors will the court take into account in assessing Harry's damages?

A.E.B.

14. (*a*) What is meant by the repudiation of a contract? What are the rights of the parties in this event?

(*b*) Mrs P orders from B 200 copies of a wedding announcement in respect of her daughter's forthcoming marriage. Two days after placing the order and before B had started printing the cards Mrs P cancels the order since the marriage has been called off. If B ignores the cancellation and prints the announcements, will he be entitled to claim the agreed price from P? Give reasons.

A.E.B.

15. (*a*) Explain and illustrate the differences between liquidated damages and penalties.

(*b*) Z agreed with B, a builder, that B should build a house for Z for £8000, the house to be ready for occupation by 1 May 1971. The parties further agreed that for every day's delay in giving Z possession of the house, B would pay Z £10. For various reasons the house is not ready until 31 May 1971. Z who has had to store his furniture and accommodate his large family in a nearby hotel claims from B by way of damages his actual expenses over this period amounting to £400. B offers to pay £300, *i.e.* 30 days at £10 per day. Advise the parties. *A.E.B.*

16. (*a*) Discuss the rules applied by the court in deciding whether to grant (i) specific performance, (ii) an injunction as remedies for breach of contract.

(*b*) H has agreed to become coach of the X Golf Club at a salary of £2000 a year. Shortly after taking up his post H receives a more attractive offer from another club and he leaves the X club without notice to take up this new appointment. State, with reasons, whether the X Club will be able to obtain an injunction to restrain H from taking up the new post. *A.E.B.*

17. Jerry Builders Ltd. entered into a contract with X to install new machinery at his factory and to complete the work not later than 1 January 1970. The contract stated that the company would pay X £50 per week compensation for any delay in completing the work beyond the final date of 1 January 1970.

There was a delay of ten weeks which caused X a trading loss of £5000. Can X recover the amount of this loss from the company? *Bankers.*

18. (*a*) What is the measure of damages recoverable for a breach of contract?

(*b*) What remedies other than an action for damages are available when a contract is broken? *Bankers.*

19. (*a*) What is the measure of damages recoverable for a breach of contract?

(*b*) Showem & Co., the London theatrical producers, engaged Terry, an actor, to play a leading part in a musical play at a London theatre. Later they refused to allow him to play the part. The actor alleges that his professional reputation has suffered as a result, whereas it would have been enhanced by a successful performance of the part. Apart from any salary payable, has he a good claim for damages? *Bankers.*

QUASI-CONTRACT

(*a*) What is meant by a quasi-contractual liability? Illustrate your answer by suitable examples.

(*b*) Croesus who is about to undertake a voyage round the world commissions Balbus to redecorate Croesus' mansion during his absence. Croesus has selected the wallpaper to be used and has agreed on a price for the complete job. When Balbus inspects the luxurious premises he decides that the wallpaper selected by

Croesus would not match the period furniture in the rooms and he therefore, without consulting Croesus whose whereabouts are not known to him, uses more expensive Japanese handpainted wallpaper. When Croesus returns he is annoyed about Balbus' action which he considers to represent a slight on his (Croesus') artistic taste and he refuses to pay for either the wallpaper or the work done. Advise the parties.

A.E.B.

INDEX

A

ACCEPTANCE:
  Communication of, 12
  Manner of, 15
  Postal, 14
  Tentative, 10
ACCORD AND SATISFACTION, 31, 190
AGENCY:
  Apparent, 184
  Characteristic of, 175
  Creation of, 175
  Estoppel, by, 176
  Necessity, of, 177
  Ratification, by, 178
  Termination of, 183
AGENT:
  Appointment of, 175
  Capacity of, 175
  Duties of, 180
  Necessity, of, 177
  Rights of, 181
  Warranty of authority of, 182
AGREEMENT, 1, 2
ASSIGNMENT:
  Automatic, 171
  Equitable, 170
  Obligations, of, 171
  Statutory, 168

B

BILL OF EXCHANGE, 172
BREACH OF CONTRACT:
  Discharge by, 192
  Fundamental, 45
  Remedies for, 206
  Repudiation by, 206

C

CAPACITY, 102
CHEQUE, 172
CHOSE IN ACTION, 168
COLLATERAL CONTRACTS, 62
COLLECTIVE AGREEMENTS, 23

CONDITION:
  Precedent, 192
  Subsequent, 192
  Time of performance, as to, 61
  Warranty, distinguished from, 58
CONSIDERATION:
  Adequacy of, 28
  Definition of, 26
  Failure of, 233
  Past, 29
  Privity and, 163
  Reality of, 27
  Rules governing, 27
  Waiver, must be supported by, 31
CORPORATION, CAPACITY OF, 119
COUNTER-OFFER, 9, 19

D

DAMAGES:
  Liquidated, 216
  Measure of, 209
  Specific sum as, 219
  Unliquidated, 208
DECEIT, 92
DISCHARGE:
  Agreement, by, 189
  Breach by, 192
  Frustration, by, 196
  Manner of, 185
  Performance, by, 185
DURESS, 103

E

EQUITY:
  Assignment in, 170
  Chose in action in, 168
  Mistake in, 70, 82
  Remedies in, 222, 223
  Undue influence, 104
EQUITABLE ESTOPPEL, 32-4
EXEMPTION CLAUSES, 40-7
EXPRESS TERMS, 37-40

INDEX

F

FIDUCIARY RELATIONSHIP:
  Agency, in, 180
  Partnership, in, 101
  Presumed influence, 105
  Suretyship, 101, 155
  Trusts, 165
FRAUDULENT MISREPRESENTATION, 92
FRUSTRATION, 196
FUNDAMENTAL BREACH, 45

G

GAMING AND WAGERING, 134
GUARANTEE, 155

H

HIRE-PURCHASE, 159
HOLDER IN DUE COURSE, 173

I

ILLEGAL CONTRACTS:
  Consequences of, 129
  Examples of, 124
  Principle of, 123
  Void contracts distinguished from, 133
IMPLIED TERMS:
  Business efficacy, from, 50
  Conduct, from, 50
  Custom, from, 49
  Statute, from, 52
  Presumed intentions, 49
INDEMNITY:
  Agent's, 182
  Guarantee distinguished from, 156
INFANTS:
  Binding contracts of, 115
  Contracts of, 109
  Necessaries, contracts for, 115
  Restitution by, 113
  Void contracts of, 110
  Voidable contracts of, 113
INJUNCTION, 223
INTENTION OF PARTIES:
  Agreement and, 2, 22
  Legal relations, to create, 22
  Mistake as to expression of, 77
  Presumed, 49

L

LIMITATION OF ACTIONS:
  Disability, effect of, 226
  Equitable claims, 227
  Fraud, effect of, 226
  Limitation Act, 1939, 225
  Mistake, effect of, 226
  Revival of right of action, 226

M

MEASURE OF DAMAGES, 209
MEMORANDUM OF AGREEMENT, 157
MERE REPRESENTATION, 89
MISREPRESENTATION:
  Fraudulent, 92, 94
  Innocent, 92, 94
  Liability, exclusion of, 97
  Misrepresentation Act, 1967, 98
  Nature of, 89
  Remedies for, 86, 87
MISTAKE:
  Common law, at, 69
  Equity, in, 70
MITIGATION, 215

N

NECESSARIES, 115
NEGLIGENCE:
  Non est factum, effect on, 78
  Liability, exclusion of, 40
  Mis-statement, by, 98
NEGOTIABLE INSTRUMENTS, 172
NON EST FACTUM, 77
NOVATION, 189

O

OFFER:
  Acceptance of, 9
  Certainty of, 5
  Communication of, 7
  Invitation to treat distinguished from, 5
  Lapse of, 18
  Options, 17
  Rejection of, 19
  Revocation of, 16
  Termination of, 16

P

PART PERFORMANCE, 157
PENALTY, 217

INDEX

PERFORMANCE:
  Discharge by, 185
  Part, 157
  Substantial, 187
  Tender of, 189
  Time of, 61
PLACE OF CONTRACTING, 15
POSTAL ACCEPTANCE, 14
PRINCIPAL
  –Agent relationship, 175
  Obligations of, 181
  Ratification by, 178
  Rights of, 180
  Third parties, liability to, 179
  Undisclosed, 180
PRIVITY OF CONTRACT, 153
PUBLIC POLICY:
  Illegal contracts, 123, 144
  Void contracts, 137

Q

QUANTUM MERUIT:
  Breach, remedy for, 220
  Quasi-contract, remedy in, 234
QUASI-CONTRACT, 231

R

RATIFICATION, 178
RECTIFICATION, 84
REMEDIES, 206–225
REPRESENTATION, 89
REPUDIATION, 115
RESCISSION:
  Duress, for, 103
  Misrepresentation, for, 94
  Mistake, for, 82
  Undue influence, for, 104
RESTRAINT OF TRADE, 138
RESTRICTIVE TRADE PRACTICES ACTS, 145
REVOCATION:
  Agent's authority, of, 183
  Offer, of, 16

S

SEVERANCE:
  Illegal contracts, of, 129
  Void contracts, of, 144
SIMPLE CONTRACTS, 1
SPECIFIC PERFORMANCE:
  Refusal of, 84
  Remedy for breach, 222
SPECIALITY CONTRACTS, 3
STATUTE OF FRAUDS, 156
SUBJECT TO CONTRACT, 10

T

TENDER:
  Definite offer, as, 11
  Standing offer, as, 11
TENDER OF PERFORMANCE, 189
TERMS:
  Certainty of, 39
  Conditions, 58
  Construction of, 40
  Exemption clauses, 40
  Express, 37
  Fundamental, 45
  Implied, 37
  Warranties, 58
TIME OF PERFORMANCE, 61
TRUST, 165

U

UBERRIMA FIDES, 99
ULTRA VIRES, 120
UNDUE INFLUENCE, 104
UNENFORCEABLE CONTRACTS, 155–158

V

VALIDITY OF CONTRACT, 67
VICARIOUS PERFORMANCE, 171
VOID CONTRACTS, 133

W

WAGERS, 134
WARRANTY, 58